# Painting the Musical City

SMITHSONIAN INSTITUTION PRESS
Washington and London

# PAINTING

# THE MUSICAL

# CITY

## Jazz and Cultural Identity in American Art, 1910–1940

DONNA M. CASSIDY

Permission is gratefully acknowledged to reproduce excerpts from the following texts: "The Judgment Day," from *God's Trombones* by James Weldon Johnson, Copyright 1927 The Viking Press, Inc., renewed © 1955 by Grace Nail Johnson. Used by permission of Viking Penguin, a division of Penguin Books USA Inc.; "O Black and Unknown Bards," from *Saint Peter Relates an Incident* by James Weldon Johnson, copyright renewed © 1963 by Grace Nail Johnson. Used by permission of Viking Penguin, a division of Penguin Books, USA Inc. For permission to cite many documents in public collections, thanks are due to the Archives of American Art, Smithsonian Institution, for the Joseph Stella Papers and the Abraham Walkowitz Papers; to Valena Minor Williams, Conservator, Aaron Douglas Collections, for the Aaron Douglas Papers; to the Yale Collection of American Literature, Beinecke Rare Book and Manuscript Library, Yale University, New Haven, Conn., for the Société Anonyme Collection and the Alfred Stieglitz Archive.

Production Editor: Duke Johns
Designer: Kathleen Sims

Library of Congress Cataloging-in-Publication Data
Cassidy, Donna.
    Painting the musical city : jazz and cultural identity in American art, 1910–1940 / Donna M. Cassidy.
        p.   cm.
    Includes bibliographical references and index.
    ISBN 1-56098-677-8 (alk. paper)
    1. Music in art.  2. Jazz–History and criticism.  3. Art, Modern–20th century–United States.  4. Art and society–United States–History–20th century.  5. Popular culture–United States–History–20th century.  I. Title.
    ML85.C37   1997
    704.9'4978'0973–dc21                              96–44169

British Library Cataloguing-in-Publication Data is available

Manufactured in the United States of America
04  03  02  01  00  99  98  97   5  4  3  2  1

∞The paper used in this publication meets the minimum requirements of the American National Standard for Information Sciences—Permanence of Paper for Printed Library Materials ANSI Z39.48  1984.

For permission to reproduce illustrations appearing in this book, please correspond directly with the owners of the works, as listed in the individual captions. The Smithsonian Institution Press does not retain reproduction rights for these illustrations individually, or maintain a file of addresses for photograph sources.

For Michael

# Contents

# Color Plates

Plate section follows page 46

# FIGURES

# Acknowledgments

Like many youngsters who take music lessons, I toyed with the idea of making a career as a concert pianist. But when I chose basketball camp over performing in a recital I realized that my music career was to be short-lived. Rather unexpectedly, my graduate studies in art history led me back to music. I selected Arthur Dove's *George Gershwin—I'll Build a Stairway to Paradise* as a research topic for a seminar on the William H. Lane collection at the Museum of Fine Arts in Boston. I had remembered the song from a high-school variety show, and became intrigued by the artist who had managed to capture this jazzy tune in paint. My seminar paper grew into a dissertation on the musical analogy and American modernism and now, many years later, has become this book.

I am grateful to the individuals who have supported and nurtured the project during its varied stages. In the beginning I was encouraged by my fellow graduate students, by Theodore E. Stebbins, Jr., who directed the Lane collection seminar, and by my dissertation committee at Boston University. Very special thanks go to my advisors Patricia Hills and Arlette Klaric and a committee member, Jonathan Ribner, who left me with thoughtful questions and comments that proposed new directions for the development of the topic in its post-dissertation life.

I have been fortunate to work in a community in southern Maine that has provided the intellectual climate essential for transforming my thesis into a book. Three summers of faculty-development workshops in the American and New England Studies Program at the University of Southern Maine fostered the revision and rethinking of my work. They helped me discover new ways of seeing art and cultural history, and I extend special thanks to my colleagues Ardis Cameron and Joseph Conforti, who were so influential in this process. I spent another two summers as a scholar at institutes for Maine teachers entitled "Changing Visions: Early Twentieth-Century Modernism in American Art and Culture," funded by the National Endowment for the Humanities and the Maine Collaborative. My planning meetings with the Collaborative director, Vicki Bonebakker, the teachers' provocative questions, and presentations by other scholars were crucial in reshaping my ideas. I wish to express my gratitude to Marcus Bruce, Christopher Castiglia, Linda Docherty, Marianne Doezema, Larry Lutchmansingh, Michael Marlais, Mark Polishook, Lois Rudnick, Elliot Schwartz, Gail Scott, Howard Segal, and Cecelia Tichi for sharing their work and ideas with me; their approaches to the study of the period inform this book in both subtle and direct ways.

Many other scholars, colleagues, and staff members either commented on parts of the manuscript or provided information necessary for the book's completion. I'm indebted to those named here and extend my apologies to any whose names I have overlooked: Robert Baldwin, William Camfield, Magda Carranza, Stephanie Clopton, the late William Dove, David C. Driskell, Elizabeth Gibbens, Jürgen Heinrichs, Linda Henderson, the late John Marin, Jr., Olivia Mattis, Ann Lee Morgan, Francis Naumann, Christopher Reed, Sheldon Reich, Marie Urskine, Adriana Williams, Valena Minor Williams, and Judith Zilczer.

Several staff members of the University of Southern Maine played key roles in this project. The USM Library—and particularly Interlibrary Loan Services—were fundamental to my research: Adrienne Andrews tirelessly and resolutely pursued the locations of hard-to-find newspapers and magazines; David Vardeman responded quickly and graciously to my last-minute and sometimes frantic requests. John Bowman of Media Services photographed magazine reproductions illustrated in the book. The squad of work-study students in the Art Department office, under the direction of Patti Volland, performed clerical tasks from photocopying to faxing. The American & New England Studies Program also supported this project: Dorothy Sayers assisted with requests for photograph permissions and copyrights and Pamela Frothingham, Peg Kearney, and Deb Springer contributed research and word-processing skills. I am also indebted to several groups within the university for financial assistance with research, photography, and production costs: the Faculty Senate, the College of Arts and Sciences Faculty Professional Development Committee, the American & New England Studies Program, and the Art Department.

I would like to thank the staffs of the following libraries and archives for their help: Archives of American Art, Boston and Detroit offices; Bowdoin College Library; Beinecke Rare Book and Manuscript Library, Yale University; the Research and Fine Arts Libraries, Boston Public Library; Mugar Library, Boston University; Lamont, Widener, and Fine Arts Libraries, Harvard University; Motion Picture, Broadcasting and Recorded Sound Division, Library of Congress; and the New York Public Library. My appreciation also extends to the many museums that provided me with the opportunity to view works in storage and to the private collectors who allowed me to reproduce works in their collections. I am especially grateful to Michael Scharf, who gave me access to his collection of twentieth-century American art and to the Estate of Norman Lewis, Howard University Art Gallery, Joslyn Art Museum, the National Urban League, the Phillips Collection, Philadelphia Museum of Art, the Romare Bearden Estate, Rose Art Museum, the Schomburg Center for Research in Black Culture, and the Whitney Museum of American Art for their generosity.

The staff at the Smithsonian Institution Press have been particularly helpful in the long publication process. Amy Pastan's enthusiasm for my topic helped to sustain me through a rewrite of the manuscript, and Duke Johns kept me on schedule during the copy editing and production phases. Their guidance, and that of the readers for the Press, shaped the final form of the book.

Finally, I want to thank friends and family members who have encouraged me. They have housed me during research travels and reassured me when I was finding it difficult to carry out research and writing in the midst of a heavy teaching schedule. No one has been more supportive than my husband, Michael Lawrenson. He read several early versions of the book and accompanied me on numerous research trips, including one away from the cool coast of Maine to the sweltering summer heat and humidity of Washington, D.C. It is to Michael, who helps keep music in my life, that this book is dedicated.

# INTRODUCTION

Historians have often adopted musical language to characterize early twentieth-century American culture. The epithet *Jazz Age* has been used to describe the social and sexual rebellions of the 1920s and *Swing Era* has served as a label for the following decades. While these phrases tend to sanitize and homogenize our view of these periods, it is telling that commentators have turned to musical modifiers to describe them. During the first decades of the century, with the advent of the phonograph, radio, and new entertainment venues, music became one of the most prominent, accessible, and experimental arts; it not only defined American popular culture but even shaped developments in the visual arts.

As art historians have demonstrated, music played a central role in the formation of American modernism.[1] While the limits and boundaries of modernism remain open to debate, one indisputable aspect of this art is its rebellion against academic art and the Victorian middle-class mores it represented. In early twentieth-century America, numerous visual artists rejected what they perceived as the standardized art of the academy in favor of a direct, emotional approach to art making. They turned to subjects that they considered authentic or real, in contrast to the unoriginal, unemotional art and culture of bourgeois society. Music offered a retreat from that art and culture and a paradigm for a novel form of visual representation. Analyses of music and its correspondence to painting filled the pages of period art journals, newspapers, and the so-called little magazines. Such discussions not only brought innovative avant-garde and popular music to the attention of readers but explored the characteristics of this art form in general. Critics and artists praised the nonrepresentational quality of music and offered it as a model for nonobjective painting, then in its infancy. Also considered mystical and emotive, music had great value for early twentieth-century artists who desired to create a new visual form with these same features.

While these ways of seeing the function of music in American modernism are important, they limit our understanding of this art and music's place in it. This fascination with the musical analogy and musical abstractions was not solely a formalist enterprise. Music served as an important cultural marker for American modernist painters, who adopted the themes of the musical city, jazz, and the jazz musician to represent modern, urban America. This little-examined interplay among music, modernist art, and cultural identity in the United States from 1910 to 1940 constitutes the subject of this book.

The search for a distinctive, indigenous cultural expression has been an ongoing concern in the history of the visual arts in the United States. Identifying Americanism or an American tradition in the arts, however, is not a simple task. Americanism is not an abstraction or reification. Rather, notions of national identity are invented under specific historical and social circumstances; the term not only changes over time but may take on multiple meanings at any given moment.[2] Debates about the nature of national identity arise especially during periods of rapid social change, as during the decades after the Revolutionary War and Civil War. In the early twentieth century America was transformed by mass immigration, an increasing population shift from rural to urban, economic depression, and the political instability surrounding the two World Wars. The cultural crisis provoked by these changes was countered by an opposing cultural insistence on seemingly stable notions of nationhood. In this context, inventing an American identity became a central concern of the visual arts.

The cultural critic Van Wyck Brooks wrote in *The Wine of the Puritans* (1908): "We must put aside anything that tends to make us self-conscious in this matter of American tradition and simply be American, teach our pulses to beat with American ideas and ideals, absorb American life, until we are able to see that in all its vulgarities and distractions and boastings there lie the elements of gigantic art."[3] Yet for Brooks's modernist colleagues in the visual arts, constructing a native art was a very conscious and deliberate process. The national identity forged by Alfred Stieglitz's circle of artists and the New York Dadaists appeared seamless, yet it was full of contradictions. They claimed their art as American yet used a style created in Europe and drew on an iconography of the city and the machine validated by Europeans. The dilemma for these artists was that, embracing the modern styles of Cubism and Expressionism, they were perceived as imitating European artists and thus being un-American. How then were they to make their art American?

Artists, writers, and critics adopted varied strategies to give their efforts, however foreign in source, a native flavor—in effect, to reinvent the prevailing avant-garde styles as American. Some, like those connected to the journal *The Seven Arts,* sought a usable past—an American artistic and intellectual tradition on which to build a new nationalism. Others looked to the present to identify unique features of the nation, as members of Robert Henri's and Stieglitz's circles did in singling out the skyscraper as an indigenous object. American modernists appropriated music, like these other subjects, to stamp their works as both modern and native. Musical language and sources served to glorify modern—and especially urban—America and to aestheticize, sanitize, and contain this quickly changing and chaotic society. Musical forms frequently served as convenient devices for constructing national identity. As the cultural historian Werner Sollors has demonstrated, the notion of a multiethnic America as a polyphonic symphony or an orchestration became popular in the decades after Israel Zangwill's 1908 play, *The Melting Pot*.[4] A musical analogy also helped the critic and writer Waldo Frank imagine an ideal American society: "In a symphony, each note rises and speaks and disappears forever. Many notes are grouped to make melodies and themes; are interwoven to fill chords; and these, too, tide and fall. All the innumerable notes lift their instant voices, and pass, and only the symphony remains. Such would be our nation; save that its creator would not be 'outside' the music. He would be the individual note, itself—the group of notes, building the structure of the Whole by knowing the Whole and by living it, personally, in its several parts."[5] This book examines a similar relation between music and cultural identity in the work of five American modernists: John Marin, Joseph Stella, Arthur Dove, Stuart Davis, and Aaron Douglas.

The first two chapters discuss the image of the musical city, which appeared in numerous early twentieth-century cultural productions, from Broadway musicals to avant-garde art. Prewar artists turned to music as they sought the language—both visual and verbal—to communicate the intensity of urban life; in both visual and written texts they envisioned the modern American city, with its dynamism, motion, speed, as melodic and polyphonic. Chapter 1 analyzes the musical city in John Marin's art, with

close attention to his 1911–13 cityscapes. For Marin, music was "rhythm—beat—balance—timing—the life flow—life's dancing."[6] He strove for this energy in his paintings and preferred subjects, such as the city, that he considered especially dynamic or musical. In a 1913 catalog Marin described the power and magnetism of New York's skyscrapers as a "great music being played"; in his letters and essays of the 1920s he wrote about New York, with its staccato pulse and noise, as a city of music and jazz. Seeing the city musically allowed Marin to understand it in a new way: he looked beyond surface appearances to an underlying reality and painted musically—that is, in a vibrant, linear style. His paintings and writings about the musical metropolis were central to his work; in particular, they helped constitute his art as both modern and American. His work, in turn, identified this music of the city with the spirit of America—restless, dynamic.

In chapter 2 I address another sort of urban music in the New York cityscapes of the American modernists: city sounds. Early twentieth-century avant-garde composers aestheticized these new sounds and visual artists, perhaps attracted by the quasi-representational quality of machine and noise music, began to paint these sounds. Thus, just as the composer George Antheil incorporated mechanical noise into his works, the artist Charles Demuth created visual equivalents of sirens screeching in city streets. Chapter 2 focuses on this urban music and its relation to the art and writings of Joseph Stella, who rhapsodized about the city's polyphony and painted the noise music of New York in such works as *The Voice of the City of New York Interpreted* (1920–22; plate 4). Varied sources, from Walt Whitman to the Italian Futurists, brought this multisensual aspect of the modern city to the attention of this modernist. Stella, an immigrant, associated his musical language not only with that of Whitman, an earlier American writer, but also with the music of a fellow immigrant, Edgard Varèse. Like Varèse, Stella framed New York as *the* modern city and the hub of a new civilization, filled with novel sights and sounds, or what he called polyphony and music. For him, painting the city and its music became part of his quest to identify his art as both modern and American.

Mechanical in its sounds, jazz also became associated with the city and modern America. Period commentators packaged this popular music, African American in origin, as the most original American art and, like many twentieth-century composers, modernist white and black painters appropriated this cultural product as inspiration for their own native expressions. Jazz shaped both Arthur Dove's and Stuart Davis's abstract art and its nationalist content, which is the focus of chapter 3. Their abstract, musical paintings—for example, Dove's *George Gershwin—Rhapsody in Blue, Part II* (1927; plate 6) and Davis's *Hot Still Scape for Six Colors—Seventh Avenue Style* (1940; plate 5)—evoked the music's speed and dynamism. These white painters saw jazz as expressive of American modernity, a national spirit, the urban environment, the commercial culture. Their view of jazz was informed by the whitening, commercializing, and sanitizing of this music in the 1920s and 1930s. Dove's and Davis's images of jazz participated in this process, as their paintings helped to constitute jazz as the modern American art—urban, energetic, disconnected from African American culture.

For African American artists the musicians of jazz take center stage, as in Aaron Douglas's *Aspects of Negro Life: Song of the Towers* (1934; plate 8), the subject of chapter 4. Like many modernists, Douglas saw equivalents between the formal components of his art and those of music; he wrote about his distinctive decorative style as a visualization of African American music. Jazz iconography also functioned as part of Douglas's representation of the contemporary African American scene and of Harlem as the modern black city. Through images drawn from jazz, particularly the figure of the jazz musician, Douglas constructed a

racial identity. W. E. B. Du Bois, one of the leaders of the New Negro movement, argued in 1903 that blacks in the United States experienced a "double-consciousness," a divided self, or sense of "two-ness,—an American, a Negro," and longed to merge this duality.[7] This notion of a complex racial identity shaped the agenda and products of the Harlem Renaissance. These artists and intellectuals did not desire to separate themselves from the so-called dominant culture but sought to negotiate a position, or identity, as both "a Negro and an American." This negotiation can be seen in *Song of the Towers.* Here, Douglas fixes jazz within African American culture: he embodies this music in the saxophonist, a figure who refers to other types in black art, literature, and music, such as the preacher or the writer of spirituals. But he also presents jazz as it appeared in the wider popular culture—as an urban music that represented liberation and that was American. For Douglas and his viewers, jazz and the jazz musician stood for this double-layered racial identity, simultaneously African American and American.

The book follows a chronological sequence and traces changes in the expression of nationalism in art from the early efforts of the gallery director Alfred Stieglitz to articulate a nationalist program for his artists in the 1910s to the more defined post-World War I Americanism of Stella and Dove to the urgent debates about national and racial identity of the 1930s, as expressed by Davis and Douglas. Included are the perspectives of the immigrant Stella and the African American Douglas, who envisioned national identity from their position as marginalized outsiders. These five artists also represent a range of approaches to music, modernism, and cultural identity. Marin adopted a musical language to talk about his expressionistic art and perceptions of the city; through music he ordered, contained, and explored this novel experience. Marin did not refer to a particular type of music in his writings about his 1911–13 cityscapes; he did, however, explicitly transfer this urban musicality to a jazz idiom in his later cityscapes and writings. Stella similarly used a general musical terminology to talk about the American city and his own cityscapes, but adapted his language from specific musical forms— Futurist noise music and the music of his friend Varèse. Dove, Davis, and Douglas appropriated jazz as a metaphor for the urban experience. They turned to this music because of their commitment to modernism but also because of their commitment to forming a distinctively American or African American art. In their estimation jazz was the perfect paradigm for a native brand of modernism: as a music it was abstract, and as jazz it was American.

Numerous studies of American modernist art have focused on representations of the city and several short analyses have linked this art and music. The relationship of modernism to nationalism too has been studied extensively, although these studies generally ignore the role of music.[8] This book makes connections among three important concerns for American modernists— music, urbanism, and national identity. It also offers new readings of American modernism by juxtaposing painters with composers (for example, Stella and Varèse) and examining canonical modernists such as Marin, Dove, and Davis in relation to one another and to African American artists, such as Douglas. This study not only inserts African American artists into American modernism but posits the importance of black culture in its formation. As Paul Gilroy's 1993 study *The Black Atlantic,* among others, has argued, black culture significantly contributed to modernity and to Western notions of modernism.[9] This book, with its attention to the appropriation of jazz and the jazz musician by both white and black artists, maintains that African American culture played an important role in the emergence of modernist art in the pre–World War II United States. It thereby introduces into discussions of this art the issue of race and its relation to the construction of national identity.

I want to address briefly the interpretive problems that arise in dealing with musical abstractions as a theme in the visual arts and to describe my approach to these problems. Multiple parallels exist—or rather, have been identified by commentators—between music and the visual arts. The vocabularies used to talk about the two arts intersect: we can discuss the color of sounds as well as color in the visual realm. We can identify similar moods, feelings, or associations (what interpreters may label the *Zeitgeist*) between a musical composition and a painting, as in the Impressionism of Claude Debussy's music and Claude Monet's canvases. Artists and composers also translate or interpret one another's themes, as Igor Stravinsky did in *The Rake's Progress* (1951), inspired by William Hogarth's prints of the same name, and as A. P. Ryder did in *Siegfried and the Rhine Maidens* (1888–91), based on Richard Wagner's opera *Götterdämmerung.* Critics may compare the structures or central organizing principles of musical compositions to those of paintings, linking, for example, Charlie Parker's jazz improvisations to Jackson Pollock's drip paintings. While we may accept such parallels, we should also recognize differences among the arts, particularly in their formal languages and the nature of their materials. Music, for example, involves a progression of notes and rhythmic patterns over time, while painting is constructed as a two-dimensional form and can be apprehended at one point in time.

We must also examine musical analogies in context. In the early twentieth century visual artists were drawn to music as a model because it was nondiscursive, evocative. Academic artists had emphasized narrative and illustration in their work and looked to poetry and literature as paradigms; modernists, in contrast, rejected the depiction of external appearances and therefore embraced music as a less literal model. American modernists often gave their works musical titles, some even derived from specific musical types or compositions. Max Weber produced at least twelve abstract pastels with such musical titles between 1912 and 1917, including *Interior with Music* (1915); Dove assigned musical titles to two early abstractions, *Music* and *Sentimental Music* (figs. 52, 53). Pamela Colman Smith created images that she had envisioned at concerts, as in *Beethoven Sonata No. 11* (fig. 1); Joseph Stella sketched his recollection of a specific performance in *Der Rosenkavalier* (fig. 24), inspired by Richard Strauss's opera; and Francis Picabia visualized the early jazz sounds that he had heard in New York clubs in *Negro Song* and *Negro Song II* (figs. 29, 30). As music became available to wider audiences through the radio and phonograph, it continued to inspire painters. In the late 1920s and 1930s jazz recordings provided a source for Dove's *George Gershwin—Rhapsody in Blue, Part I*, while songs from the radio inspired *The Moon Was Laughing at Me* and movie music *Swing Music (Louis Armstrong)* (figs. 55, 61, plate 7). But without their titles, would we know that these are paintings about music? Visual artists turned to music as a paradigm because it was evocative and seemed to possess no fixed narrative. How then can we pin down the meanings of these music paintings? How do we read them?

Colman Smith offered this explanation of her musical watercolors: "They are not pictures of the music themes—pictures of flying notes—not conscious illustrations of the name given to a piece, but just what I see when I hear music."[10] This is synaesthesia, an association or correlation between two senses, as when a certain sound evokes an image or color in the mind. Her figurative images express her impression of the music. Artists sometimes propose systems of correspondences between the visual and the musical. Like the Orphist Robert Delaunay, the Synchromist painters Stanton Macdonald-Wright and Morgan Russell established connections between

color and sound. For them, pitch in music was equivalent to luminosity in painting and musical tone was parallel to color saturation. In his essay *Concerning the Spiritual in Art* (1912), Wassily Kandinsky devised parallels between music and painting, between the timbre of musical instruments and specific colors and shapes. Such written texts were, and still are, crucial in interpreting musical qualities in the visual, and in revealing how a particular visual artist may define the musical.

Marsden Hartley, for instance, produced several music paintings in Germany in 1912–13, including *Musical Theme No. 2 (Bach Preludes et Fugues)* and *Musical Theme (Oriental Symphony)* (figs. 2, 3). How ought we to understand these works and their musical references? He explained: "It's a new theme I'm working on—did you ever hear of anyone trying to paint music—or the equivalent of sound in color? . . . There is only one artist in Europe working on it [Kandinsky] and he is a pure theorist and his work is quite without feeling—whereas I work wholly from the intuition and the subliminal."[11] For Hartley "painting music" meant painting equivalents of sound in color but also painting with feeling and a sense of the otherworldly. Explaining his new works to his patron Alfred Stieglitz, Hartley described their mystical quality and his initial inspiration from Kandinsky.[12] References to his musical paintings as subliminal and intuitive recall passages in *Concerning the Spiritual in Art* in which Kandinsky discusses music as heavenly and abstract. The glowing, vibrating colors and upward-moving triangles in these works follow Kandinsky's formal prescriptions for a spiritual art, while the themes of Johann Sebastian Bach and the Orient reinforce their mystical content.[13] By examining Hartley's sources and his own writings and paintings, we can begin to appreciate what the musical meant for him.

In this study I read the musical in the work of each of the five artists by looking at the context in which he created and wrote. I examine written language—letters, essays, reviews—to explore how each defined music and the musicality of the visual. Each artist, however, presents challenges in interpreting this notion of "visual music." For Marin and Stella musical language became part of their invention of the city and of modern America. Their essays about the city as musical raise questions as to whether their painted representations of the city possess an equal musicality. Dove drew a more direct connection, making musical paintings from specific compositions, such as Gershwin's *Rhapsody in Blue.* Having literal sources for his paintings allows us to explore the process by which he translated the musical to the visual. Douglas's *Song of the Towers* represents music on two different levels: in the abstract patterns of form and color and in the figure of the jazz musician. Through its double reference to music, this painting typifies the tension between figuration and abstraction in American modernism of the period.

As an important element of early twentieth-century American culture, music, and especially jazz, exerted a powerful influence on the visual arts. Painters saw in music those qualities that they wanted to achieve in their own work. Confined by the limits of their medium, Marin, Stella, Dove, Davis, and Douglas turned to music to help them construct a new art in an American modernist mode. This book is not an exploration of music itself, or of musicology, but examines modernist visual art through its representations of music and the idea of the musical city. By this means we may understand modernism as an art engaged with the culture of early twentieth-century America, especially with the issues of ethnicity, race, and national identity.

Figure 1

Pamela Colman Smith, *Beethoven Sonata No. 11,* 1907. Watercolor, 13½ × 9 in. (34.3 × 22.9 cm). New Haven, Yale University (Yale Collection of American Literature, Beinecke Rare Book and Manuscript Library).

Figure 2

Marsden Hartley, *Musical Theme No. 2 (Bach Preludes et Fugues),* 1912. Oil on canvas mounted on Masonite, 24 × 20 in. (60.9 × 50.8 cm). Madrid, © Fundacion Coleccion Thyssen–Bornemisza. (All rights reserved).

Figure 3

Marsden Hartley, *Musical Theme (Oriental Symphony),* 1912–13. Oil on canvas, 39⅜ × 31¾ in. (100 × 80.6 cm). Waltham, Mass., Rose Art Museum, Brandeis University (Gift of Mr. Samuel Lustgarten, Sherman Oaks, Calif.).

While these powers are at work pushing, pulling, sideways, downwards, upwards, I can hear the sound of their strife and there is great music being played.

And so I try to express graphically what a great city is doing.

John Marin, 1913

Everything became alive each a playing with and into each other like a series of wonder music instruments

It became a music—they the buildings—they the people too a dancing

To capture—to capture a bit of it—I have tried

John Marin, 1950

# 1. DYNAMISM, MOTION, SPEED

## JOHN MARIN AND THE "GREAT MUSIC" OF THE CITY

The use of music as a trope in early twentieth-century art criticism and writing was widespread and varied: it signified the abstract, scientific, emotive, spiritual. American modernist painters saw these sometimes contradictory qualities as essentially expressive of their own concerns. Music also provided an aesthetic model for them because it expressed a modern tempo. For many commentators, new musical forms, from avant-garde noise music to jazz and ragtime, conveyed the sensations and energetic pulse beat of modern America. Some critics were particularly interested in the temporal quality of music, discussing it generally as dynamic and involving the passage of time. As such, music functioned as a powerful metaphor for modernity. As cultural historians have argued, a sense of speed and dynamism pervaded modern experience.[1] New technologies and machines, from the telegraph and telephone to the automobile and electricity, transformed everyday life and perceptions of reality, and nowhere were these changes more profound than in urban America. Modernist

Figure 4

Chorus line, still from the Busby Berkeley film *42nd Street,* 1933. New York, Museum of Modern Art (Stills Library).

artists turned to music as they sought the language to picture this new world and to order the modern city, with its kinetic rhythms and raucous sounds. This art also offered painters a paradigm for representing simultaneity, the modern construct of consciousness that posited that time and space shaped sensations of material reality. In simultaneity past and present merge and objects constantly move and metamorphose. As an environment of intense motion, the modern city became the ideal space for modernist artists to explore simultaneity. Music and the city were wedded together and to notions of modernity and national identity.

From 1910 to 1940 the image of the musical metropolis appeared in numerous cultural products, from Broadway musicals to avant-garde art. The chorus girls who performed in the title number in

Busby Berkeley's 1933 film *42nd Street* (fig. 4) sported costumes in the form of skyscrapers, creating the effect of a dancing skyline. Two decades earlier, the painter John Marin (1870–1953) had subtitled his etching of the Woolworth Building *The Dance* (fig. 5). In critical discourses of the period, music was often presented as abstract and invisible, and Marin used the term music to describe similar features of the city. Along with many of his contemporaries, he envisioned the urban environment, with its invisible forces—its power, magnetism, dynamism—in musical terms, referring to New York's skyscrapers as a "great music being played" and New York itself as a city of jazz. Marin's images and writings about the musical city played a central role in defining his art as both modern and American.

*Marin's Music and His Vision of the City*

Musical analogies made frequent appearances in Marin's writings, revealing his passion for an art form that had been nurtured in him since childhood.[2] The painter enjoyed different kinds of music, including that of Bach, Beethoven, Mozart, Haydn, Chopin, Purcell, and Orlando Gibbons, as well as jazz, the music of vaudeville bands, and Gershwin. He often listened to music on the radio and frequently attended concerts; he went to performances in New York by the pianist Rosalyn Tureck, who also played at the painter's New Jersey home, and admired the pianists Artur Rubinstein and Rudolf Serkin.[3] Playing the piano was Marin's chief avocation. A Steinway grand piano graced his Cliffside, New Jersey, residence while another could be found on a glassed-in porch at his summer home in Cape Split, Maine. Herbert J. Seligmann, the artist's friend and Maine neighbor, remembered Marin's unusual, improvisational piano playing (fig. 6): "I have come to his house, and waited outside, as he explored the structure of a Beethoven sonata, repeating and replaying the chords as it pleased him, then going off on his own improvisations. . . . His playing was as peculiar to himself as his painting."[4]

This avocation shaped Marin's perceptions of his vocation. In essays and letters he often enlisted musical analogies to describe both the process and product of painting. Like many of his contemporaries, he explained the abstract components of his art with comparisons to music: "[I] demand that they have the music of themselves so that they do stand of themselves as beautiful—forms—lines—and paint on beautiful paper or canvas."[5] As a pianist Marin saw an affinity between the performance of music and the act of painting, as both depended on intuitive movement of the fingers and hands:

> Bach is finger patterns finger juxtapositions—as the fingers look well in their different positions they

make the music sound well. To play this music takes an unbelievable concentration and absorbing. In playing the piano one's head should be lowered one's eyes intent on fingers and at the same time a looking right into the piano—sometimes as it were crouched right on the instrument. The music should course right down through the tips of the fingers right into the instrument. . . .

> That time with me—vague glimpses—I feel that I am on the threshold of something relating to it—how to hook up music with art.[6]

Marin experienced the same unity with his paint materials that he felt when playing the piano. He wrote of the artist's tools as musical instruments and on occasion even painted with both hands, just as he played the piano.[7]

For Marin, music and painting also evidenced similar laws of balance and rhythm. The "backbone principle," or balance of movement, was the foundation of all art: "You try to see your objects in their movement—positions—you seek for (back bones) of these swaying objects—these you must hold to for all you are worth. All good writing—All good music—All good painting—obeys this principle."[8] The structure of thirds governed this tenet in both arts: the primary colors red, yellow, blue in painting corresponded to the three major triads in harmony.[9] Rhythm or action in painting was also allied with music: "The rhythmic flow [in painting] shows that you have music aboard. Yes I would have it that the painter who has not music—is not for me—Who has not the rhythmic flow as had Mozart as had Bach is not for me."[10] Marin's favorite musical forms, from eighteenth-century polyphony to jazz, are characterized by the combination of several independent musical lines or melodies that differ rhythmically but fit together harmoniously. Marin had visualized this complex "rhythmic flow" of varied rhythms and voices through color and line in his paintings.[11]

Figure 5

John Marin, *Woolworth Building (The Dance),* 1913. Etching, 12¾ × 10⅜ in. (32.4 × 26.4 cm). Philadelphia Museum of Art (Alfred Stieglitz Collection. Courtesy of the John Marin Estate/ Kennedy Galleries, New York).

Figure 6

Herbert J. Seligmann, *Marin Playing the Piano,* n.d. Ink on paper, 11 × 8½ in. (27.9 × 21.6 cm). Washington, D.C., © 1995 Board of Trustees, the National Gallery of Art (John Marin Family Papers, gift of John Marin, Jr. Courtesy of the John Marin Estate/Kennedy Galleries, New York).

It is with the aid of Marin's commentaries on his own art that we can read his painting as musical. Music is abstract, suggestive, immaterial; its meanings cannot easily be pinned down. It was this uncertainty and fluidity of meaning in music that appealed so much to Marin and his contemporaries. The art critic Samuel Swift of the *New York Sun* described Marin's nonrepresentational art as an "approach in a way to the sister art of music, in which definite meanings may not be attached to the materials out of which one builds his composition."[12] Marin identified specific parallels between music and painting and his words direct viewers to read the rhythm, balance, and action of his images, embodied in line and color, as a kind of silent, visual music.

In particular, Marin's words have encouraged viewers to read the painter's images of New York City as musical. (A videotape produced for the 1981 Kennedy Galleries exhibition "John Marin's New York" included an original jazz score played as background for the painter's urban scenes.)[13] But how did this wedding of music and the city emerge within Marin's art? Marin wrote about the visual elements of color and line as musical. A key feature of his cityscapes is the dynamic line that appears as broken diagonal marks in his 1911–13 watercolor series and as curving calligraphic lines in his oil paintings of the 1950s. Viewed in the context of Marin's own words, the linearity of these works can be seen as musical. Marin also considered his cityscapes to be representations of New York's hustle and bustle, itself a type of music, as his son later explained: "My father was a loner who loved the sights, sounds, the architecture and excitement of New York. . . . The people, buildings, ferryboats, the El, subways and bridges of the teeming city made music; and John Marin loved music."[14] Writing about his urban art in 1950, he echoed the syncopated musicality of the city in his prose:

They—the drawings—were mostly made in a series of wanderings around about my City—New York—with pencil and paper in—sort of—Short hand-writings as it were—Swiftly put down—obeying impulses of a wilful intoxicating mustness—of the nearness—nay—of the being in it—of being a part of it—of that—which to my Eye went on—of the rhythmic movements of people on Streets—of buildings a rearing up from sidewalk—of a mad wonder dancing to away up there aloft—for

Everything became alive each a playing with and into each other like a series of wonder music instruments

It became a music—they the buildings—they the people too a dancing

To capture—to capture a bit of it—I have tried[15]

Marin connected urban dynamism, music, and a visual-art style early in his career, in some of his first New York watercolors. In particular, his 1911–13 cityscapes and accompanying writings were crucial in shaping a contemporary and historical understanding of his art as modern, musical, urban, and American.

The emergence of New York as an important theme in Marin's art coincided with his return to the city after a four-year stay in Europe. The painter had gone to Paris in 1905 but returned to New York in December 1909, returning briefly to Europe in May 1910. Later that same year he permanently resettled in the United States. In Paris he had painted some of that city's signature buildings, among them the Cathedral of Notre-Dame; during his 1909–10 visit to New York, he discovered equivalent American landmarks in the new skyscrapers and joined other artists who were looking to the burgeoning metropolis as a subject.[16] Chief among these were the New York Realists, who painted city streets and new buildings in such works as John Sloan's *Election Night* (1907), Robert Henri's *West Fifty-Seventh Street, New York* (1902), and George Bellows's *Pennsylvania Station*

*Excavation* (1907–9). Photographers associated with the circle of Alfred Stieglitz, Edward Steichen, Alvin Langdon Coburn, and Stieglitz himself, also seized upon the urban environment as a fruitful subject. As early as 1903 the critic Sadakichi Hartmann wrote an essay acclaiming New York's skyscrapers as heralds of a new aesthetic in *Camera Work,* a "little magazine" published by Stieglitz; other articles followed, advertising the city and its towers—Daniel Burnham's Flatiron Building (1902), Ernest Flagg's Singer Building (1908)—as appropriate topics for visual artists.[17] *Camera Work* reproduced numerous photographic cityscapes, including Stieglitz's *The 'Flat-iron'* (1902–3), Steichen's *The Flatiron—Evening* (1905), and Coburn's *New York* (1907); the October 1911 issue, with its reproductions of Stieglitz's landmark New York photographs, ensured the centrality of the theme for this group.[18]

By 1909 Marin was close to the Stieglitz circle,[19] and his own 1909–10 New York cityscapes focused on the same sites that appear in the group's photographs: views down Fifth Avenue, the bustling harbor, the Brooklyn Bridge, and recently constructed skyscrapers. He painted the Singer and Flatiron buildings, among others, portraying more than the external features of these urban monuments. He was working toward a new direction in his work, as he explained to Stieglitz: "As you have no doubt been told by [Paul] Haviland the skyscrapers struck a snag for the present at least so we had to push in a new direction. Haviland, Steichen, and [Arthur B.] Carles saw the new direction, and [it] may be a step forward."[20] What was this new direction? At this time Marin's cityscapes begin to show a shift away from the muted colors and soft, atmospheric, Whistlerian manner typical of his early works, toward the brighter colors of the Post-Impressionism that he had seen in Paris. These works also reveal an emerging interest in depicting the city's underlying forces. The titles of the Parisian scenes on view in Marin's 1910 exhibition at Gallery 291 (also

called the Little Galleries of the Photo-Secession) argue his concern with both the dynamism and the invisible structural forces operating in urban architecture: *Moving Spots (Pont des Arts), Movement (Pont de Lalma), Thrust of the Bridge (Pont Alexander), Sweep of the Bridge (Pont Alexander),* and *The Swirl.*[21] At the same time Marin began to paint New York with increasing abstraction, fragmentation of form, and a manner suggesting movement, as can be seen in the agitated pencil lines in *New York Skyline, Boats in Foreground* (1910) and the broken, vividly colored brushstrokes in *Buildings* (fig. 7). The ineffable forces of energy and excitement were especially evident in the nearly abstract 1910 *Spirit of New York* (fig. 8), in which a watercolor wash seems to dissolve the city's structures. It was not external form but something else that Marin painted here, something beyond appearance—the spirit of the city.

Marin further explored New York's underlying spirit in works of the next two years, and fifteen of these cityscapes were exhibited at Gallery 291 from January 20 to February 15, 1913. These watercolors—*The Brooklyn Bridge, Movement, Fifth Avenue,* and the Woolworth Building series (figs. 9–13)—are key works in the development of Marin's modernist style. Here again he focused on technological marvels like the Brooklyn Bridge and new skyscrapers like the Singer and Woolworth Buildings.[22] In these watercolors New York's architecture swirls, soars, and totters, creating a chaotic, topsy-turvy urban scene. Since the literal description of external appearances concerns Marin little, he shatters the surfaces of objects, dematerializing form. While the large, hazy color areas typical of his Whistlerian works still appear in some of his 1911-13 work, atmosphere gives way to line as the dominant visual element, and a new visual language begins to emerge. In contrast to the rigid linear grids of Analytical Cubism, Marin's watercolors comprise broad strokes of watercolor wash and unpainted areas of white paper, so that buildings and bridges appear

Figure 7

John Marin, *Buildings,*
1910. Watercolor on ivory
paper, laid on white wove
paper, 12 × 9 in. (30.5 ×
22.7 cm). Art Institute of
Chicago (gift of Georgia
O'Keeffe to the Alfred
Stieglitz Collection,
1956.373. Photograph ©
1994, The Art Institute of
Chicago. All rights
reserved. Courtesy of the
John Marin Estate/
Kennedy Galleries, New
York).

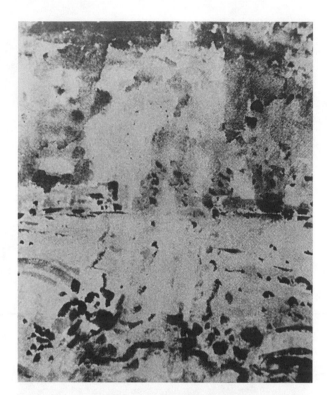

Figure 8

John Marin, *Spirit of New York,* 1910. Watercolor on paper, 15½ × 13 in. (39.4 × 33 cm). Location unknown (reproduced in Sheldon Reich, *John Marin: A Stylistic Analysis and Catalogue Raisonné,* part II, Tucson: University of Arizona Press, 1970, 350. Courtesy of the John Marin Estate/Kennedy Galleries, New York).

Figure 9

John Marin, *The Brooklyn Bridge,* 1912. Watercolor on paper, 18½ × 15½ in. (47 × 39.4 cm). New York, Metropolitan Museum of Art (Alfred Stieglitz Collection, 1949, 49.70.105. All rights reserved. Courtesy of the John Marin Estate/ Kennedy Galleries, New York).

Figure 10

John Marin, *Movement, Fifth Avenue,* 1912. Watercolor on paper, 17 × 13¾ in. (43.3 × 35 cm). Art Institute of Chicago (Alfred Stieglitz Collection, 1949.554. Photograph by Kathleen Culbert–Aguilar. © 1994, The Art Institute of Chicago. All rights reserved. Courtesy of the John Marin Estate/ Kennedy Galleries, New York).

Figure 11

John Marin, *Woolworth Building, No. 28,* 1912. Watercolor over graphite on paper, 18½ × 15⅝ in. (47 × 39.7 cm). Washington, D.C., © 1995 Board of Trustees, the National Gallery of Art (gift of Eugene and Agnes E. Meyer. Courtesy of the John Marin Estate/ Kennedy Galleries, New York).

light, airy, and hovering on the paper's surface. This new style is markedly dynamic, exuberant, and distinctive. *The Brooklyn Bridge* (fig. 9) is not covered with descriptive details; instead, the whole environment is energized by black streaks and diagonal brushstrokes in the sky, repeated black dabs in the pathway, and ascending curves of the support wires and Gothic archways. In *Movement, Fifth Avenue* (fig. 10) the right side of the street tilts to the left, the left to the right, and the street curves up in defiance of the laws of nature and perspective. Marin transforms the solid forms of the street and buildings into fluid washes, disintegrating their material presence and bringing inanimate forms to life.

This process is also evident in Marin's numerous studies of Cass Gilbert's Woolworth Building, in construction from 1911 to 1913. In *Woolworth Building, No. 28* (fig. 11) jumbled buildings, people, and trees in the foreground suggest the confusion of the city below. The tower is vertically centered, with diagonal lines and color patches radiating from this central axis. The relative stability of the Woolworth Building seen here is disrupted in other versions of the same scene. Fractured contours, scrambled forms, and broken brushstrokes evoke the city's vitality in *Woolworth Building, No. 29* and *No. 31* (plate 1, fig. 12). The pink skyscraper in *No. 29* seems to have lifted itself off its foundation to dance and sway to the traffic rhythm at its foot—a posture the building also assumes in *No. 31.* In the latter hardly a vertical or horizontal line exists: myriad short dabs and diagonal lines signify trees, buildings, automobiles, and streets, while the contours of the building itself bend inward and upward. In *Woolworth Building, No. 32* (fig. 13) Marin represents the structure as an upward-sweeping ellipse that culminates in a towering pinnacle.

Marin, of course, did not invent this visual language or approach to representation; he was amply influenced by the European modernist avant garde.[23] The tilted, fragmented, and distorted forms of his

Figure 12

John Marin, *Woolworth Building, No. 31, 1912.* Watercolor over graphite on paper, 18½ × 15⅝ in. (47 × 39.7 cm). Washington, D.C., © 1995 Board of Trustees, the National Gallery of Art (gift of Eugene and Agnes E. Meyer. Courtesy of the John Marin Estate/ Kennedy Galleries, New York).

Figure 13

John Marin, *Woolworth Building, No. 32, 1913.* Watercolor over graphite on paper, 18⅜ × 15⅝ in. (46.7 × 39.7 cm). Washington, D.C., © 1995 Board of Trustees, the National Gallery of Art (gift of Eugene and Agnes E. Meyer. Courtesy of the John Marin Estate/ Kennedy Galleries, New York).

Figure 14

Alvin Langdon Coburn, *Singer Building,* 1910. Gum platinum print. Rochester, N.Y., courtesy of George Eastman House.

1911–13 cityscapes clearly owe a good deal to the experiments of Robert Delaunay's Eiffel Tower paintings, to the Futurists' studies of segmented motion, and to the innovations of Cézanne, Picasso, and Braque. In addition, contemporary experiments in abstract art by the Americans Max Weber, Marsden Hartley, and Arthur Dove undoubtedly encouraged Marin to move toward a nonrepresentational mode.

Images by photographers of the Stieglitz circle that convey the passage of time perhaps informed Marin's cityscapes as well. Stieglitz's 1910 prints *The City of Ambition* and *Old and New New York,* which appeared in the October 1911 edition of *Camera Work,* present the Manhattan skyline and its skyscrapers in a rising mist, creating the effect of an organic and mysterious city, burgeoning and living. Alvin Langdon Coburn's *Singer Building* (fig. 14), reproduced in *Camera Work* (October 1910) as an advertisement for his book *New York,* suggested motion through the diagonal street, blurred forms, and light streaks formed by passing trams. Marin may well have been familiar with Coburn's book, since the subjects and vistas in his 1910–13 cityscapes—looking down Broadway to the Singer Building and the Brooklyn Bridge, for example—are similar to Coburn's photographic views. The painter's *Buildings* (fig. 7) and *Broadway, Singer Building* (1912) particularly recall the photographer's *Singer Building.*[24]

Like Marin, Coburn was concerned with picturing New York's verticality and vigor. His 1911 *Camera Work* article, "The Relation of Time to Art," praised photographers' ability to visualize the dynamic metropolis. He identified New York as the quintessential modern city, full of rush and turmoil, where "time and space are of more value than in any part of the world." In Coburn's estimation, photography was the art medium best suited to represent the contemporary, scientific age because it could capture fleeting instants of time and the flux of the urban environment. Comparing photography to painting, he proposed that we shall find that the essential difference is not so much a mechanical one of brushes and pigments as compared with a lens and dry plates, but rather a mental one of a slow, gradual, usual building up, as compared with an instantaneous, concentrated mental impulse, followed by a longer period of fruition. Photography born of this age of steel seems to have naturally adapted itself to the necessarily unusual requirements of an art that must live in skyscrapers, and it is because she has become so much at home in these gigantic structures that the Americans undoubtedly are the recognized leaders in the world movement of pictorial photography.

Just imagine any one trying to paint at the corner of Thirty-fourth street, where Broadway and Sixth avenue cross![25]

We may imagine that Marin took Coburn's statement as an explicit challenge, for he did indeed paint Broadway and other rush-hour hot spots and found a way to suggest in paint the instantaneity, the fleeting and momentary changes in the city that Coburn so loved.[26]

Drawing on both European modernism and contemporary American photography, then, Marin formed his own singular modernist manner, composed of brilliant colors, bouncing curves, and streaking diagonals. He was able to use this same linear style in his etchings of the urban scene, *Woolworth Building (The Dance)* and *Brooklyn Bridge No. 2 (Song of the Bridge)* (figs. 5, 15). The use of *Song* and *Dance* as subtitles for these prints was apt, for in his January 1913 exhibition catalog essay Marin enlisted a musical analogy to explain his cityscapes to viewers:

Shall we consider the life of a great city as confined simply to the people and animals on its streets and in its buildings? Are the buildings themselves dead? We have been told somewhere that a work of art is a thing alive. You cannot create a work of art unless the things you behold respond to something within you.

Therefore if these buildings move me they too must have life. Thus the whole city is alive; buildings, people, all are alive; and the more they move me the more I feel them to be alive. . . .

I see great forces at work; great movements; the large buildings and the small buildings; the warring of the great and the small; influences of one mass on another greater or smaller mass. Feelings are aroused which give me the desire to express the reaction of these "pull forces," those influences which play with one another; great masses pulling smaller masses, each subject in some degree to the other's power. . . .

While these powers are at work pushing, pulling, sideways, downwards, upwards, I can hear the sound of their strife and there is great music being played.

And so I try to express graphically what a great city is doing.[27]

Although the Cubist and Futurist sources for Marin's text have been discussed elsewhere,[28] his use of the term *great music* to describe his vision of the city has been virtually ignored. How may we read this phrase? What did Marin mean by it? What did it signify to viewers looking at Marin's art in 1913?

Marin's description of architectural forces as music in his essay suggests that he was familiar with the common linkage between music and architecture as sister arts in modern Western art theory.[29] Marin had himself studied architecture, and the art historian Abraham Davidson has proposed that his apprenticeship as an architect helped mold his vision of the city's buildings as alive and filled with tensions.[30] Conceivably this background also shaped his vision of the city's buildings as musical. The notion of architecture as "frozen music" and of music as "liquid architecture" was a classic statement of Western aesthetics. Mathematical principles of musical intervals were used by the Renaissance architects Leon Battista Alberti and Andrea Palladio and in subsequent French academic theory.[31] Theoreticians claimed that architecture and music shared a mathematical, abstract ordering.

Figure 15

John Marin, *Brooklyn Bridge No. 2 (Song of the Bridge)*, 1913. 10¾ × 8⅞ in. (27.3 × 22.5 cm). Philadelphia Museum of Art (Golden Collection. Courtesy of the John Marin Estate/ Kennedy Galleries, New York).

This invisible great music of the city also alludes to the discussion of music as an ideal abstract art, common in modernist criticism. Several critics even used this musical analogy to explain Marin's 1911–13 cityscapes. Forbes Watson of the *New York Evening Post* claimed, "Mr. Marin does not present the world objectively but rather expresses his own emotions in beautiful color notes, almost abstractly as if music were his medium."[32] But while such comparisons between music and painting, based on the abstract and emotive qualities of both arts, were prevalent at this time, so too were references to the invisible forces of objective reality and the simultaneity of experience as musical. Marin's notion of the underlying forces of the city as musical intersected with meanings circulating in modernist art and philosophy.

Like many members of the Stieglitz circle, Marin was intrigued by new concepts of art and experience. *Camera Work* frequently published essays on antiphotographic art theories and discussions about the underlying forces of objective reality.[33] Another central theme in this influential little magazine was the critique of positivism and materialism. At the turn of the century many thinkers began to distrust external reality. The rise of spiritualism, occultism, the notion of the fourth dimension, non-Euclidean mathematics, and psychology marked this inward-turning search for an essential reality beyond appearances.[34] Marin's art makes this same turn. As is evident from his 1913 catalog essay, the invisible underlying forces of New York are the subject of his 1911–13 watercolors. That the painter selected the phrase *great music* to define these forces and movements is not surprising, given the popularity of this trope in the period's critical discourse. For many, music functioned as an apt metaphor to explain new concepts of reality and experience that were defined by the elements of time and motion.

Popular in New York avant-garde circles, the French philosopher Henri Bergson wrote about the continuity and simultaneity of experience in musical terms.[35] In *An Introduction to Metaphysics* (1903) he theorized that there were different ways of knowing objective reality: relative knowledge viewed things from the outside; absolute knowledge viewed from within. Experiencing the world was a dynamic process: past, present, and future were interconnected, not distinct; the world was constantly moving and changing, and objects were not isolated phenomena perceived at discrete moments. Bergson characterized this complex apprehension of both time and reality as *durée,* pure duration, or stream of consciousness—a "continuous flux, a succession of states, each of which announces that which follows and contains that which precedes it."[36] He used numerous metaphors to express this knowledge of the inner life of things and of the fluid nature of experience and time. In *Time and Free Will* (1910) he compared *durée* to music:

> Pure duration is the form which the succession of our conscious states assumes when our ego lets itself live, when it refrains from separating its present state from its former states . . . it is enough that in recalling these states it does not set them alongside its actual states as one point alongside another, but forms both the past and present states into an organic whole, as happens when we recall the notes of a tune melting, so to speak, into one another.[37]

Bergson also characterized life's rhythms in musical language in an essay published in the January 1912 issue of *Camera Work,* entitled "What Is the Object of Art?": "Others delve yet deeper still . . . they grasp something that has nothing in common with language, certain rhythms of life and breath that are closer to man than his inmost feelings, being the l iving law—varying with each individual—of his enthusiasm and despair, his hopes and regrets. By setting free and emphasizing this music, they force it upon our attention. . . . And thus they impel us to set in motion, in the depths of our being, some secret chord which was only waiting to thrill."[38]

Bergson was not alone in adopting music as a metaphor for the continuity, simultaneity, and dynamism of experience, and vice versa. Early twentieth-century critics and artists often identified these musical qualities as elements that painters should and could emulate visually through pattern and color. A 1908 *Camera Work* article characterized progression over time—a combined sense of time and motion—as inherently musical: "The element of time enters as an all-important factor, much of the effect produced depending upon the relative duration of the different sounds, and upon the spacing between them."[39] The critic J. Nilsen Lauvrik, writing in "Is It Art? Post-Impressionism, Cubism, Futurism," claimed that Wassily Kandinsky's attempt to produce "color music" failed because music was dynamic, while painting was static.[40] Kandinsky approximated the musical element of movement through color contrasts in his paintings and stated, in *Concerning the Spiritual in Art* (1912): "[The painter] naturally seeks to apply the methods of music to his own art. And from this results that modern desire for rhythm in painting, for mathematical, abstract construction, for repeated notes of colour, for setting colour in motion."[41]

Similarly, the art critic Willard Huntington Wright discussed rhythm, motion, and time in musical terms in his book *Modern Painting: Its Tendency and Meaning* (1915). For Wright music was abstract, based on dynamic force, the "rhythmic movement of all nature"; a painter, he thought, should emulate this musical rhythm. Time, also integral to music, was more difficult for the painter to express: "Could painting extend itself into time and present singly and in sequence the visions of objective nature, dramatically synthesized with colour and line, it could perhaps influence people to emotion in the way music does. But the musical quality of time-extension is impossible in painting. And since a picture presents a simultaneous vision . . . it is incapable of working from a prelude to a finale like music." Although Wright believed

Figure 16

Stanton Macdonald-
Wright, *"Conception."
Synchromy,* 1915. Oil on
canvas, 30 × 24 in. (76.2 ×
61 cm). New York,
Whitney Museum of
American Art (gift of
George F. Of, 52.40. ©
1995 Whitney Museum of
American Art).

it impossible for the painter to capture time, he did
recognize elements of time, or duration, in some contemporary paintings: the Cubists broke up natural
objects "for the sake of extending the aesthetic appreciation into time like music," and the Synchromist
painter Morgan Russell incorporated the "quality of
duration" in his works, since he "sought to have his
picture develop into time like music."[42]

The Synchromist painters Russell and Stanton
Macdonald-Wright (Willard Wright's brother) defined
the musicality of their art as color set in motion and
united with the expression of the passage of time. In
the introduction to a catalog for their 1913 exhibition
at the Bernheim-Jeune Gallery in Paris they explained
the connection of music to color in their work, calling it "color motion," or "color music": "These 'color
rhythms' somehow infuse a painting with the notion
of time: they create the illusion that the picture devel-
ops, like a piece of music, within the span of time,
while the old painting existed strictly in space."[43]
Russell identified motion as a key ingredient in music
and in his own art, declaring that he wanted to
"[k]eep the 'music' at all costs—the palpitation or
undulation."[44] The Synchromists emulated "color
music"—that is, displays of moving colored lights—
in their paintings by using complementary and contrasting colors to create the optical effect of movement. Macdonald-Wright's *"Conception." Synchromy*
(fig. 16) is a mass of abstract, dynamic color forms that
appear to melt into one another like the shifting tints
in a color-music display. These artists looked beyond
the confines of easel painting to create a dynamic,
musical visual form. As early as 1912 Russell was planning a kinetic light machine that would make patterns
in colored light over time, just as a musical instrument
uses sound over time.

This concept of visual music as color and form in
motion found an audience in the popular culture.
Performances of an instrument called the color organ
attracted the interest of artists and the public alike.

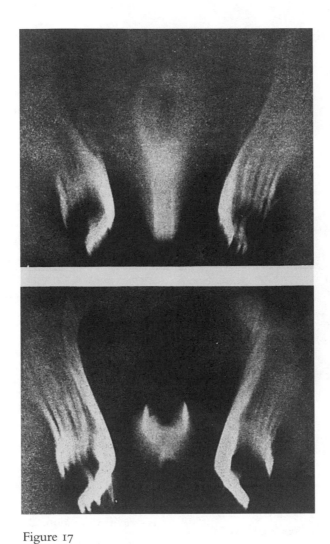

Figure 17

Francis Brugière, photo-
graph of images produced
by Thomas Wilfred's color
organ, 1922 (reproduced in
Stark Young, "The Color
Organ," *Theatre Arts* 6, no.
1, January 1922, 24).

Figure 18

Georgia O'Keeffe, *Blue and Green Music,* 1919. Oil on canvas, 23 × 19 in. (58.4 × 48.3 cm). Art Institute of Chicago (Alfred Stieglitz Collection, gift of Georgia O'Keeffe, 1969.835. Photograph © 1994, The Art Institute of Chicago. All rights reserved. © 1997 The Georgia O'Keeffe Foundation/Artists Rights Society [ARS], New York).

These concerts consisted of displays, called "color music," that combined color and light with the musical elements of time and movement. At least two versions of this machine were designed, by Thomas Wilfred and A. Wallace Rimington, who built upon late nineteenth-century experiments with light and color. The performer played abstract patterns of colored light, projected on a screen, by pressing keys identified with specific colors (fig. 17); this color organ did not produce any sound, but was sometimes accompanied by piano music or an orchestra. Rimington first demonstrated his color organ in 1895 in London and later published his theories in *Colour Music—The Art of Mobile Colour* (1911). *The Literary Digest* publicized his invention in a June 1913 article, making his ideas known in the United States. New York concert-goers witnessed other performances that showcased color music. On March 20, 1915, the first complete production of Alexander Scriabin's experimental *Prometheus: The Poem of Fire* (1908–10), a combination of orchestral music and projected displays of color, was staged in New York—an event that received a great deal of press attention and stimulated further color-music experiments.[45]

For the Synchromists, movement from one tone to the next and the resulting passage of time were key elements in music that they strove to incorporate in visual art. Indeed, for many early modernists concerned with the relationship of art to music, dynamism, rhythm, and optical motion were central concepts. Repeated curves and swirling lines in Max Weber's *Interior with Music* (1915) create a sense of motion. According to the painter, this work visualized the movement of sound in space: "There are moments when our senses seem to take on the functions of each other. To hear is to see, to see is to touch, and so it seems that the audible tones of music float and interlace or blurr [*sic*] in space as do volumes of smoke or even vapors or aromas. Here is an expression of a conception of music as it wafts in space and

Figure 19

Max Weber, *Interior of the Fourth Dimension,* 1913. Oil on canvas, 29¾ × 39½ in. (75.6 × 100.3 cm). Washington, D.C., © 1995 Board of Trustees, the National Gallery of Art (gift, partial and promised, of Natalie Davis Spingarn in memory of Linda R. Miller and in honor of the 50th Anniversary of the National Gallery of Art).

is encased or seized in rhythmic architectural contour."[46] Georgia O'Keeffe's 1919 abstract music paintings also presented motion and energy as key elements.[47] In *Blue and Green Music* (fig. 18), curves rise upward and outward from the lower right, while diagonals and curves ripple like sound waves. Patterns on the canvas evoke the movement of music.

Such were the ideas circulating in avant-garde culture in the early 1910s. Marin's use of the phrase *great music* to describe his experience of New York and his cityscapes intersected with these notions— Bergsonian *durée,* the visual representation of time, dynamism, and movement. In the context of such ideas we can read not only the subject of Marin's cityscapes as a great music, but his painterly style itself: rhythmic, linear, agitated. While Marin's musical works predated many of the paintings of the Synchromists,

Weber, and O'Keeffe, like them he perceived a connection between music and dynamism and informed his painting with the musical quality of motion. Unlike the Synchromists and O'Keeffe, however, Marin never produced completely abstract music paintings; instead, he used music to represent his idea of the city.

Marin was not alone in seeing the city as musical. His image of New York as a great music parallels Weber's writings about the fourth dimension and the Brooklyn Bridge. In a 1910 essay Weber characterized the fourth dimension as the subjective perception of reality or the "sense of space magnitude" in and around objects that could arouse the imagination and stir the emotions. For him, this state was comparable to an invisible phenomenon—to "color and depth in musical sound."[48] Weber portrayed this musical fourth dimension in his cityscapes: in *Interior of the Fourth*

Figure 20

Abraham Walkowitz,
*Metropolis No. 2,* 1923.
Watercolor on paper, 29¾
× 21¾ in. (75.6 × 55.3 cm).
Washington, D.C.,
Hirshhorn Museum and
Sculpture Garden,
Smithsonian Institution
(gift of Joseph H.
Hirshhorn, 1966.
Photograph by Lee
Stalsworth).

*Dimension* (fig. 19) he painted New York's port and architecture as a network of interpenetrating transparent planes like those in *Interior with Music*. In a 1912 essay on the Brooklyn Bridge, he personified the urban environment:

> This morning I was on the old Bridge of this New York. Midst din, crash, outwearing, outliving of its iron and steel muscles and sinews, I stood and gazed at the millions of cubes upon billions of cubes pile upon pile, higher and higher.... Lulled into calm and meditation (I gazed) by the rhythmic music of vision (sight) I gazed and thought of this pile throbbing, boiling, seething, as a pile after destruction, and this noise and dynamic force created in me a peace the opposite of itself.[49]

Like Marin, Weber perceived the city as a living organism, full of power, rhythm, energy, and clashing forces; and both artists understood this dynamism, this invisible fourth dimension, as musical.

Abraham Walkowitz, a contemporary of Marin and Weber, also wrote about New York's musicality and transformed the city's skyscrapers and rushing crowds into "symphonies of line" and "improvisations" in his paintings. Like his modernist colleagues in both the United States and Europe, Walkowitz sought to express the spirit of objective reality and to produce an art based on emotion. He explained the undated drawing *Two Blind Men Looking at New York* as "the equivalent of what one feels going through from the Battery to Times Square, showing the buildings each saying 'I must be higher,' while a suggestion of airplanes hovers overhead and the people crowd like mosquitoes in the streets below."[50] His fragmented, non-naturalistic cityscapes *Metropolis No. 2* and *New York Improvisation* (figs. 20, 21) express the frantic rhythm and architectural magnitude of New York.

Like Marin, Walkowitz described his cityscapes and the spirit of New York in musical terms. He wrote of the city's inhabitants as "the human symphony, the

Figure 21

Abraham Walkowitz, *New York Improvisation,* 1915. Watercolor and charcoal on paper, 23 × 16⅛ in. (58.4 × 41 cm). Washington, D.C., Hirshhorn Museum and Sculpture Garden, Smithsonian Institution (gift of Joseph H. Hirshhorn, 1972. Photograph by Lee Stalsworth).

dark, the light, the big, the small."[51] His notebooks contain comments that mingle the musical with the visual:

> —1917—symphonic summations—abstract—tinkle of blues, yellows—flashes of scarlet—chinese breadth and precision of line—titanic majesty of city scenes— —park scenes—like master violinist—vibrates with life[52]

The titles of many of his cityscapes use musical terms. In the 1940s he wrote a book entitled *Improvisations of New York: A Symphony in Lines;* in the introduction Konrad Bercovici wrote, "Walkowitz's paintings and drawings are the only ones that have captured the spirit, the life, the music, and the captiousness, the massive coquetry of the giant of all giants we call New York."[53]

Along with Weber and Walkowitz, Marin used musical language to come to terms with the experience of the modern city. In the early twentieth century, music was understood as abstract, dynamic, full of motion, a metaphor for underlying reality or spirit, Bergson's *durée*—qualities that informed Marin's explanations and perceptions of the city and his own cityscapes. Curves, diagonals, and loose, gestural washes in *Woolworth Building (The Dance)* and *Movement, Fifth Avenue* (figs. 5, 10) signified the energetic spirit, the great music, of New York. Looking beyond appearances and dematerializing the metropolis, Marin constructed an urban vision that was romantic and celebratory, erasing surface dirt and ignoring social problems. To see the city as musical— as immaterial, as an art form—was to define this environment benignly, as contained, balanced, and ordered. In fact, according to Marin the goal of his 1911–13 cityscapes was to picture the invisible forces of the metropolis and thereby to balance them: "Within these frames must then be a balance a controlling of these warring pushing pulling forms."[54] The musical language that the painter used in his cityscapes was a tool to contain and structure the chaotic modern experience of the city, for the artist as well as for his viewers. The notion of the great music of the city that Marin presented in his paintings in turn shaped perceptions of New York itself, offering something beyond the visible city—the music or spirit of New York that was equated with an American identity.

## Marin's Musical City and National Identity

Some of Walkowitz's cityscape titles combined musical and patriotic language, as in *I Glorify New York: A Symphony in Lines* (c. 1912).[55] New York, the quintessential modern city, stood for the whole of America. Marin's musical cityscapes were also tied to the issue of national identity. He painted his 1911–13 watercolors of New York at a time when the Stieglitz circle was just beginning to discuss the formation of American identity as part of its mission, and Marin's works contributed to identifying nationalism in modernist terms. Many viewers certainly would have read the subject matter of these watercolors—New York's streets and skyscrapers—as American; furthermore, the musical language that Marin and his associates used to discuss his art also constituted these images as native expressions. The musicality of these New York images—their energy, restlessness, dynamism—was recognized by contemporary critics as characteristically American, while the language that Marin used to explain these works—power, force, great music— intersected with nationalist discourses of the period. This urban music, then, as much as the architectural icons of the Woolworth Building and the Brooklyn Bridge, defined the modernity and Americanism of Marin's art.

The search for an indigenous artistic and cultural expression has been an ongoing, highly self-conscious concern in the history of the visual arts in the United

States, assuming a different complexion in each historical period. Identifying Americanism, or an American tradition in the arts, however, is not a simple task. Americanism is not something abstract or reified; rather, notions of national identity are invented or developed under specific historical and social circumstances and are therefore subject to constant change. Artists and critics have debated, defined, and redefined what qualities and what aesthetic traditions are typically American. Moreover, just as nations create sanctioned histories to give meaning and shape to the present and future, artists invent traditions to endow their works with social and cultural relevance.[56]

The period between the turn of the century and World War II was one of cultural and social crisis in which a stable notion of national identity was both greatly desired and anxiously questioned. Marin's patron Alfred Stieglitz was an active and influential participant in this process of identity formation. He had initially founded Gallery 291 to exhibit photography as fine art and to present European avant-garde art to the New York public; these goals were hardly nationalistic. In the early 1910s, however, he began to exhibit the emerging American modernists at his gallery and in the later part of the decade he made a commitment to support only American artists. The European artists Francis Picabia and Marcel Duchamp and the critic and writer Waldo Frank encouraged Stieglitz to support native modernism. By 1916 an observer could remark that Stieglitz's goal as both photographer and art patron was the promotion of an indigenous expression: "The real American life is still unexpressed. America remains to be discovered. Stieglitz wanted to work this miracle."[57] Cultural nationalism clearly became much more central to Stieglitz's agenda in the 1920s and 1930s, as it did in the New York art world generally. In 1923, for example, he wrote to encourage Paul Rosenfeld to complete his book *Port of New York:*

Yes, you have struck it—why it's so important: America without that damned French flavor!—It has made me sick all these years. No one respects France [more] than I do. But when the world is to be France I strenuously hate the idea quite as much as if the world were to be made "American" or "Prussian." I'm glad you have made the discovery for yourself,—That's why I continued my fight single-handed at 291—That's why I'm really fighting for Georgia [O'Keeffe]. She is American. So is Marin. So am I. Of course by American I mean something much more than is usually understood—if anything is usually understood at all! . . . But there is an America. Are we only a marked down bargain day remnant of Europe?—Haven't we any of our own courage in matters "aesthetic"? Well, you are on the true track and there is fun ahead.[58]

Stieglitz's nationalist conversion was part of a larger aesthetic and cultural transformation.[59] National identity became a recurrent concern in the art criticism of the 1910s and was at the center of commentaries on two major exhibitions at this time. The 1913 New York Armory Show, which brought European modernism crashing onto the American scene, not only forced the public's attention to the new styles but also prompted a debate about American modernism.[60] Where, critics wondered, were the native equivalents of Picasso and Picabia? This exhibition sharpened American artists' already strong sense of inferiority to Europe.[61] They fought back in 1916 with the Forum Exhibition in New York. This show's organizers, which included Christian Brinton, Robert Henri, Stieglitz, John Weichsel, and Willard Huntington Wright, brought together 193 works by contemporary American artists to spark interest in native modernism and to draw focus away from the European brand.[62] Yet, for all their efforts, they could not deny that the work of these artists depended on foreign sources. How could modernists work in a European-originated style and still be American? This was the dilemma for the American avant garde: how to define a national identity in an art based on the European models of Cubism and Expressionism.

Artists, writers, and critics adopted numerous strategies to give their efforts, however foreign in source, an American stamp. Some looked to the past, singling out native qualities in earlier artists and linking their own works with this tradition. Founded in 1916 by James Oppenheim, Waldo Frank, and Van Wyck Brooks, the magazine *The Seven Arts* called for an art directly related to American life and independent of European models; it promoted the concept of a "usable past," a tradition in the arts on which to build a "new Americanism."[63] In his essays and books Brooks presented the nineteenth-century writings of Edgar Allan Poe, Nathaniel Hawthorne, Ralph Waldo Emerson, Henry David Thoreau, and Walt Whitman as the material of the usable past. For him, these writers formed a tradition of individualism and anticommercialism, and both this tradition and these qualities provided a model for contemporary artists. Similarly, Paul Rosenfeld, also a *Seven Arts* contributor, saw the true American artist as a composite of Emerson's American scholar and Whitman's poet, whose main duty was to beat out the "rhythms of his age."[64]

While defining a usable past and an American tradition was one aspect of cultural nationalism, the definition of a usable present was another. Important in the cultural nationalist campaign was the packaging of certain aspects of modern American life as distinctive and unique. This task was taken up in the pages of the little magazines. In *291* Marius de Zayas noted: "In politics, in industry, in science, in commerce, in finance, in the popular theatre, in architecture, in sport, in dress—the American has known how to get rid of European prejudices and has created his own laws in accordance with his own customs. But he has found himself powerless to do the same in art or in literature."[65] Writers and artists promoted popular art and commercial and technological inventions—objects ironically "discovered" and validated by Europeans—as sources and models for an indigenous art. Robert Coady's short-lived magazine *The Soil* (1916–17) championed not only modern and African art but vernacular culture as expressive and representative of the nation.[66] The journal's five issues were filled with articles on manifestations of this culture—Charlie Chaplin, Bert Williams, the art of window dressing and prestidigitation, the Nick Carter serial, the ball field, the prize ring. Indebted to *The Soil, Broom* (1921–24) examined what its writers considered the most significant American cultural products—popular art forms such as movies and bill posters—and emphasized the importance of American society and culture to twentieth-century artists. In "The Great American Bill-poster," Matthew Josephson directed American artists to look away from "approved European methods" in creating art and instead to "plunge hardily into that effervescent revolving cacophonous milieu . . . , where Billposters enunciate their wisdom, the Cinema transports us, the newspapers intone their gaudy jargon; where athletes play upon the frenetic passions of baseball crowds, and sky-scrapers rise lyrically to the exotic rhythm of jazz bands."[67]

Like many of his contemporaries, Marin wished to create an art expressive of modern America. After his 1910 European trip the painter remained in the United States for the rest of his life, inspired by the American city and landscape and constructing, with Stieglitz's assistance, an image of himself as a native painter. He declared in 1911, "I feel the place for an American to work is in America and I am going to stay there."[68] In the 1920s and 1930s he wrote extensively of his commitment to an indigenous art. He advised young painters, "Yes you may be Americans that and nothing else and if you are not just that—that is if you are still close to Europe—well let's hope your children may."[69] For him, simply painting so-called American subjects did not produce a native art: "I do have scorn for those who just by giving the American locale—hoist themselves upon us as Artists—just because they use the—American locale."[70] An indigenous art must, he felt, be compounded of an American subject and something less easy to describe, an American sensibility. The nationalist content, or intention, of Marin's 1911–13 cityscapes, however, is difficult to determine. At this time, Stieglitz's nationalist program was still in formation; Marin's writings are not a useful guide, since many of his statements about Americanism date from the 1920s or later. How important was national identity in Marin's early art? Did critics see his early cityscapes as explicitly American? Did the painter's writings about them shape perceptions of his art as nationalistic?

Despite his later claim that subject was not a defining feature of national identity, it was by painting such themes as the city, the skyscraper, and the landscape—themes contemporary critics labeled American—that Marin gained an identity as an native artist. If his style was "still close to Europe," both he and Stieglitz sought to distance his art from such foreign associations. He identified himself as an American artist not only by painting native scenes but by expressing his personal response to such locales: he cultivated an Americanism by painting the modern city through his own subjectivity. Since he was American, so too would his art be—or so he believed.[71] Marin's focus on individuality and feeling as key to an American identity was self-serving: the emphasis on these qualities in his paintings masked the European sources of his style.

The art historian Timothy Robert Rodgers has analyzed the early aesthetics of the Stieglitz circle:

"Ideal," "truth," "spiritual," etc., had no fixed meaning when applied to art. . . . Consequently, writers and artists often used this terminology simply to substantiate their activities and artistic prejudices. . . . For

American artists such as Marin, these notions allowed them to avoid analytical thought and systematic procedures in their attempt to come to terms with European art, while sheltering from criticism their art of imitation.[72]

*Musical* might be added to this list of vague terms. Among its many and fluid meanings, Marin's term *great music* was associated with Americanism, with urban dynamism—a quality increasingly marked as both modern and American by contemporary critics. By painting the city in an energetic manner, Marin gave his art—perhaps unwittingly—a native stamp.

American critics played an important role in this process. Themselves having a vested interest in identifying an American style, they were at some pains to distinguish Marin's energy and rhythms as peculiarly indigenous. They immediately wrote about his cityscapes both as expressive of the new America and as musical, clearly taking their cue from the painter's own 1913 catalog essay. J. Nilsen Lauvrik of the *Boston Transcript* commented on Marin's 1911–13 cityscapes: "The chaotic hurly-burly of New York is given a pictorial rendering . . . one gains a powerful impression of this city of amazingly tall towers, of gigantic structures towering above puny ones and of the rush and go that constitutes the tumultuous pulse beat of New York."[73] J. Edgar Chamberlain saw this energy as musical:

And the Woolworth Building studies are not intended as records of fact. Did you ever brood over this great hastening metropolis, with all its peoples blown everyday on a hurricane of money-making impulse, until it seemed to you that the whole city, skyscrapers and all, had joined in a mad dance of eager life? . . . Mr. Marin has done this in these sketches. . . . Then, in another sketch, the great building seems to begin to join the dance in which all New York is swinging away.[74]

In avant-garde circles New York was singled out as particularly representative of modern America. As early as 1903 Sadakichi Hartmann had described the Flatiron Building as "typically American in conception as well as execution," while Stieglitz wrote of it as the "bow of a monster ocean steamer—a picture of a new America in the making."[75] A contemporary article in *Current Opinion* presented the skyscraper and "Negro Song" as indigenous American art products. Picabia considered New York's skyscrapers expressive of modernity, as did art and cultural journals of the 1910s, typified in Arthur Cravan's 1916 poem, "New York":

New York! New York! I should like to inhabit you!

I see there science married

To industry

In an audacious modernity,

And in the palaces,

Globes,

Dazzling to the retina.

By their ultraviolet rays;

The American telephone,

And the softness

Of elevators . . .[76]

For Waldo Frank New York's skyscrapers and fast pace represented the conflicting forces of materialism and spirituality: the inhabitants—the business-minded New Yorkers—lacked a spiritual life, while the city's buildings (material form) embodied dynamic America (its spirit). He wrote in *Our America:* "New York is a resplendent city. Its high white towers are arrows of will: its streets are the plowings of passionate desire. A lofty, arrogant, lustful city, beaten through by an iron rhythm."[77] This iron rhythm, or urban vitality, was equated with the national spirit. In 1925 a critic wrote of the American spirit as "restless, centrifugal, perilously poised," and located it in urban skyscrapers and jazz music.[78]

In the context of such ideas it was logical that critics and viewers should read Marin's cityscapes as specifically American, not merely modernist. The tendency to view art in nationalist terms was increasing everywhere, as the modernist style was associated with the progressive and competitive energies of nations. The "great forces at work," "great movements," the "warring of the great and the small," "these powers" that Marin described in his 1913 catalog essay both destroyed and created, and had their parallels in European movements, also intensely conscious of national identity. In 1912 Benjamin de Casseres wrote of the new art as a "healthy anarchic spirit," embodied in the works of the German composer Richard Wagner: "It is a glorious age and a glorious anarchic world of color, motion vibration and scintillating creative-destructiveness!" The critic presented an image of the universe much like Marin's: "A universe that wavers and totters and flows and blends, that melts and reappears eternally."[79] The Italian Futurists used a similar language of anarchic, rebellious energy—a language that was intensely nationalistic and that would inform their fascist agenda in the years ahead.[80] Marin may or may not have intended his work to assume such nationalistic inflections; in the context of the ideas circulating in the Stieglitz circle it undoubtedly did. His representation of New York's dynamic forces formed an image of the city as the heart of a new world in creation, a modern America. Marin used a vocabulary of power—the power of the city, a power associated with modernity—and envisioned it not as destructive but aesthetic: it was music. His 1911–13 cityscapes and 1913 catalog essay were infused with the emerging cultural nationalism of the time. His subject matter—the skyscrapers, the new New York— became the icons of modern America, while the great music of the city took on an American identity in its connection to native characteristics, nationalist terminology, and eventually the unique American musical product, jazz.

*From Great Music to Noise Music and Jazz*

The nexus of New York, music, and nationalism continued in Marin's works in the 1920s and 1930s. In his writings he continued to use musical language to describe the city. He marveled at the varied materials and buildings of New York, with its "lights brilliant noises startling and hard   pace setting   in all directions—through-wires—people movements." Contemporary life overwhelmed the senses with "the eye with so much to see and the ear to hear—things happening most weirdly upside down." For him, "the seeing eye and the hearing ear become attuned then comes expression/taut, taut/loose and taut/electric/staccato."[81]

Marin's later cityscapes approximate this description of New York. In *Lower Manhattan (Composing Derived from the Top of the Woolworth)* (fig. 22) the yellow sun at bottom center radiates from the compositional midpoint, and the buildings seem to explode outward from it in a staccato rhythm of broken black lines. *Broadway Night* (plate 2) illustrates the metropolitan center as an amalgam of light, noise, and jazz: people and automobiles jostle in the foreground as numbers, signs, and theater marquees flash invitingly; dazzling reds, yellows, greens, and blues create an optical pulse, and zigzags and diagonals add to this dynamism. Like his earlier works, these cityscapes embody visual dynamism and convey the experience of the modern urban environment, with its myriad

Figure 22

John Marin, *Lower Manhattan (Composing Derived from the Top of the Woolworth)*, 1922. Watercolor and charcoal with paper cutout attached with thread, on paper, 21⅝ × 26⅞ in. (54.9 × 68.3 cm). New York, Museum of Modern Art (acquired through the Lillie P. Bliss Bequest. Photograph © 1995 The Museum of Modern Art, New York. Courtesy of the John Marin Estate/Kennedy Galleries, New York).

noises and sounds, as overwhelming. By the 1920s new theaters and bars along Broadway and in Harlem brought the sounds of popular music into the heart of the city. Marin described New York as "the land of Jaz—Lights and movies—the land of the money spenders" and commented: "Yesterday I heard a bird singing—Well I might go down in Africa and hear a—lion roar—down the street—the honk of an automobile down to the city—a jaz band."[82]

While it is unclear just what kind of music Marin had in mind when he adopted the term *music* to describe his early cityscapes, his use of music in later art and writings derived from a specific form: the new urban sound of jazz.[83] Jazz drew on the "noise music" of the city, the aestheticized urban cacophony associated with modernity and Americanness. Like Marin, art musicians turned to the city, specifically its noises and machine sounds, to create a new modern music. Ragtime and jazz often included effects that imitated the sounds of urban, mechanized life: blaring car horns, rattling streetcars and trains, grinding gears. Like modernist painting, the new music both absorbed and challenged the lessons of classical traditions. For listeners these popular musical forms, with their fast rhythms, syncopations, irregularity, and dominant percussion, matched the hurried pace and dynamism of modern life.[84] For visual artists the music of the city helped define their art as urban, modern, and American and shaped the construction of a national identity.

Life in ancient times was silent. In the nineteenth century, with the invention of machines, Noise was born. Today Noise is triumphant, and reigns supreme over the senses of men. . . . Every manifestation of life is accompanied by noise. Noise is therefore familiar to our ears and has the power to remind us immediately of life itself.

Luigi Russolo, 1913

New York . . . Clamorous with lights, strident with sounds—that's Broadway, the White Way. . . . It is an immense kaleidoscope—everything is hyperbolic, cyclopic, fantastic. . . . And the multicolored lights of the billboards create at night a new hymn of praise. Far away on the horizon, they radiate a silvery, daybreak clangor, or ring out in deep tones the hour of royal sunset. . . . A constant roar from the subterranean depths of the sleepless city, marking its deep breath and rhythm, is a ceaseless commentary and setting for this poem.

Joseph Stella, n.d.

# 2. PAINTING SOUND, DISCOVERING AMERICA

## JOSEPH STELLA, THE NEW ART, AND NOISE MUSIC

New kinds of sounds transformed cities in early twentieth-century America: machines screeched, the hundred languages and musics of immigrant communities clashed one with another, and popular music flooded from the doorways of cafés and clubs. Henry W. Nevinson, in the *Atlantic Monthly,* remarked on this cacophony: "Noise . . . is a modern creation. . . . In the last fifty years, what an immense advance man had made upon those primitive sounds. Think of the express train as it yells and roars. . . . Think of a cotton mill, a printing press, an iron foundry!"[1] To contain and order this noise, commentators used the familiar language and structure of music. At the turn of the century the writer Henry Blake Fuller, for instance, compared Chicago's "downtown racket" to "the music of a battle hymn," while the critic Sadakichi Hartmann described New York as having a "pernicious habit of industry, yelling and writhing," a "madd'ning roar," and "much brass and tympani."[2] The German composer Kurt Weill imagined the myriad languages of the New York immigrant neighborhoods as operatic.[3]

Noise was transformed and normalized in other ways. As a pervasive part of the modern scene, it became a subject for musicians, writers, and visual artists. Ordinary sounds ornamented musical compositions, as did the steam whistles and clattering typewriter scripted into Erik Satie's *Parade* (1917); listening to mechanical sounds, composers such as Edgard Varèse and, later, John Cage came to redefine music and created novel musical instruments. These composers were attracted to the urban cacophony because its random, dissonant sounds challenged long-held notions of Western art music. They rejected academic conventions and concepts of beauty as inconsistent and inadequate to express modern experience.

Like their counterparts in music, early twentieth-century painters rebelled against artistic conventions and rejected the standardized art of the academy—both the classicism and the academic realism popular at the turn of the century. Modernist painters desired to experience and communicate an intense "real life" to counter the sense of unreality imposed by the routines of modern life and restrictive, normative culture.[4] Many artists found revitalization in the expressive distortions and liberated color and brushwork of Fauvism, Expressionism, and Cubism. This new visual language was able to signify intense feeling; some artists used their newfound emotional freedom to describe the modern city of skyscrapers, immigrant working-class neighborhoods, and centers of the new leisure culture, such as Broadway. For many artists, representing the simultaneity of modern life required that they find a way to picture its new sounds. A 1912 article in the *Nation* proposed that painting sound would be the art of the future,[5] and numerous American painters took up this challenge to "illustrate" noise in their representations of the contemporary scene. Arthur Dove transmuted the whistles and shrieks of cogs and sprockets into metallic paint and yellows, reds, and blues in *Factory Music* (1923); Charles Demuth overlaid fragmented forms,

diagonals, and fire-engine reds in *I Saw the Figure Five in Gold* (fig. 23) to convey the confusion of the howling sirens, gongs, and rumbling wheels described in William Carlos Williams's 1921 poem "The Great Figure."[6]

Painting the noise of the city—in short, its music—became a concern for another American modernist: Joseph Stella (1877–1946). An amateur musician, Stella produced various types of music paintings throughout his career.[7] In *Der Rosenkavalier* (1913–14; fig. 24) the artist transformed a specific contemporary musical score into a kaleidoscope of brilliant colors and shattered forms; later, in *Tropical Sonata* (1920–21), he used a more general musical title to emphasize the decorativeness of a landscape image. Connections among the arts and senses informed Stella's cityscapes too. He created synaesthetic visions of the modern metropolis, translating the sounds in and around New York—especially those he heard at the Brooklyn Bridge—into visual form. Both historical and contemporary sources shaped his musical metropolis. He adopted conventions to represent sound and music from the European Futurists and the Cubists, especially Francis Picabia. Futurist musicians considered urban noise—from clattering streetcars to pounding machinery—musical, and writers associated with the movement encouraged visual artists to paint these sounds into their multisensual urban images. For these painters machinery, technology, and their sounds embodied modernity.

For modernists like Stella, painting the city and its music also became part of their quest to identify their art as modern and American. As the art historian Anna C. Chave has argued, the greatest dilemma for American artists of the time was how to formulate "an indigenous mode of expression, a new art for the New World."[8] Although hardly native or American, Futurism and Cubism offered Stella a way to value the modernity of American culture. Just as the Stieglitz circle painters and their supporters constructed

Figure 23

Charles Demuth, *I Saw the Figure Five in Gold,* 1928. Oil on composition board, 36 × 29¾ in. (91.4 × 75.6 cm). New York, Metropolitan Museum of Art (Alfred Stieglitz Collection, 1949, 49.59.1. All rights reserved).

Figure 24

Joseph Stella, *Der Rosen-kavalier,* 1913–14. Oil on canvas, 24 × 30 in. (76.2 × 61 cm). New York, Whitney Museum of American Art (gift of George F. Of, 52.39. © 1995 Whitney Museum of American Art).

their own history of American art and placed their work in that tradition, Stella identified native precursors to modernism to give his own efforts a nationalist stamp. In particular, he located his musical metropolis in an American context. His essays on New York refer to urban sounds and sights in musical terms, recalling Walt Whitman's writings. The poet's vision of the nation and the city was synaesthetic: he praised the urban scene as an appropriate subject for artists and called city noises a grand opera. Whitman was a cultural hero for Stella and an exemplar of the ideal American artist; the painter consciously emulated Whitman and associated his own art with the poet's.

Stella's image of America was also shaped by the fact that he was an immigrant discovering and, in a sense, creating a new world and identity. He wrote about his hope in the new American civilization and its arts: "My belief in the artistic future of America is not based on sentimentality or patriotism. I know what America can produce and have faith in what it will produce."[9] Stella shared this vision with another immigrant, the French-born composer Edgard Varèse. Stella's *The Voice of the City of New York Interpreted* of 1920–22 (plate 4) and Varèse's contemporary musical ode to America, *Amériques* (1918–21), presented the United States as the new world—a construct pervasive after World War I, when commentators on both sides of the Atlantic saw the nation as the new civilization and Europe as the old. Stella turned to new conceptions of painting and music, defining his art as modern and American by presenting the musical city as the embodiment of the new world.

*Visualizing Noise: Futurism, Francis Picabia, and Stella*

The Italian-born Stella immigrated to the United States in 1896 and resided with his brother on New York's Lower East Side. The following year marked the beginning of his formal art training, with study at the Art Students League and then at the New York School of Art. The Realist approach to art that defined the curriculum at these schools influenced Stella's early work and his initial vision of the city. Using this Realist lens, he saw New York in particular ways: he described its external features and largely focused on the human inhabitants, as is evident in his illustrations and drawings for the magazines *The Outlook* and *The Survey* (1905–6). An excursion to Europe from 1909 to 1912, however, changed his artistic outlook and the way he framed the urban environment. During this trip, the painter not only discovered European modernism, but in a sense also discovered modern America.

In 1909 Stella returned to Italy, visiting his native village of Muro Lucano, near Naples, as well as Rome, Florence, and Venice, and two years later arrived in Paris, where he soon learned about the new art. Stella later recalled this experience in an autobiography: "At my arrival [in Paris], Fauvism, Cubism and Futurism were in full swing. There was in the air the glamor of a battle, the holy battle raging for the assertion of a new truth. My youth plunged full in it."[10] In Paris he associated with avant-garde artists, including Henri Matisse and Pablo Picasso, became acquainted with Futurism at the February 1912 exhibition at the Bernheim-Jeune Gallery, and, together with his friend Amedeo Modigliani, may have viewed the unexhibited works of the Futurist painter Gino Severini.[11]

Stella's interest in modernism continued after his 1912 return to New York. The following year he participated in the Armory Show, which further stimulated his fascination with the new art.[12] He had ample opportunities to learn more about Futurism; although no Futurist art was exhibited in the United States until the middle of the decade,[13] numerous journals, magazines, and books printed Futurist manifestoes, beginning in 1909, when an English translation of the first manifesto, by Filippo Tommaso Marinetti, appeared in the April–July issue of *Poesia*.[14] On occasion, contemporary art books and journals mentioned Futurist music.[15] The movement, both artistic and literary, was a conscious attempt to express the energy, speed, and fragmentation of the modern world. It used some of the faceting techniques of Cubism and the multiple, repeated images of stop-action photography. For Stella, Futurism offered a new language and way of seeing that consciously opposed itself to Realism: "Futurism strives to be absolutely free of any tradition: its effort chiefly lies in creating a new sort of language apt to express the feelings and the emotions of the modern artist."[16] This art broke with tradition both stylistically and in its focus on emotions, rather than the literal rendition of physical appearances. Stella quickly embraced this new art; his writings and paintings after 1912 clearly evidence the influence of Italian Futurism.

One of Stella's initial essays in modernism, produced upon his return to New York, was a music painting—*Der Rosenkavalier*, inspired by Richard Strauss's 1911 opera of the same name (fig. 24). Its shattered forms and brilliantly colored geometric wedges mark it as Futurist. Stella used radiant colors and dynamic shapes and lines as equivalents of sound: whirling spirals and dazzling pinks, greens, and whites evoke Strauss's romantic music and the opera's sweet themes, as well as its costumes, staging, and lighting.[17] Here, the intangible forms of music helped Stella to explore a world beyond appearances and surface realities—a world of feeling.

That Stella turned to music as a means to experiment with an abstract, emotional art was not surprising. Many contemporary critics and artists characterized music as the most emotive of the arts. In his 1911 article on Rodin's *Balzac,* Sadakichi Hartmann presented music's affective power as an appropriate model for the other arts: "In our age Music is the grand source of instant inspiration—no wonder that the other arts try to exercise many of the same sensuous, emotional, and intellectual gratifications."[18] Gabrielle Buffet called for a nondecorative, nonobjective art, as emotive as music: "These works do not form any part of Decorative Art (as has been alleged) for they form a unity, wholeness, in themselves, and awaken an emotion of the same kind as that which music evokes."[19] For many American modernists, music provided a model for the visual arts not only because it was abstract but because of its expressive power. Arthur Dove gave the title *Sentimental Music* (fig. 53) to one of his early abstractions; and Georgia O'Keeffe saw a parallel between music's affective power and her own abstract paintings: "Tell me— do you like my [*Music*]—I didn't make it to music—it is just my own tune—it is something I wanted very much to tell someone—and what I wanted to express was a feeling like wonderful music gives me."[20]

The Futurists often used musical analogies to describe their painting. They expressed intense emotion through intense color: "The time has passed for our sensations in painting to be whispered. We wish them to sing and re-echo upon our canvases in deafening and triumphant flourishes."[21] Umberto Boccioni wrote that he wanted to do a series of paintings in which "color becomes a sentiment and a music in itself."[22] The Futurists formulated a lexicon for translating sound, especially noise and mechanical, urban clamor, into painted form. In his essay "The Painting of Sounds, Noises, Smells" (1913), Carlo Carrà prescribed visual signs for sounds and smells: "THE PAINTING OF SOUNDS, NOISES, AND ODOURS DENIES . . . Greys, browns . . . the pure horizontal, the pure vertical . . . The right angle . . . The cube . . . [and] WANTS . . . Reds, Reeeds that screeeeeeeam . . .

greeeeeens that shrieeeeeek . . . The dynamic arabesque . . . The sphere, the whirling ellipse . . . the spiral and all the dynamic forms which the . . . artist's genius can discover."[23] Intense color contrasts and dynamic lines and forms served as visual equivalents for sound in Luigi Russolo's *La Musica* (fig. 25). Here, brilliant greens, reds, and oranges shriek and blare from the canvas, curves imply music's flow, and resonating white circles with blue-violet edges suggest sound waves or music's vibration. In *Der Rosenkavalier* (fig. 24), one of Stella's first essays in Futurism, the intense colors and dynamic forms seem to follow Carrà's directives for painting sound.

The Futurists unequivocally embraced the new and modern. They praised the city and industrialization in visionary terms, as Marinetti, the group's spokesperson, exclaimed in his 1909 manifesto: "We shall sing of the great crowds in the excitement of labour, pleasure and rebellion; of the multicoloured and polyphonic surf of revolutions in modern capital cities . . . of the greedy stations swallowing smoking snakes; of factories suspended from clouds by their strings of smoke; of bridges leaping like gymnasts over the diabolical cutlery of sunbathed rivers."[24] Futurist manifestoes called upon artists to communicate *all* aspects of the modern experience, and painters evolved visual means for representing contemporary life in its many aspects, especially its sounds. Carrà evoked abrupt, staccato city noises in the shattered forms and short broken lines of *What the Streetcar Said to Me* (1911), while similar visual clues signal the shouts of workers in Boccioni's *The Noise of the Street Enters the House* (1911).[25]

American painters such as Stella discovered the value of their own urban environment through these European artists and found ways to make the Futurist technique their own. Just as the Futurists wrote about the "multi-coloured and polyphonic surf of revolutions in modern capital cities," Stella rhapsodized about the new polyphony of modern America that he discovered on his return from Europe: "When in 1912, I came back to New York I was thrilled to find America so rich with so many motives to be translated into a new art. Steel and electricity had created a new world. A new drama had surged from the unmerciful violation of darkness at night, by the violent blaze of electricity and a new polyphony was ringing all around with the scintillating, highly-colored lights. . . . A new architecture was created, a new perspective."[26] For Stella, the musical term *polyphony* (that is, when several voices or melodies moving independently fit together harmoniously) defined the modern urban condition, its confusion and simultaneity, its multilayered visual and aural stimuli. Stella first visualized polyphony in *Battle of Lights, Coney Island, Mardi Gras* (1913–14; fig. 26), which he began in spring 1913 as a response to the Armory Show.

Coney Island was an emblem of modernity and American culture: its amusement parks, Steeplechase Park, Luna Park, and Dreamland, brought together a mix of popular pastimes, including bathing, bands, dance halls, and vaudeville. Like African American music and dance, prize fighting, popular literature, and movies, these parks, with their egalitarian amusements and grand scale, challenged Victorian manners and combined the modern and the exotic in a peculiarly American broth.[27] Luna Park (fig. 27), for example, offered a Japanese garden, Chinese theater, wild animals, and re-creations of famous disasters, among other attractions. For one contemporary visitor, its architecture was "an enchanted, storybook land of trellises, columns, domes, minarets, lagoons, and lofty aërial flights. And everywhere was life. . . . It was a world removed—shut away from the sordid clatter and turmoil of the streets."[28] Coney Island presented an alternate reality, separate from everyday life, where social conventions were relaxed and a holiday atmosphere reigned. Yet it also replicated and packaged the confusion and chaos of modern life as entertainment. The parks provided a seaside escape from the city, yet

Figure 25

Luigi Russolo, *La Musica,* 1911–12. Oil on canvas, 86½ × 55 in. (220 × 140 cm). London, Estorik Collection.

Figure 26

Joseph Stella, *Battle of Lights, Coney Island, Mardi Gras,* 1913–14. Oil on canvas, 76 × 84 in. (193 × 213.4 cm). New Haven, Yale University Art Gallery (bequest of Dorothea Dreier to the Société Anonyme Collection).

its rides borrowed their designs from industrial and urban machinery: the Switchback Railway (forerunner of the roller coaster), the Flip-Flap Railway, and the Helter Skelter, or Human Toboggan.

The spectacle of this exotic yet modern realm drew artists, including John Sloan, George Bellows, and Stella. *Battle of Lights* describes the frenetic mood that Stella perceived in Luna Park: "I built the most intense dynamic arabesque that I could imagine in order to convey in a hectic mood the surging crowd and the revolving machines generating for the first time, not anguish and pain, but violent, dangerous pleasures. I used the intact purity of the vermilion to accentuate the carnal frenzy of the new bacchanal and all the acidity of the lemon yellow for the dazzling lights storming all around."[29] In *Battle of Lights* Stella adapts European modernism—the dynamism, geometric shapes, and brilliant colors typical of Cubism and Futurism—to evoke the experience of walking through Coney Island's Luna Park, with its electric lights, fireworks, raucous crowds, and nonstop hubbub. Commotion and confusion rule in this chaotic world: yellow dabs flicker like the electric lights of the Park's tower; curves, spirals, and circles mimic the rotating Ferris wheels and roller coasters; fragmented human figures dance and sway to music from cabarets, dance halls, and vaudeville bands; and letters from partially visible electric signboards flash in the center. We can

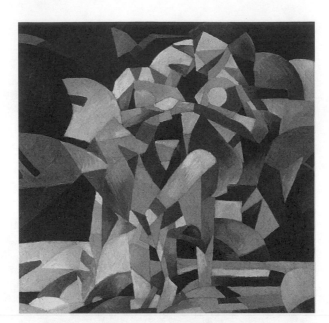

Figure 28

Francis Picabia, *Dances at the Spring,* 1912. Oil on canvas, 47½ × 47½ in. (120.7 × 120.7 cm). Philadelphia Museum of Art (Louise and Walter Arensberg Collection. © 1997 Artists Rights Society [ARS], New York/ADAGP/SPADEM, Paris).

Figure 29

Francis Picabia, *Negro Song (Chanson Negre),* 1913. Watercolor on paper, 26 × 22 in. (66.3 × 55.9 cm). New York, Metropolitan Museum of Art (Alfred Stieglitz Collection, 1949, 49.70.15. © 1997 Artists Rights Society [ARS], New York/ADAGP/SPADEM, Paris).

Plate 1

John Marin, *Woolworth Building, No. 29, 1912*. Watercolor on paper, 18⅞ × 15½ in. (48 × 39.4 cm). Washington, D.C., © 1996 Board of Trustees, the National Gallery of Art (gift of Eugene and Agnes E. Meyer. Courtesy of the John Marin Estate/ Kennedy Galleries, New York).

Plate 2

John Marin, *Broadway Night,* 1929. Watercolor on paper, 21⅜ × 26⅝ in. (54.3 × 67.6 cm). New York, Metropolitan Museum of Art (Alfred Stieglitz Collection, 1949, 49.70.143. All rights reserved. Courtesy of the John Marin Estate/Kennedy Galleries, New York).

Plate 3

Joseph Stella, *The Brooklyn Bridge,* 1919–20. Oil on canvas, 84 × 36½ in. (214.5 × 194 cm). New Haven, Yale University Art Gallery (gift of the Société Anonyme Collection).

Plate 4

Joseph Stella, *The Voice of the City of New York Interpreted,* 1920-22. Five panels, oil and tempera on canvas, 99 × 270 in. (251.5 × 685 cm), variable. Newark, N.J., Newark Museum (purchase 1937, Felix Fuld Bequest Fund. Photograph by Armen).

Plate 5

Stuart Davis, *Hot Still Scape
for Six Colors—Seventh
Avenue Style,* 1940. Oil on
canvas, 36 × 45 in. (91.4 ×
114.3 cm). Boston, Museum
of Fine Arts (gift of the
William H. Lane Foun-
dation and the M. and M.
Karolik Collection, by
exchange. © 1996/All
rights reserved. © 1996
Estate of Stuart Davis/
Licensed by VAGA, New
York).

Plate 6

Arthur Dove, *George Gershwin—Rhapsody in Blue, Part II*, 1927. Oil on metal, 20½ × 15½ in. (52 × 39.4 cm). Collection of Michael Scharf.

Plate 7

Arthur Dove, *Swing Music
(Louis Armstrong),* 1938.
Emulsion, oil, and wax on
canvas, 17½ × 26 in. (44.7 ×
65.8 cm). Art Institute of
Chicago (Alfred Stieglitz
Collection, 1949.540.
Photograph © 1996, The
Art Institute of Chicago. All
rights reserved).

Plate 8

Aaron Douglas, *Aspects of Negro Life: Song of the Towers,* 1934. Oil on canvas, 108 × 108 in. (274.3 × 274.3 cm). Art and Artifacts Division, Schomburg Center for Research in Black Culture, New York Public Library, Astor, Lenox and Tilden Foundations. (Photograph by Manu Sassoonian.)

Figure 30

Francis Picabia, *Negro Song II (Chanson Negre II)*, 1913. Watercolor on paper, 21¾ × 25¾ in. (55.8 × 66 cm). Private collection. (© 1997 Artists Rights Society [ARS], New York/ ADAGP/SPADEM, Paris).

read the swirling lines and contrasting colors in *Battle of Lights* in both visual and aural terms: as signifying the dynamic experience of being in Coney Island and as equivalents of sounds. Each mark thus has a dual and simultaneous meaning.

While the Futurists were the most direct source for Stella's style, the French painter Francis Picabia also influenced him. Picabia was a follower of Picasso's and Braque's Cubism. He brought the musical analogy to the pages of New York's newspapers and to the city's art scene. In New York in 1913 he exhibited four canvases at the Armory Show, including *Dances at the Spring* (1912; fig. 28), and became a well-known figure among the avant garde. In his published statements he rejected Realism as outdated and advocated music as a

paradigm for a new art: "Does [the composer] attempt a literal reproduction of the landscape scene, of its details of form and color? No; he expresses it in sound waves. . . . And as there are absolute sound waves, so there are absolute waves of color and form."[30] Picabia's own abstract paintings illustrated his theories and examples of his "painted music," such as *Negro Song (Chanson Negre)* and *Negro Song II (Chanson Negre II)*, were exhibited at Gallery 291 (figs. 29, 30). Picabia also praised New York as a modern, Cubo-Futurist city and, like the Futurists, wrote about it in musical terms: "I hear every language in the world spoken, the staccato of the New Yorker, the soft cadences of the Latin people, the heavy rumble of the Teuton, and the ensemble remains in my soul as the ensemble of some

great opera."[31] As Stella began painting *Battle of Lights,*
Picabia's presence in New York reaffirmed all that he
had learned in Europe about modernism: the importance of abstraction, of painting feelings and experiences (like sounds), and of the city as the ultimate
modern subject.

The shattered, wedge-shaped forms of *Battle of
Lights* show some affinity to Picabia's *Dances at the
Spring* and stronger connections between Picabia's
music paintings and Stella's art are evident in works
of the second part of the decade, when both were
associated with the circle of the collectors Walter and
Louise Arensberg in New York. Stella may have seen
Picabia's *Music is like painting* (fig. 31) at the 1917
Society of Independent Artists exhibition in New
York or at the Arensberg apartment, where the exhibition was organized. This work illustrated the theory
that painters could use line or color to translate music
into two-dimensional form: five diagonal lines stretch
from the bottom of the paper with curves springing
to their right and left; on these curves, red, orange,
yellow, green, blue, and violet color bands describe a
spectrum.[32] Stella's later musical landscapes—his
Serenades, Nocturnes, Scherzos, Sonatas—certainly
argue Picabia's influence. *Song of the Nightingale* (fig.
32) contains hazy blues, curved shapes, and a linear
network similar to that in *Music is like painting,* while
*Serenade: Christmas Fantasy (La Fontaine)* (fig. 33), with
its curves and spectrum, also recalls Picabia's work.[33]
Stella's synaesthetic visions of the Brooklyn Bridge
and New York replicate this static, ordered representation of sound as well as the mechanistic imagery
popular among artists connected with the Arensberg
circle and the New York branch of the Dada movement, such as Charles Demuth, Marius de Zayas, and
Man Ray. The painter's association with the Arens-
bergs drew him into an international community of
artists and intellectuals fascinated by the modern
metropolis and technology, including the image of
the musical city.

In the late 1910s Stella came into direct contact
with American industry and technology. In 1916 he
moved to an area of Brooklyn near the great bridge
and in 1918 depicted Pittsburgh and Bethlehem,
Pennsylvania factories as part of a *Survey* magazine
series illustrating the industrial power behind
America's contribution to World War I. This new
study of industrial issues prompted the painter to turn
to the Brooklyn Bridge as a subject. Stella was fascinated with the bridge throughout his career, producing numerous sketches and at least six paintings of it:
*The Brooklyn Bridge* (1919–20; plate 3), *The Bridge,*
from *The Voice of the City of New York Interpreted*
(1920–22; fig. 38), *American Landscape* (1929), *The
Bridge* (1936), *Brooklyn Bridge, Variations on an Old
Theme* (1939), and *The Old Bridge* (1941).

As in *Battle of Lights,* Stella painted the sights and
sounds around the Brooklyn Bridge together. His
friend August Mosca wrote, "Always [Stella] loved the
noises of the city—his studio on Fourteenth Street
was his favorite because he loved the daily and constant procession of people and autos."[34] Sound certainly entered his written representations of the
Brooklyn Bridge, even his initial impressions of it: "To
realize this towering imperative vision in all its integral possibilities, I lived days of anxiety, torture and
delight alike, trembling all over with emotion as those
railings in the midst of the bridge vibrating at the
continuous passage of the trains. . . . Upon the swarm-
ing darkness of the night, I rung all the bells of alarm
with the blaze of electricity scattered in lightnings
down the oblique cables, the dynamic pillars of my
composition."[35] He later described the noise around
the bridge in his 1929 essay, "The Brooklyn Bridge (A
Page of My Life)":

It was the time when I was awakening in my work
an echo of the oceanic polyphony (never heard
before) expressed by the steely orchestra of modern
constructions. . . .

Meanwhile the verse of Walt Whitman—soaring above as a white aeroplane of Help—was leading the sails of my Art through the blue vastity of Phantasy, while the fluid telegraph wires, trembling around, as if expecting to propagate a new musical message . . .

Seen for the first time, as a weird metallic Apparition under a metallic sky, out of proportion with the winged lightness of its arch, traced for the conjunction of WORLDS, supported by the massive dark towers dominating the surrounding tumult of the surging skyscrapers with their gothic majesty sealed in the purity of their arches, the cables, like divine messages from above, transmitted to the vibrating coils, cutting and dividing into innumerable musical spaces the nude immensity of the sky, it impressed me as the shrine containing all the efforts of the new civilization of AMERICA—the eloquent meeting point of all the forces arising in a superb assertion of their powers in APOTHEOSIS. . . .

Many nights I stood on the bridge . . . here and there lights resembling suspended falls of astral bodies or fantastic splendors of remote rites—shaken by the underground tumult of the trains in perpetual motion, like the blood in the arteries—at times, ringing as alarm in a tempest, the shrill sulphurous voice of the trolley wires—now and then strange moanings of appeals from tugboats, guessed more than seen, through the infernal recesses below.[36]

Stella perceives the bridge through all his senses: its vibrating cables, tumultuous trains, the voice of the trolley wires, the moaning of the tugboats that pass beneath it. The bridge is animated through the language of sound and motion. For Stella, musical language—the "oceanic polyphony," the "steely orchestra," the "new musical message" of the telegraph wires, musical spaces of the sky—functioned as a device to describe the mystical, overwhelming presence and power of the structure itself.

Given the centrality of sounds and musical metaphors in his essays, we may assume that Stella also tried to convey this musical experience of the bridge

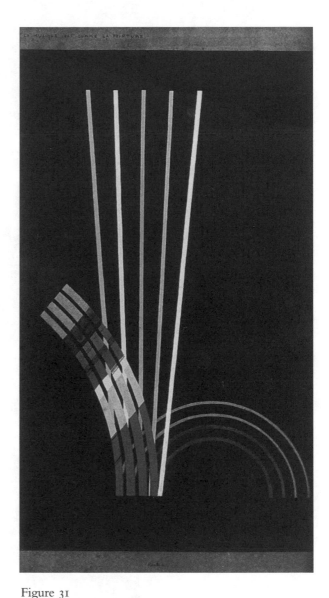

Figure 31

Francis Picabia, *Music is like painting,* 1913–17. Watercolor and gouache on Isorel, 48 × 26 in. (120 × 67 cm). Private collection. (© 1997 Artists Rights Society [ARS], New York/ ADAGP/SPADEM, Paris).

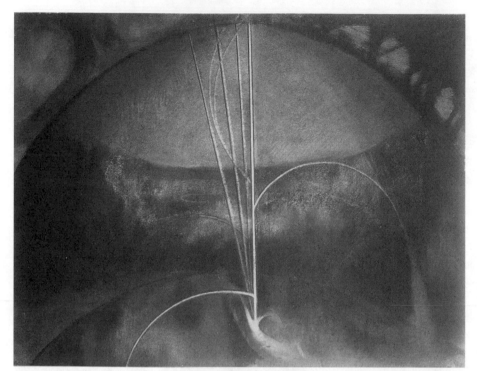

Figure 32

Joseph Stella, *Song of the Nightingale,* 1918. Pastel on paper, 18 × 23⅛ in. (45.8 × 58.6 cm). New York, Museum of Modern Art (Bertram F. and Susie Brummer Foundation Fund. Photograph © 1995 The Museum of Modern Art, New York).

Figure 33

Joseph Stella, *Serenade: Christmas Fantasy (La Fontaine),* 1937. Oil on canvas, 43⅛ × 37⅛ in. (109.6 × 94.3 cm). Washington, D.C., Hirshhorn Museum and Sculpture Garden, Smithsonian Institution (gift of Joseph H. Hirshhorn, 1966. Photograph by Lee Stalsworth).

in his visual representations. In *The Brooklyn Bridge* (plate 3) he combined views of the bridge's walkway, roadway, and underground tunnels. The literal lines of cables and steel rods and the invisible lines of light beams and directional lines crisscross the composition, multiplying perspectives, after the manner of the Cubists and Futurists. With their directives for painting sound in mind, we can read Stella's curving lines and bright colors as signifying the flow of urban noise. In particular, curves to both sides of the bottom Gothic arches and to the left of the red central arch and red oval can be seen as representations of the sounds surrounding the bridge. Stella's comments in fact suggest that he saw the visual element of line as an illustration of sound; he explained in a 1944 letter, for example, that the stringent lines of the Brooklyn Bridge's cables contrasted with the "fluctuating, swirling curves of sound and light."[37] Hazy, atmospheric colors perhaps convey the depth and resonance of sounds like the vibrating colors in Russolo's *La Musica* (fig. 25). Reds, yellows, and greens could signal traffic noise and the hum of the bridge as well as the subway "ringing as alarm" and the "shrill sulphurous voice of the trolley wires."

Noise from the modern environment also became part of *The Voice of the City of New York Interpreted* (1920–22; plate 4). Considered Stella's most ambitious work, its five panels are monumental in scale, measuring 8¼ feet high at the center point and 22½ feet wide. He described this project's evolution: "Continually I was wandering through the immense metropolis, especially at night, in search of the most salient spectacles to derive from the essentials truly representative of her physiognomy. And after a long period of obstinate waiting, while I was at the Battery, all of a sudden [there] flashed in front of me the skyscrapers, the port, the bridge with the tubes and subways."[38] These features form the individual panels of *New York Interpreted*. The central panel, *The Skyscrapers* (fig. 34), depicts Manhattan with hyperextended buildings soaring vertically and glowing with a gray light. Flanking this image are paintings of the White Way glittering with the flickering neon lights, motion, and sounds of New York's theater district (figs. 35, 36). The built-up harbor in *The Port* (fig. 37), with its overlay of cables, smokestacks, and towers, stands in contrast to the calm inlet and incoming ships. At the other end, in *The Bridge* (fig. 38), the heavy lines of the arches and four main cables of the Brooklyn Bridge frame the towers of Manhattan in the distance. Predellas of subways and tunnels visually connect the polyptych's separate panels.

The importance of sound in *The Voice of the City of New York Interpreted* is evident from the title. In addition, Stella's writings about the work relied on musical analogies. For the painter, the ordered composition paralleled a musical form: "I used the skyscrapers, the port, the bridge, and the white waves [*sic*] as the five movements in a big symphony—a symphony free in her vast resonances, but firm, mathematically precise in her development."[39] He told one critic in 1924, "The recapitulation of verticals as a 'leitmotif' [in *New York Interpreted*] has the effect of a symbol of the new battle of contemporary mankind to erect to unexplored heights."[40] Like a recurring theme in a musical composition, the vertical repeated through the five panels unifies them and reiterates the theme of the city's immense scale and verticality. Stella used a second leitmotif to link the paintings: "The larger purpose of the interpretation is to show the beating heart, the life-giving dynamo, from which the movement in the . . . panels, like the blood in the veins to the heart, permanently flow[s] back."[41]

Stella thus used music to explain the formal structure of this polyptych and his ordering of the city. He constructed other relations between his cityscapes and music; for example, between light and sound. The city, he wrote, was filled with noise and "strident with sounds," and the dazzle of myriad urban lights created a kind of visual music—the billboard's "new hymn."

Figure 34

Joseph Stella, *The Skyscrapers,* from *The Voice of the City of New York Interpreted,* 1920–22. Oil and tempera on canvas, 99¾ × 54 in. (253.4 × 137.2 cm). Newark, N.J., Newark Museum (purchase 1937, Felix Fuld Bequest Fund).

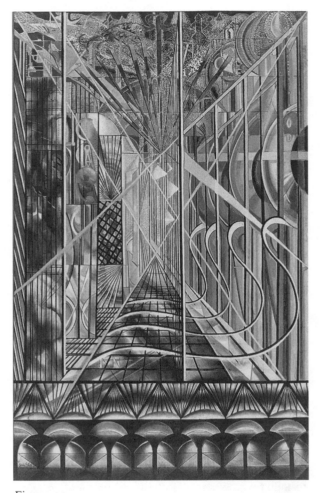

Figure 35

Joseph Stella, *White Way I,*
from *The Voice of the City of
New York Interpreted,*
1920–22. Oil and tempera
on canvas, 88½ × 54 in.
(224.8 × 137.2 cm).
Newark, N.J., Newark
Museum (purchase 1937,
Felix Fuld Bequest Fund).

Figure 36

Joseph Stella, *White Way II,*
from *The Voice of the City of
New York Interpreted,*
1920–22. Oil and tempera
on canvas, 88½ × 54 in.
(224.8 × 137.2 cm).
Newark, N.J., Newark
Museum (purchase 1937,
Felix Fuld Bequest Fund).

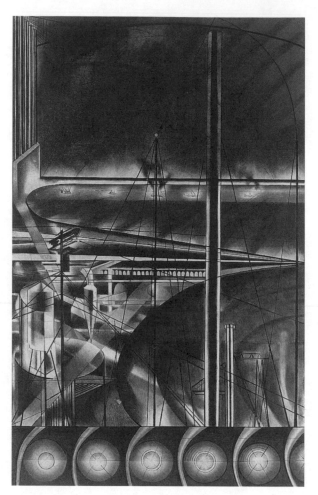

Figure 37

Joseph Stella, *The Port,*
from *The Voice of the City
of New York Interpreted,*
1920–22. Oil and tempera
on canvas, 88½ × 54 in.
(224.8 × 137.2 cm).
Newark, N.J., Newark
Museum (purchase 1937,
Felix Fuld Bequest Fund).

The city's electric lights were "delicate and harsh," "shrieking, attacking themselves," and "merging into a sudden, extravagant, grandiose polyphony, as a new creator of a new music." *New York Interpreted* embodied this new music. For Stella the White Way raged "madly in the whirlwind of the simultaneous mimic advertisement animated by the polychromatic riot of a new poliphony [*sic*]"; *White Way I* and *II* recorded "the sensations produced by the confusion of light and sound as one emerges from the subterranean passages to the street above." *The Skyscrapers* represented "an interpretation of the city's colossal skyscrapers blended together in a symphony of lights in the shape of a high vessel's prow." *The Port* was musical as well: "Here and there and upon the blue green of the whole, funnels and factories and ships ring the bell of a new religion."[42]

Stella also signified urban noise through color and line in *New York Interpreted.* As in *The Brooklyn Bridge,* we can read forms as equivalents of sounds, intersecting with other musical images. Reds and greens in the lower part of *The Skyscrapers* suggest the subway's roars and screeches. The reverberating oval in the right foreground of *The Port* seems to be an equivalent of the foghorns of the harbor; its hazy colors may refer to sound waves, as in *The Brooklyn Bridge* and Russolo's *La Musica.* S curves in *White Way I* evoke movement or the flow of sound in Times Square, just as curves suggest music in Russolo's work and Picabia's *Music is like painting;* musical notes on the vertical shafts in *White Way II* function as literal signifiers of the music of Broadway stages and clubs. Intense colors in these two paintings also indicate loud or sharp sounds, like Carrà's shrieking and noisy colors. In *The Bridge,* too, we can interpret the reds, greens, and curves as equivalents of the noises eddying around the Brooklyn Bridge.

While there are clear connections between visual forms and sounds in *Battle of Lights, The Brooklyn Bridge,* and *New York Interpreted,* Stella's interest in

Figure 38

Joseph Stella, *The Bridge,* from *The Voice of the City of New York Interpreted,* 1920–22. Oil and tempera on canvas, 88½ × 54 in. (224.8 × 137.2 cm). Newark, N.J., Newark Museum (purchase 1937, Felix Fuld Bequest Fund).

painting noise may not be reduced to mere illustration. Like many early twentieth-century artists, he adopted a nonrepresentational style to invent or conjure correspondences to experience; he wanted an art that was evocative, not illustrative. He used the new visual language of abstraction to signify living and being in the modern city—its possibilities, its multisensual overload, its dizzying perspectives. For Stella, a new art was needed to realize this new culture: "We, in this epoch, experience many sensations and emotions that the ancients could not feel. A true art is always more or less the reflection of everything that is going on during its epoch, and therefore cannot live on the crumbs of the past."[43] He adopted both the modernist language of painted forms and the literary language of essays to come to terms with the complexity of this new environment. For Stella, the musical in both paintings and prose served to explain his encounters with the modern city, including its noises and sounds.

### Noise Music and American Cultural Identity

Stella's cityscapes and writings about New York in musical terms were not an isolated phenomenon. As discussed in chapter 1, both Marin and Walkowitz represented the modern city as musical. Their musical cityscapes glorified American modernity and helped to constitute their art and identity as American, much as did Stella's operatic, polyphonic images of Coney Island, the Brooklyn Bridge, and New York.

Stella's perceptions of America were shaped not only by aesthetic conventions but by both his status as an immigrant and the historical context in which he worked. He saw a new value in this country in the late 1910s. World War I had ravaged and disrupted old-world European society; afterward, the United States played the leading role as inheritor of Western civilization. As Romain Rolland wrote: "My faith is great

in the high destinies of America. And it is clear to me that the events of today make more urgent than before that these be realized. On our old Continent, civilization is menaced. It becomes America's solemn duty to uphold the wavering torch."[44] After the war, the United States was in a position to expand industrially, whereas European countries, having borrowed heavily from the United States during the war, had few resources for modernization.[45] Modernization came to be equated with Americanization.

Like many of his contemporaries, Stella looked to the technological achievements of modern America as emblems of the new world. In the presence of the Brooklyn Bridge at night he "felt moved, as if on the threshold of a new religion or in the presence of a new DIVINITY."[46] He used old frames to see these new things. He constructed *New York Interpreted* (plate 4) as a religious icon: the five-panel polyptych with predella is modeled on the Italian altarpieces that Stella had admired in his native country, while its soaring Gothic arches and vertical structures associate modern urban forms with medieval Christian architecture.[47] For Stella, the sounds of this new religion could be heard in the bells of factories and the ships of New York harbor.[48] While the painter remained ambivalent about urbanization and technology and often wrote about its hellish dark side, like many American artists of the postwar decade he attached great hope to the machine. Stella transformed urban chaos into the symmetrical, well-ordered space of *New York Interpreted* and, in the end, sanitized the city and modernity. He also envisioned the city as musical—full of noise and sounds, operatic, polyphonic. While his visual language was European in its roots, he used the language of the new and the musical in his essays to identify his art as American, drawing from contemporary and historical sources in painting, poetry, and music.

Stella's effort to identify his art as modern and American was deliberate. As an immigrant he needed

to form an American identity, especially in the context of postwar anti-immigration fervor and prevalent
Anglo anxiety about the stability of so-called native
values. Like other early twentieth-century artists,
Stella looked to an earlier American culture for the
ancestors of his own work. In a period often characterized as antitraditional, many artists sought to establish a national tradition and often created one to
serve their own needs and vision.[49] As discussed in
chapter 1, writers for *The Seven Arts* defined and promoted a "usable past" as a basis for a "new Americanism." Walt Whitman, in particular, became the
hero and guiding force of this journal and one the
major sources of that past.[50] He taught many artists to
see America in a certain way. As Malcolm Cowley
claimed: "Before Walt Whitman America hardly existed, to him we owe the pioneers, the open spaces, in
general the poetry of square miles."[51] The poet wrote
directly about American life, sex, and emotions, called
for cultural independence from Europe, and praised
the ordinary in American life; in short, his goals were
similar to those of many modernists. Indeed, Whitman was mythologized during this time as the
"patron saint of American modernism" and seen as
the "quintessential avant-garde artist—the non-
conformist, the lonely individualist, the iconoclast, the
embattled radical, the outsider."[52]

Whitman also offered a precedent for these artists'
interest in the noises and musicality of the city. Not
only did he exalt American life through a series of
poetic songs—"Song of Myself" and "Song of the
Open Road," for instance—but music directly influenced his work. He identified this art as an important
source for poetry: "Music, in the legitimate sense of
that term, exists independently of technical music . . .
just as poetry exists independently of rhyme. . . . I
advise each and every young person early to com-
mence the study of music, and persevere in its practice
and enjoyment all their days."[53] Whitman had a passion for music: he wrote music criticism for the

Figure 39

Joseph Stella, *Portrait of Walt
Whitman,* 1920. Location
unknown.

*Brooklyn Star,* included popular ballads and arias from his beloved Italian operas in his own singing repertoire, and was an avid concert-goer. The poet's enthusiasm for opera in particular shaped his poetry. He compared *Leaves of Grass* (1855) to a grand opera and around 1859 penned an anonymous defense of "Out of the Cradle Endlessly Rocking": "Walt Whitman's method in the construction of his songs is strictly in the method of the Italian opera."[54]

Early twentieth-century artists and writers were undoubtedly aware of Whitman's interest in music through contemporary publications about the poet and through his verses. An analysis of musical analogies in Whitman's work appeared in Basil de Sélincourt's *Walt Whitman: A Critical Study* in 1914, and Louise Pound published the essay "Walt Whitman and Italian Music" in the *American Mercury* in 1925.[55] Whitman's poetry was compared to music in *The Seven Arts:* "Free verse is the merger of these values for while it has variety of rhythm and tune, as in prose, it has an undercurrent of similar beat. The pulse is there, coming at uneven intervals, but speeding up, lifting, emotionalizing the flight of the song. A good example is Whitman's 'When Lilacs Last in the Dooryard Bloom'd.' "[56] But equally important, Whitman presented common sounds as a type of music in his own writing, directing the poet—as well as the painter and musician—to embrace all sensual experience. For him the "music" of America included the city's rhythms and sounds, envisioned, for instance, in this passage from *Leaves of Grass:*

I hear all sounds as they are tuned to their uses. . . .
    sounds of the city and sounds out of the city. . . .
    sounds of the day and night; . . .
The ring of alarm-bells. . . . the cry of fire. . . . the
    whirr of swift-streaking engines and hose-carts
    with premonitory tinkles and colored lights,
The steam-whistle. . . . the solid roll of the train of
    approaching cars;

The slow-march played at night at the head of the
    association, . . .

I hear the violincello or man's heart's complaint,
And hear the keyed cornet or else the echo of sunset.
I hear the chorus . . . it is a grand-opera. . . . this
    indeed is music![57]

Whitman characterized New York as musical in his 1871 essay, "Democratic Vistas": "The splendor, picturesqueness, and oceanic amplitude and rush of these great cities . . . the tumultuous streets, Broadway, the heavy, low, musical roar, hardly ever intermitted, even at night."[58]

Whitman's musical metropolis became a model for Stella, who described the poet as his inspiration and as the creator of "oceanic polyphony."[59] Following Whitman's precedent, Stella represented the city as musical in his essays on New York and the Brooklyn Bridge: he spoke of the "new polyphony," "hymns of electric lights," the "triumphant song of a new religion," and the whining, humming, and moaning of traffic on the bridges, waterways, and roadways—a portrayal of the city that evokes Whitmanesque language. Stella had read Whitman before coming to the United States and his interest in the poet was nurtured at the New York School of Art, where his teacher, Robert Henri, often quoted *Leaves of Grass* in his classes. Henri encouraged students to embrace life with Whitman's vigor and to follow the poet's vision of America—free-thinking, individualistic, anti-materialistic.[60] Stella's continuing admiration for the poet is evidenced in his tribute, *Portrait of Walt Whitman* (fig. 39), as well as in his writings. He praised Whitman's hymn celebrating the "Redemption of Art," considering him the guardian of a "new sacred fire of inspiration" who opened up "illimited fields for future harvests" in American art.[61] He also appreciated Whitman as a forerunner of modern artists, even calling him a Futurist: "America which is so young and energetic and has the great futurist work first achieved by Walt Whitman."[62]

Stella used the term *futurist* to describe not only the Italian modernists but all antitraditionalists; by using this word, however, he linked Whitman to those European modernists who had sought a new language, thus presenting two related models for American artists.[63] But did Stella himself see these connections between the Italian Futurists and Whitman? The art historian Marianne W. Martin has argued that Whitman was a conscious intellectual source for the Italians; clearly, Marinetti's language in the *Initial Manifesto of Futurism* resonates with a Whitmanesque lushness and passion: "We shall sing of the great crowds in the excitement of labour, pleasure and rebellion; of the multicoloured and polyphonic surf of revolutions."[64] Did Stella recognize this similarity too? While the painter admitted the influence of the Italian artists on his work, he also sought an American precedent. By linking his vision of the city with Whitman's, Stella attempted to transform his art into a native expression—to mask the European old and to reveal the American new.[65]

Stella's art and writing about the city were also interpreted or read as American in other ways. His use of the phrase "new polyphony" would have been understood at the time as referring to American cultural identity, since musical terms were often used to explain the concept of multicultural America in early twentieth-century discourse. The cultural historian Werner Sollors has pointed out that "ethnic literature abounds in musical imagery, so that the notion of a multi-ethnic harmony, a polyphonic symphony, has become cliché since David Quixano's compositions in Zangwill's *Melting-Pot* and Horace Kallen's problematic definition of American civilization as an orchestration of mankind."[66] In Israel Zangwill's 1908 play *The Melting Pot,* the protagonist, David Quixano, is a composer who creates an "American symphony" inspired by the melting pot, "America as God's

Crucible, the great Melting-Pot where all the races of Europe are melting and re-forming!"[67] In response to Zangwill, Horace Kallen's essay "Democracy versus the Melting-Pot" (1915) offered a different musical model for American pluralism: "As in an orchestra every type of instrument has its specific *timbre* and *tonality* . . . ; as every type has its appropriate theme and melody in the whole symphony, so in society, each ethnic group may be the natural instrument, its temper and culture may be its theme and melody, and the harmony and dissonances and discords of them all make the symphony of civilization."[68] Even commentators across the Atlantic imagined the American melting pot in musical terms. Romain Rolland wrote:

> You have a second task—one more difficult and more remote. It is to establish from all these free-moving personalities within your States a tie that shall be as a blood-bond. Their lives are of many moods and colors. Build them into a great cathedral. Their voices are unconscious and spontaneous and discordant. Compose from them a Symphony. Think of the rich foundation of your country. It is made up of all races; it has flowed in to you from all continents. May this help you to understand the essential spirits of these peoples whose sum must be America. . . . You must make of your culture a symphony that shall in a true way express your brotherhood of individuals, or races, of cultures banded together.[69]

For this French writer, as for so many cultural critics of the time, the model for the American symphony was in Whitman's poetry.

Stella created visual images of this pluralistic, or polyphonic, America. In 1918 he produced sketches for *The Survey* illustrating the contribution of civilian workers to World War I. *The Survey*'s goal in this four-issue series (1918–19) was to show "how Slav and Italian, foreign born and native born, have worked shoulder to shoulder."[70] Stella made a drawing of this

Figure 40

Joseph Stella, *The New Race of the New World* (illustration reproduced in *The Survey* 41, November 30, 1918, 262).

ideal worker in *The New Race of the New World,* which appeared in *The Survey* on November 30, 1918 (fig. 40). This image of a single worker, however, could not evoke the complexity of multiethnic America as well as did Stella's cityscapes, whose simultaneity represented the "new polyphony" of modern America.

Stella also shared this interest in the musical city with avant-garde musicians. Just as he assimilated music into his visual metropolis, Futurist composers appropriated urban sounds into their music. The impulse to aestheticize noise and redefine art was the same in both branches of the modernist movement. Noise was a central topic of discussion for Futurist musicians, who, like the painters and poets, rebelled against the past—in their case, against the hold of the music academies and opera on the Italian music scene. They embraced the modern world and its music, as Balilla Pratella proclaimed: "All forces of nature, tamed by man through his continued scientific discoveries, must find their reflection in composition—the musical soul of the crowds, of great industrial plants, of trains, of transatlantic liners, of armored warships, of automobiles, of airplanes. This will unite the great central motives of a musical poem with the power of the machine and the victorious reign of electricity."[71] Luigi Russolo praised the pleasing sounds of the "deep, solemn breathing of a city at night":

Let us wander through a great modern city with our ears more attentive than our eyes, and distinguish the sounds of water, air, or gas in metal pipes, the purring of motors (which breathe and pulsate with an indubitable animalism), the throbbing of valves, the pounding of pistons, the screeching of gears, the clatter of streetcars on their rails, the cracking of whips, the flapping of awnings and flags. We shall amuse ourselves by orchestrating in our minds the noise of the metal shutters of store windows, the slamming of doors, the bustle and shuffle of crowds, the multitudinous uproar of railroad stations, forges, mills, printing presses, power stations, and underground railways.[72]

Inspired by modern sounds, Pratella and Russolo proposed a new music of noise, atonality, microtones, and rhythmic irregularity in their numerous manifestoes—*Il Manifesto dei musicisti futuristi* (1910), *Il Manifesto tecnico della musica futurista* (1911), *La Distruzione della quadratura* (1912), written by Pratella and edited by Marinetti, and, most important, *L'Arte dei rumori* (1913), by Russolo. Russolo predicted that the "motors and machines of industrial cities may some day be intelligently pitched, so as to make of every factory an intoxicating orchestra of noises."[73] Pratella's own musical compositions, such as *Inno alla vita, Musica futurista per orchestra* (1913), celebrated in sound the speed and machinery of the modern age: he introduced six groups of noise instruments, or *intona-rumori*—booms, whistles, whispers, screams, and other voices of men and animals—and invented new music makers, such as the *scoppiatore,* a crackler that imitated the sound of an internal combustion engine.[74]

Though the Futurist music movement was short-lived, ordinary noise found its way into much other avant-garde music: Charles Ives's *Central Park in the Dark* (1906), with its imitation car horns, subway roars, and jazz bands; Erik Satie's *Parade* (1917), with its pistol shots, rattle, steam whistles, and typewriters; Arthur Honegger's *Pacific 231* (1923), with its sound of a train leaving a railroad station; George Antheil's *Ballet mécanique* (1924), with its airplane propellers, electric bells, and motor horns; and George Gershwin's *An American in Paris* (1928), with its taxi horns.[75] For American and European composers alike, these machine sounds not only provided a shock to the ears—and an attack on romantic music and musical conventions of beauty and harmony—but also placed their work instantly as modern. While composers on both sides of the Atlantic produced this music, by the 1920s *modern* was frequently equated with *American*.[76]

Visual artists were attracted to these new sounds for similar reasons: to challenge aesthetic conventions and undermine the snobbery of high art by embracing the ordinary and the modern. But noise and machine music held appeal for visual artists not only because of its modernity but because of its semirepresentational quality. In compositions like *An American in Paris* abstract musical sounds were combined with literal sounds to create an aural portrait of the city. Artists like Stella undoubtedly saw this music as a parallel to their own efforts to fashion an art that combined real experience with the aesthetic issues of abstraction. Stella was familiar with this new music. Futurist music was much discussed in contemporary art journals, little magazines such as *Broom,* and the popular press. If he did not know these specific sources, he certainly received a musical education from his friend Varèse (fig. 41), who experimented with new sounds and noise to produce modernist, American compositions.

As a leading member of the avant garde, Varèse was committed to what he called the "liberation of sound." The French-born composer had studied at the Paris Schola Cantorum and Conservatoire but found both institutions too limiting. From 1907 to 1915 he associated with modernist writers, visual artists, and musicians in Paris and Berlin, including Guillaume Apollinaire, Auguste Rodin, Amedeo Modigliani, Robert Delaunay, Erik Satie, and Arnold Schoenberg. In December 1915 Varèse immigrated to New York, where he sought out centers of experimental art: in 1916 he met Stieglitz, frequented Gallery 291, and became an intimate of the Arensberg circle.[77] He seems to have had very few composer friends, preferring companions from the other arts, especially painting and sculpture. As he later stated, he saw the visual arts as meeting the challenge of the modern world in a way that music did not: "It is many years now since painting freed itself from the constraints of pure representation and description and from academic rules. Painters responded to the world—the completely different world—in which they found themselves, while music was still fitting itself into arbitrary patterns called forms, and following obsolete rules."[78] Varèse's admiration for the visual arts shaped his work. He described his music in highly visual terms, talking about "movement of sound masses" and their collisions and sound movements projected onto "other planes, moving at different speeds and at different angles."[79]

The musicologist Olivia Mattis has traced in detail Varèse's use of Cubism, Futurism, and Dada to frame his own thinking about a new music.[80] While he was certainly familiar with Futurism and Marinetti's writings, he felt a particular affinity for Cubism, whose focus was on spatial thinking, escape from traditional perspective (parallel to tonality in music), multiple viewpoints, and a radical subordination of subject matter to style. Varèse was also drawn to the notion of a fourth dimension, stimulated, perhaps, by Cubist experiments in simultaneity: "We actually [currently] have three dimensions in music: horizontal, vertical, and dynamic swelling or decreasing. I shall add a fourth, sound projection—the feeling that sound is leaving us with no hope of being reflected back, a feeling akin to that aroused by beams of light sent forth by a powerful searchlight—for the ear as for the eye, that sense of projection, of a journey into space."[81]

The composer Ferruccio Busoni helped Varèse to formulate his ideas about a new music and musical simultaneity. In his essay "Sketch for a New Aesthetic of Music" (1907) Busoni advocated abandoning the twelve-tone scale and program music and developing instruments to create innovative sounds, especially microtonal pitches.[82] Similarly, Varèse envisioned a revolution of new sounds created by new musical instruments. For him, music had to express its time and place: "Speed and synthesis are characteristics of our own epoch. We need twentieth century instruments to help us realize them in music."[83] He was in search of a continuum of sound, in opposition to the

discrete tones produced by traditional instruments such as the piano. Varèse turned to science and technology as well as ordinary machines found at flea markets to explain and produce his idea of spatial music and a musical continuum:

> When I was a student at the Paris Conservatoire, I came across a definition of music that was the first to satisfy me completely, suggesting as it did a new and freer conception of music. Hoene Wronsky, physicist, chemist, musicologist, and philosopher of the first part of the nineteenth century, defined music as "the corporealization of the intelligence that is in sounds." Looking back, it seems to me that it was this definition which started me thinking of music as organized sound instead of sanctified and regimented notes. I began to resent the arbitrary limitations of the tempered system, especially after reading at about the same time, Helmholtz's description of his experiments with sirens in his *Physiology of Sound.* Wanting to experiment myself, I went to the *Marché aux Puces,* where for next to nothing you could find just about anything, and picked up two small [sirens]. With these I made my first experiments in what later I called spatial music. The beautiful parabolas and hyperbolas of sound the sirens gave me and the haunting quality of the tones made me aware for the first time of the wealth of music outside the narrow limits imposed by keyboard instruments.[84]

Varèse developed these ideas after his 1915 arrival in New York in *Amériques* (1918–21), *Offrandres* (1921), *Hyperprism* (1922–23), *Octandre* (1923), and *Intégrales* (1924). In these compositions he experimented with instrumentation; he tended to avoid strings in favor of high woodwinds and brass and expanded the orchestra's percussion section. *Hyperprism,* for instance, first performed in New York in March 1923, was scored for sixteen percussion instruments, including a siren and a string drum that produced a lion's roar. Because of his interest in ordinary modern sounds, such as sirens, he was often associated with the Futurists. Although he was familiar with the Futurists' writings, he did not see himself as a noise musician and indeed criticized what he considered the Futurists' mere imitation of sounds. Varèse believed that the composer must transmute noise into organized sound, into music. Most important, he wanted to create simultaneous sound masses, or spatial music, with these new sounds and instruments. He later said: "One of the greatest assets that electronics has added to musical composition is that of metrical simultaneity. My music being based on movements of unrelated sound masses, I have long felt the need and anticipated the effect of having them move simultaneously at different speeds."[85]

Despite Varèse's attempt to move away from literal sound imitation or representation, his music still conjured up concrete images of the urban environment. Georgia O'Keeffe wrote of *Intégrales* in a letter to the composer: "It is as good as Broadway at night and that is one of my great excitements!"[86] A satirical cartoon responding to the first performance of *Hyperprism* at the Klaw Theater in New York on March 4, 1923 (fig. 42), represents Varèse's music as a cityscape, with whistles blasting, cars and trains crashing, and buildings crumbling. Paul Rosenfeld, a music critic and the composer's friend, thought that the percussive sounds of *Hyperprism* recalled "fragments and vistas of the port and the industrial landscape invested with new magic," while, on another occasion, he noted:

> Still another [reason for using percussion] is to be found in what may be termed "skyscraper mysticism." This is a feeling of the unity of life through the forms and expressions of industrial civilization, its fierce lights, piercing noises, compact and synthetic textures: a feeling of its immense tension, dynamism, ferocity. . . .
>
> Varèse in particular among composers would seem to be subject to this feeling, he is somewhat

the mystic of the sounds of sirens, horns, gongs, and whistles afloat in the air of the great industrial centers.[87]

Such descriptions of Varèse's music vividly recall images and forms in Stella's works. This connection is more than coincidental. The two artists were close friends during the years following the Armory Show and throughout the twenties, as Stella's sympathetic portrait of Varèse (fig. 41) attests.[88] Both were connected to the Arensberg circle and the New York Dadaists, and they traveled together to Paris in 1928. In a number of works painter and composer addressed similar subjects. Varèse's poem "Oblation" (1916–17), reportedly composed after an evening spent drinking with Picabia on the Brooklyn Bridge, mentions the bridge and New York skyscrapers and is nearly contemporary with Stella's painting *The Brooklyn Bridge* (plate 3). In 1921 Stella joined the administrative council of Varèse's International Composers' Guild, an organization in operation from 1921 to 1927 that staged performances of contemporary music.[89] The composer's wife, Louise, later wrote of Stella and his relation to the composer: "At that time [about 1921] our friend the Italian painter Joseph Stella was living on Fourteenth Street near our apartment. Stella and Varèse were very fond of each other, in spite of occasional breaches in their friendship due to Stella's neurotic susceptibility. . . . That spring, however, relations were extremely warm and he and Varèse were often together during my absence."[90] This friendship provided a forum for the exchange of artistic ideas.

As expatriate Europeans Stella and Varèse shared a similar aesthetic background. Both had participated in Parisian avant-garde circles in the early 1910s and had brought common interests—the city, its dynamism, engineering marvels—to their new life in New York. Louise Varèse commented: "Stella and Varèse had a kindred—a creative—passion for New York and

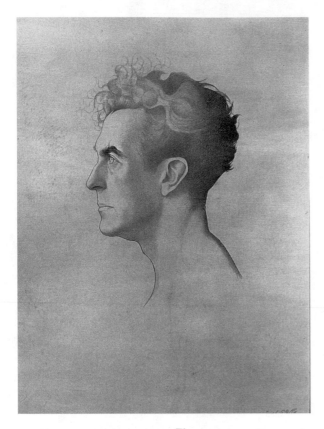

Figure 41

Joseph Stella, *Portrait of Edgard Varèse,* c. 1922. Silverpoint on paper, 22 × 16 in. (55.9 × 40.6 cm). Baltimore Museum of Art (Purchase Fund, BMA 1963.114).

Stella's five paintings, *The Skyscrapers, White Way, The Port,* a second *White Way,* and *Brooklyn Bridge,* are its magnificent multiple portrait. These are reproduced in a brochure Stella gave me."[91] Varèse, for his part, was enamored of such engineering feats as the Hoover Dam and the George Washington Bridge.[92] Both Stella and Varèse viewed technology and the American city as a world of powerful contrasts, at once spiritual and materialistic. Impressed with bridges and skyscrapers, Stella called these structures ghostly apparitions and shrines of a new religion; he described *New York Interpreted* as "highly spiritual and crudely materialistic alike."[93] Similarly, Varèse's music is simultaneously eery and haunting, metallic and shrill, reflecting his interest in the concrete worlds of science, engineering, and astronomy, as well as the ineffable realms of the fourth dimension, mysticism, and alchemy.

Both men also imagined America as the new world. While Stella painted icons of this new civilization, Varèse envisioned his own modern America through sound. His fascination with things American began while he was still in Europe: he based an early work, *Martin Pas,* on a Native American folktale, was familiar with James Fenimore Cooper's Leatherstocking tales, and praised the American inventor of the dynamophone, Thaddeus Cahill. As Olivia Mattis notes, "America represented two concepts for the composer: industrial sophistication ('the future') and the undiscovered primitive West ('the source')."[94] When Varèse first came to the United States he had acted as an ambassador and promoter of French music and culture. He soon, however, became Americanized. In 1928, when he returned to Europe, touring with the Pan-American Association of Composers, he was an advocate of American modernist music, in particular the work of the composers Charles Ives, Carl Ruggles, and Henry Cowell.

Varèse's Americanization began before this European tour, with *Amériques.* The composer's first orchestral work completed in New York, *Amériques* demonstrated his new ideas and announced his break with European music. This work is marked by an innovative use of varied sounds—the first version calling for some 142 instruments. The final rendition, which lasts about thirty-five minutes, is scored for two piccolos, three kinds of flutes, three oboes, an English horn, a heckelphone, five clarinets, three bassoons, two double bassoons, eight horns, six trumpets, five trombones, two tubas, two harps, strings, and a group of twenty-one percussion instruments including a whip, siren, and lion's-roar drum. In this work Varèse drew upon the ordinary sounds of the New York environment to create a music based on a continuum of pitch, not discrete tones. Louise Varèse explained: "He listened to the 'parabolas and hyperbolas' of the fire-engine sirens with their haunting music. . . . He now elevated one to the rank of music instrument in the score he was working on, to which he was to give the title *Amériques: Americas, New Worlds*."[95]

For Varèse, *Amériques* represented new artistic discoveries as well as his own personal exploration of America. He once referred to this work as *Americas, New Worlds,* but stressed that this piece was not intended as a literal sound picture of the noises of modern life, nor was the title "purely geographic." It was instead "symbolic of discoveries—new worlds on earth, in the sky, or in the minds of men."[96] It was an abstract interpretation of New York: "If anything, the theme is a meditative one, the impression of a foreigner as he interrogates the tremendous possibilities of this new civilization of yours. The use of strong musical effects is simply my rather vivid reaction to life as I see it, but it is the portrayal of a mood in music and not a sound picture."[97] The Cuban writer Alejo Carpentier spoke of *Amériques*'s significance to Varèse:

North America impressed [Varèse] with a sensation of vastness and extent. . . . For him, New York is neither

jazz nor "musical comedy," nor even Harlem dives. He stands apart from those ephemeral characteristics of this new world, but feels himself profoundly moved by the tragic meaning which he perceives in the implacable rhythm of its labor, in the teeming activity of the docks, in the crowds at noon, in the bustle of Wall Street. . . . *Amériques* begins to ripen. . . . He will not attempt to create a score that will convey the external or picturesque side of American life, but rather throw himself courageously into the discovery of new horizons.[98]

*Amériques,* like other Varèse compositions, became identified with the machine and urban America, especially in the post–World War I context. Rosenfeld, for instance, defined the composer as an exemplar of the "expression of the American temperament" in music:

Varèse really found himself in America and through his music he is helping America to find herself. . . . He has accomplished with the phenomena of the great modern city and the Port of New York something analogous to what Picasso has done with the visual ones, and as little in the intention of descriptivity. Like the great modern painter, Varèse has used elfin and brutal motifs produced by sirens, steam whistles, and their overtones, all the ground bass of the monster city. . . . The first of his strident, brassy, cubistic American tone poems, *Amériques*, for giant orchestra, is something of a satire on the blatancy and overgrown monstrosity of American life. . . .[99]

Noisy, urban, shrill, haunting, American—these qualities were read into both Varèse's and Stella's work. *Amériques* as a tribute to the new world parallels *New York Interpreted:* the pieces are contemporary, produced when painter and composer were particularly close. In the early twenties, as recent immigrants, both Stella and Varèse decided—perhaps even together—to celebrate their new homeland. Inspired by

**Figure 42**

Cartoon, "Edgard Varèse's
*Hyperprism,* first per-
formed at Klaw Theater,
New York, March 4, 1923"
(reproduced in Louise
Varèse, *Varèse: A Looking-
Glass Diary, 1883–1923,*
New York: W. W. Norton,
1972).

New York's rhythm, activity, and bustle, they praised
the new world in *Amériques, New York Interpreted,* and
writings on their respective works: they extolled the
city, new sounds and sights, and simultaneity of noise
and vision in the modern urban world. Although
Stella did not hear *Amériques* performed until the late
1920s,[100] he knew and responded to Varèse's themes
and theories. In a pamphlet on *New York Interpreted* he
mentions the city's "new polyphony" and "symphony
of lights"; later, in the essay "The Brooklyn Bridge (A
Page of My Life)" (1929), he discusses the "new musical message" of the telegraph wires and "innumerable
musical spaces." Varèse in turn admired *New York
Interpreted* and even planned to use—but did not—
*The Port* as the cover for the printed score of *Octandre*
(fig. 43).

Both artists formulated their initial ideas within
the European avant garde and then reconstructed
them as emblems of America, the new world. While
*New York Interpreted* still evidences the influence of
Cubo-Futurism, in it Stella largely abandoned the
energy and dynamism of his earlier *Battle of Lights,* a
more immediate response to European modernism.
*New York Interpreted* is linked iconographically to
Futurism, but in spirit is closer to the machine style
typical of post-World War I American art, as in
Georgia O'Keeffe's *City Night* (1926) or Charles
Sheeler's *Church Street El* (1920). In *Amériques* Varèse
too transformed Futurism, Cubism, and avant-garde
music into a uniquely American idiom. Though the
composer denied the influence of Futurist noise
music, like Russolo and Pratella he used new machines and modern sounds in his compositions. With
*Amériques* he made these new sounds symbolize an
American experience—new worlds, new discoveries—attempting to detach noise music from its
European source.

Painter and composer envisioned this new world in
similar ways. The strong verticality in *New York
Interpreted* parallels the vertical dimension in Varèse's

music. The composer rejected the melodic line (the horizontal) in his works in favor of an emphasis on verticality, the blending of sounds in a continuum: "The new composers have not abandoned melody . . . there is a distinct melodic line running through their work. . . . But the line in our case is often vertical and not horizontal."[101] Responding to this concept, Rosenfeld used the phrase *skyscraper chord* to describe Varèse's music.[102]

*New York Interpreted* is organized in a sort of musical structure of gradual rise, crescendo, and subsidence: the curves of *The Bridge* and diagonal inlet in *The Port* direct the viewer into the White Way on each side; the swirls of these panels meet the upward-sweeping and soaring forms of the skyscrapers in the center, the visual climax. The multiplicity, the layering and blending of forms, sounds, and sensations in *Amériques* is the aural equivalent of this formal plan.

*New York Interpreted* and *Amériques* hover between abstraction and representation: neither was intended to be descriptive or realistic, and both fragment and re-form contemporary life and experience. Both are about the boundless possibilities of modern American society, the optimism that imbued national identity after World War I. *New York Interpreted* transforms the modern city—its commerce, popular culture, and architecture, the technological wonders of electricity and iron construction—into a religious icon and an image of power. For Stella, New York was an "imperial city," the "center of the world," representative of "titanic efforts" and "conquests."[103] Varèse shared this vision in *Amériques:*

> *Amériques!* You know, I came to this country: the opening of horizons, new things in the minds of men, in the sky, and everything. *Amériques:* it's the point of departure. You know, I came from Europe, and, you know, shit on Europe. *Amériques.* You think of freedom; you think of expanding. To be completely free. . . . Nothing can ever beat . . . the euphoria of discovery.[104]

Figure 43

Joseph Stella's *The Port,* printed as a score cover for Edgard Varèse's *Octandre.* 1920s? (reproduced in Louise Varèse, *Varèse: A Looking-Glass Diary, 1883–1928,* New York: W. W. Norton, 1972).

The affinities between *New York Interpreted* and *Amériques* suggest that at this moment Stella and Varèse formed similar and complementary ways of looking at America: Stella with his image of the city filled with sounds and a new polyphony of lights and Varèse through new spatial sounds symbolizing the new world. They, like many Europeans, admired the technology often ignored by their American colleagues. As Harold A. Loeb wrote in *Broom,* "America regarded from France is not the same America that bustles one from subway to elevator. . . . Your intellectual America, yes, it bores me, but that other America of the skyscraper, of the movies, of the streets, that is admirable."[105] Still gazing at America with European eyes, these two immigrants created an America compounded of modernity and limitless potential.

The mingling of languages—of different senses, different arts—epitomizes the struggle of early twentieth-century modernists and in some sense recapitulates the experience of immigrant America. How were artists to see, to find the language—visual, musical, verbal—to define and communicate the new, the modern, the American? Stella moved beyond the realm of the purely visual. He painted noise into his images of the modern scene: he represented the multisensual experience of places like Coney Island and New York, using a visual language originally established by European modernists but fundamentally altered by the experience of the United States. He repackaged his images of the city and its music as American, making connections with that hero of Americanism, Whitman, and sharing a vision of the new world with his fellow immigrant Varèse. His musical and visual language furthered the discourse about pluralism that was essential to America's self-definition in the 1920s. As an immigrant Stella was poised between two cultures, an outside observer in both the United States and Italy; as one critic wrote: "Two instincts clash in him, . . . two homelands crowd his creative thought. . . . Two-sided, alienated, he views the greatness of America with the eyes of a European, and the gentleness of the Neapolitan sea with the eyes of a stranger."[106] Seeing America as an immigrant, Stella celebrated its immensity, its modernity, the freshness embodied in the city, its buildings, and its sounds.

What [jazz] represents is the indefinable thing which will mark the Puritan President Coolidge, the Irish Tammany ward leader, Harry Sinclair, Babbitt and Mr. Simeon Strunsky himself, every one of them, as Americans, in any city of Europe. It represents the composite essence of them all.

That essence, if I may be forgiven for taking the liberty of attempting to describe anything so elusive, is energetic, wistful, enterprising and self-confident.

Paul Whiteman, 1926

Jazz has been a continuous source of inspiration in my work from the very beginning for the simple reason that I regard it as the one American art which seemed to me to have the same quality of art that I found in the best modern European painting.

Stuart Davis, c. 1957

# 3. Jazz Paintings and National Identity

## The Abstract Art of Arthur Dove and Stuart Davis

For Marin and Stella, painting the music of the city, its dynamism and noise, was a means of infusing their art with a native Americanism. To the general theme of the musical metropolis, modernist painters added an element that sounded a more specific note of modernity and national identity: jazz. This distinctively American music had numerous shifting and sometimes contradictory meanings in early twentieth-century culture: it had the allure of primitivism, the multicultural ingredients of the melting pot, and the raucous energy of urban mechanical sounds.

Jazz was at the center of debates about national identity. In period art and cultural journals it was frequently proposed as the American contribution to modern art. Jazz possessed a distinctly native flavor and, along with the skyscraper, was considered a unique American cultural product. As early as 1913 one writer labeled both "Negro songs" and the Woolworth Building indigenous art forms; a decade later Claude Bragdon repeated this claim, stating that the American spirit— "restless, centrifugal, perilously poised"—expressed itself best in jazz music and the skyscraper.[1]

The composer George Gershwin identified a similar affinity between jazz and the American spirit:

> I maintained years ago that there is very little difference in the music of different nations. There is just that little individual touch. One country may prefer a peculiar rhythm or a note like the seventh. This it stresses, and it becomes identified with the nation. In America this preferred rhythm is called jazz. . . . Jazz is the result of the energy stored up in America. It is a very energetic kind of music, noisy, boisterous and even vulgar. One thing is certain. Jazz has contributed an enduring value to America in that it has expressed ourselves.[2]

But how did jazz, a musical form originating in African American culture, become equated with American identity? What notion of Americanness did this music construct? What role did visual images of jazz play in this process? Definitions of *American* are made and remade under changing historical circumstances to fit the needs and interests of the time. In the early twentieth century the term was revised and re-formed in response to such social transformations as European immigration, the migration of blacks to northern cities, and the Depression. In this context musical forms served as convenient devices for reconstructing national identity, with numerous writers singling out jazz as a metaphor for the nation. Jazz, however, did not provide a static container for Americanness, as notions of national identity not only change over time but have multiple meanings at any given moment. The term *jazz* is thus subject to repeated redefinitions, of which perhaps the most salient is its (attempted) conversion from a black art form to a white one in the early modernist period. The next two chapters analyze visual representations of jazz to suggest the range of possible meanings of *American* and its ethnic and racial inflections in early twentieth-century American modernist art.[3]

This chapter focuses on jazz as an important marker of national identity in Arthur Dove's and Stuart Davis's abstract art. For these two painters, jazz was an expression of American modernity and a representation of the urban environment and commercial culture. The whitening and sanitizing of jazz in the popular culture of the 1920s and 1930s also informed their view of the music and their jazz paintings. Dove's and Davis's jazz images in turn participated in this process. While the fact that jazz was identified as American is certainly evidence of the blackening of American culture and identity, Dove's and Davis's abstract paintings, like the popular film *King of Jazz* (1930) and such performers as Paul Whiteman, made blacks invisible in the representation of jazz. Using jazz, they pictured a particular type of Americanness— urban, modern, energetic, white.

## The Cultural Meanings of Jazz

It is not an easy task to trace the development of jazz. Cultural attitudes toward race and national identity shaped early accounts of this music, its histories, and performers' and composers' biographies. Most historians do agree that jazz originated in the African American music of the urban South, emerging in the first decade of the twentieth century among black piano players in the New Orleans red-light district, Storyville. By 1907 black instrumental bands there began to use what would become identified as jazz features—"undulating slow drag," "up-tempo strut," improvisation, swing (rhythmic forward momentum of the melody), syncopation, and breaks or solos. The term *jazz,* or *jaz,* used by Southern blacks to mean "to speed things up," was adopted to describe this syncopated music of New Orleans.[4] The African American tradition of oral performance, which relied on an interaction between performer and audience (call and response), also shaped jazz. Historians and musicologists have proposed other influences: the syncopation of German and Italian immigrant marching brass bands; hymns, blues, and spirituals; minstrel music; late nineteenth-century cakewalks and "coon songs"; ragtime; and stride piano.[5]

The diffusion of jazz and growth of its popularity was closely tied to both the mass migration of southern blacks to the North and the expansion of consumerism in the 1920s.[6] The closing of Storyville in 1917 sparked an exodus of musicians from New Orleans; they brought jazz to Chicago, Kansas City, New York, Los Angeles, and port towns along the Mississippi. About six out of seven major musicians born in the South before 1915 migrated North in the years before World War II.[7] This resettlement of jazz performers and composers was part of a larger movement: over two million blacks moved northward, seeking improved economic and political conditions. As a result, northern urban markets for jazz flourished, especially in the consumer boom after World War I, as new homes for music appeared in northern cities: dance halls, movie theaters, nightclubs, and Prohibition speakeasies. Jazz also emerged at a time when phonograph recordings, radios, and motion pictures were enlarging the listening audience. In the North musicians continued to perform their improvisational music in these new venues and expanded their audiences through national concert tours and recordings.

Jazz, however, has never been a fixed musical form. It is difficult to identify a pure or authentic black jazz, since it was historically a product of hybridization and this process of intermixture continued as it moved out of the South.[8] In the North New Orleans-style jazz was modified as it responded to larger white audiences and the commercial music industry. A popular form of jazz arose in New York and flourished in the city's Harlem district in the 1920s and 1930s. New

Orleans jazz—"hot," loud, improvised—survived in some urban areas, such as Chicago's South Side, but Big Band commercial groups of the period—often composed of white musicians—created a symphonic jazz style that downplayed improvisation and the raucous, wild, and sensual sounds of the original forms.

As it became more popular and accessible, jazz drew the attention of cultural critics, who interpreted, reinterpreted, labeled and relabeled it; the music took on an extramusical life and became the center of social, political, and moral debates. Discussed in the popular press and churches, among the intelligentsia and both white and black Americans, jazz acquired numerous cultural meanings: it communicated change and rebellion; it was associated with marginal groups—blacks and musicians—and was perceived as a challenge to white cultural hegemony; and it was often viewed as the devil's music, sinful and morally corrupt.[9] Jazz became an important marker for modernist artists for many reasons. They considered it authentic, real, intuitive, vital, and modern; both primitive and progressive; and distinctly American. Jazz, in a way, was the ideal American modernist art—anti-Victorian, antibourgeois, transgressive, both primitive and modern, natural and industrial. Black culture became an important part of modernism as visual artists—both American and European—engaged in these discussions and represented jazz in their work.[10]

Modernist artists were attracted to early jazz saloons in their quest for the vital and real in American life. Stuart Davis and Glenn O. Coleman, for instance, documented their excursion to Newark's barrel houses in sketches for a 1915 article in the *New York Call*. This feature presented their journey to a black working-class community as an exotic adventure. The reporter Emanuel Julius, who accompanied the two painters, wrote of "far-off" Newark as a place where he lost his sense of direction and where "north, south, east, and west were strangers to me"; he was in a foreign, unknown land. The threesome visited a dance hall with both black and white clients, owned by a white man, where they listened to "authentic" black music.[11] Davis drew the gritty environment of these sites. He detailed the external forms of early ragtime—the barrel house, band, dancers—and its performance in a primitive locale, as in *The Back Room* (fig. 44). In similar fashion, Charles Demuth frequented New York jazz bars, most notably the Marshall's, a black-owned club on 53d Street, and Barron Wilkins' Little Savoy in Harlem.[12] These places were fashionable yet risqué, outside the sphere of middle-class respectability; as such, they had an aura of the exotic and the sexually liberated. Demuth communicates this flavor in such works as *Negro Jazz Band* (fig. 45), with its melting forms and sensual colors,

physical intimacy, and the revealing costume of the female singer.

This interest in jazz among modernists was part of a larger preoccupation with what was thought of as the primitive. The music critic Ted Gioia explains, "Jazz and primitive art were seen as closely allied: both were like a breath of fresh air, full of the vitality and exuberance missing in the more stylized extensions of purely European traditions."[13] Jazz was considered primitive because of its perceived origin in African music, as two contemporary articles, "Appeal of the Primitive Jazz" (1917) and "Why 'Jazz' Sends Us Back to the Jungle" (1918), indicate.[14] In French culture, too, where the music was very popular, fascination with jazz fused with a fascination for things African. This French avant-garde taste for African styles in art, and for qualities variously called "ethno-

Figure 44

Stuart Davis, *The Back Room,* 1913. Oil on canvas, 30¼ × 37½ in. (76.8 × 95.3 cm). New York, Whitney Museum of American Art (gift of Mr. and Mrs. Arthur G. Altschul, 69.114. © 1995 Whitney Museum of American Art. © 1996 Estate of Stuart Davis/ Licensed by VAGA, New York).

graphic," "primitive," and "untutored," dates at least to Picasso's 1907 confrontation with African art in a Paris museum, out of which came *Les Demoiselles d'Avignon*.[15] A similar impulse shaped the experimental ballet *La Création du monde,* which premiered in Paris in 1923 and combined Darius Milhaud's jazz-inspired music, a narrative written by Blaise Cendrars as a primordial creation myth, and Fernand Léger's set and costume designs, based on his interpretation of African sculpture and dance.[16]

The physical environments of jazz nightclubs reinforced these attitudes (fig. 46). Larger, mostly white-owned clubs conformed to white views of blacks as primitive, natural, and sensual, and Harlem became an "uncivilized" jungle where whites could go for an adventure.[17] These clubs were segregated: the performers were black, but the audiences were strictly white. Harlem's 133d Street, with its many nightclubs, was even called "the Jungle." Performers at the Nest, Shim Sham, Green Cat, the Paradise Inn, the Cotton Club, Connie's Inn, and other popular locales played songs with titles suggesting exotic, wild Africa; Duke Ellington alone composed "Jungle Blues" (1930), "Jungle Night in Harlem" (1930), and "Echoes of the Jungle" (1931). Murals with "primitive" themes decorated the walls of Harlem's Cotton Club, and Aaron Douglas painted *Jungle* and *Jazz* panels (1927; now lost) for the Club Ebony on 129th Street and Lenox Avenue in Harlem.[18] The Cotton Club produced lavish floor shows in which performers wore revealing shirts with palm decorations, and female dancers attached bongo drums to their hips.[19] This music and its performers were sometimes confused with other marginalized cultures, such as Native Americans and Polynesians, underscoring the notion that all non-Western cultures were generic, interchangeable, and primitive.[20]

Painted images of these night spots also presented them as exotic and erotic. In *Blues* (fig. 47) the Chicago painter Archibald J. Motley, Jr., sketched the

Figure 45

Charles Demuth, *Negro Jazz Band,* 1916. Watercolor on paper, 12⅞ × 7⅞ in. (32.7 × 20 cm). Collection of Irwin Goldstein, M.D.

Figure 46

Interior of Connie's Inn, Harlem, New York. New York Public Library (Astor, Lenox and Tilden Foundations, Photographs and Prints Division, Schomburg Center for Research in Black Culture).

packed space of Paris's Petite Café. The figures' closeness to us and to one another and the hot colors conjure up an atmosphere of physicality and liberation often associated with jazz clubs. This work is also charged with the dizzying "hotness" and overt sexuality common in Motley's jazz-club paintings, such as *Saturday Night* (1935).[21] Reginald Marsh portrayed the same sensuality in *Tuesday Night at the Savoy Ballroom* (fig. 48), which defined jazz as a music of release, natural rhythm, and the primitive. In such paintings the female figure is singled out as the object of sexual liberation (especially susceptible to the intoxicant jazz), while the physical intimacy marks the breaking down of barriers—social restrictions, racial segregation— possible in cultures and spaces outside of the white middle-class mainstream.

While representational painters delineated the primitive environments of jazz performance, abstract artists visualized the music's exoticism and attempted to recapitulate its rhythms. Dove's *Primitive Music* (fig. 49) evidences the painter's interest in non-Western art and cultures, although it is open to question whether the term *primitive* in the title refers to Native American or African American culture.[22] With its rickracks and lozenge shapes, recalling motifs in Native American art and craft designs, *Primitive Music* is usually included in Dove's Indian painting series.[23] At this time, however, the term *primitive* described numerous non-Western cultures. This painting may allude not to the drums of Native Americans but to African music, or jazz, or even the not-uncommon conflation of the two. Dove himself used the word to characterize jazz in his painting *Primitive Jazz* (1929), and one reviewer of his 1944 show associated *Primitive Music* with Africa, stating that its "angles, stresses, and rhythms . . . may well make one think of Congo drums."[24]

Figure 47

Archibald J. Motley, Jr.,
*Blues,* 1929. Oil on canvas,
36 × 42 in. (91.47 × 106.7
cm). Collection of Archie
Motley and Valerie Gerrard
Browne, Evanston, Illinois
(photograph courtesy of
the Chicago Historical
Society).

Figure 48

Reginald Marsh, *Tuesday
Night at the Savoy Ballroom,*
1930. Tempera on composition board, 36 × 48 in.
(91.5 × 122 cm). Waltham,
Mass., Rose Art Museum,
Brandeis University (gift of
the Honorable William
Benton, New York).

Figure 49

Arthur Dove, *Primitive Music,* 1943 or 1944. Gouache on canvas, 18 × 24 in. (45.7 × 60.9 cm). Washington, D.C., Phillips Collection (acquired 1944).

Defined as primitive, jazz functioned as the ultimate art of rebellion—anti-Victorian, anti-intellectual, anticivilized, intuitive, sensual. It was an art of revolt "from convention, custom, authority, boredom, even sorrow—from everything that would confine the soul of man and hinder its riding free on the air."[25] Jazz offered a way of dealing with modern life and provided an escape from war and the impersonal standardization of the machine. According to one writer, jazz was popular in the 1920s, after World War I, because it offered a "fresh joyousness" and a "temporary forgetfulness" after the horrors of war. It became a "balm for modern ennui" and a "safety valve for modern machine-ridden and convention-bound society."[26] For others, jazz was the ultimate modern art, a music of the machine.

Critics and writers both praised and criticized jazz's modernity. Harold A. Loeb hailed its contemporary flavor in *Broom:* "Ragtime is the auditory expression of the new life which has overtaken us unawares, and as long as the Mysticism of Money and the speed and the agitation of the industrial civilization which are its product last, Jazz will continue to vibrate the nerves of man." Writing in *The Negro and His Music* (1936), Alain Locke talked about jazz as the "spiritual child of this age" and the "characteristic musical speech of the modern age," as did Sadakichi Hartmann: "The Zeitgeist moves to the tune of jazz. Busy housewives move their furniture twice a month with radio accompaniment to keep up with the restlessness of the age." For Waldo Frank, too, jazz was a machine music of the modern age: "Jazz syncopates the lathe-lunge, jazz shatters the piston-thrust, jazz shreds the hum of wheels, jazz is the spark and sudden lilt centrifugal to their incessant pulse. . . . This song is not an escape from the Machine to limpid depths of the soul.

It is the Machine itself! . . . Its voice is the mimicry of our industrial havoc."[27]

The perception of jazz as a modern machine-age music was based on certain metallic, machinelike, or harsh sounds characteristic of it. Early jazz performers often used sound effects in their music: Jelly Roll Morton included automobile horns, steamboat whistles, and church bells in his works, while Duke Ellington's "You've Got Those 'Wanna Go Back Again' Blues" (1926) imitated train whistles. Jazz's cacophony and syncopated beat were likened to the clatter and rhythm of mechanical noise, and therefore appealed particularly to European modernists interested in machine culture, which they saw as progressive. The French architect Le Corbusier characterized the trumpet in a Harlem band as a turbine; the poet Blaise Cendrars wrote that his typewriter was "as fast as jazz"; the German composer Paul Hindemith instructed his students to imitate machine rhythms while playing the ragtime passage in his 1922 piano suite; and the French painter Maurice Vlaminck equated the sound of an internal combustion engine to jazz.[28] A Bauhaus student, Xanti Schawinsky, produced a work in 1924 in which a tap dancer was partnered with a machine—a parallel that Bertolt Brecht understood: "An episode in an American feature film, when the dancer Astaire tap-danced to the sounds of a machine-room, showed the astonishingly close relationship between the new noises and the percussive rhythms of jazz."[29]

Modern and mechanical, jazz also became associated with the city and the modern culture of America. Hiram Kelly Moderwell, for instance, wrote in *The Seven Arts:* "I like to think that [ragtime] is the perfect expression of the American city, with its restless bustle and motion, its multitude of unrelated details, and its underlying rhythmic progress toward a vague Somewhere."[30] Le Corbusier considered jazz a mechanical music and a music of New York's machine future: "Manhattan is hot jazz in stone and steel."[31] According to the painter Florine Stettheimer, New York had "At Last grown young/with color/with light/and jazz."[32] A jazzlike music with a mechanical beat appeared in John Alden Carpenter's *Skyscrapers* ballet (1926) to evoke the construction of a modern city.

Modernist painters made this connection between jazz and the city in their art. Marin, as we have seen, correlated urban dynamism with jazz, describing New York as "the land of Jaz—Lights and movies—the land of money spenders."[33] The brilliant contrasting colors in his *Broadway Night* (plate 2) produce the dynamism of the metropolitan center of light, noise, and music—a visual equivalent to jazz. Like Marin, Stuart Davis used color harmonies and dissonances to picture the city's energy, its "hot" jazzy quality, in *Hot Still Scape for Six Colors—Seventh Avenue Style* (plate 5). A devotee of jazz, Davis wrote of it as an integral element of modern American life: "Contemporary Culture as a Subject includes the Past in the form of the Past and Present Individual Formulations of it. . . . The latter includes New Lights, Speeds, Sounds, Communications, and Jazz in general, as the Ornaments of daily Experience."[34] Both Mark Tobey and Piet Mondrian constructed parallels between jazz and the city in their works of the early 1940s: the former used line to communicate the city's confusion, energy, and sounds in *Broadway Melody,*[35] while the latter equated the urban street with jazz in the irregular rhythms, flickering optical effects, and grid plan of *Broadway Boogie-Woogie* (figs. 50, 51).

Dynamic, machinelike, urban—these qualities defined jazz as a modern music and, moreover, as American. *Modern* and *American* became equivalent terms, especially in European eyes and in the post-World War I context. Visiting New York in the 1910s, Marcel Duchamp, Francis Picabia, and Albert Gleizes were engrossed with the city's modernity. Picabia wrote:

Figure 50

Mark Tobey, *Broadway Melody,* 1945. Tempera on board, 23⅞ × 17⅛ in. (60.6 × 43.5 cm). Ann Arbor, University of Michigan Museum of Art (gift of Mr. and Mrs. Roger L. Stevens, 1949/1.152. © 1997 Artists Rights Society [ARS], New York/Pro Litteris, Zurich).

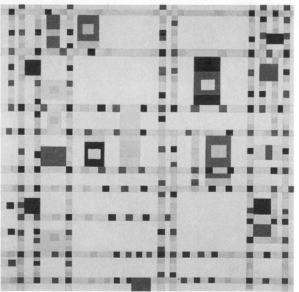

Figure 51

Piet Mondrian, *Broadway Boogie-Woogie,* 1942–43. Oil on canvas, 50 × 50 in. (127 × 127 cm). New York, Museum of Modern Art (given anonymously. Photograph © 1995 The Museum of Modern Art, New York. Courtesy of the Mondrian Estate/Holtzman Trust, Essex, Conn.).

You of New York should be quick to understand me and my fellow painters. Your New York is the cubist, the futurist city. It expresses in its architecture, its life, its spirit, the modern thought. . . .

Because of your extreme modernity therefore, you should quickly understand the studies which I have made since my arrival in New York. They express the spirit of New York as I feel it, and the crowded streets of your city as I feel them, their surging, their unrest, their commercialism, and their atmospheric charm.[36]

These European artists were quick to incorporate skyscrapers, advertising, and jazz into their works, as the purest expressions of modern American culture. When Picabia painted his impressions of the United States, he chose New York City and African American music as his subjects. His abstraction *New York* (1913) conveyed his feelings about the city, while *Negro Song* and *Negro Song II* communicated his responses to early jazz, specifically to a black singer whom Picabia had heard perform at a Harlem restaurant (figs. 29, 30).[37] This European fascination with things American was not limited to the French Cubists. As Beeke Sell Tower has demonstrated, German Expressionist artists such as Otto Dix and George Grosz considered the hectic pace and rhythm of ragtime and jazz both American and synonymous with modernity. For them, this popular music was emblematic of Americanization and American technology, although some also came to associate it with an uncultured, commercial, mechanized America, decadent and corrupt.[38]

Just as European artists framed jazz as modern and American, their colleagues in the United States began to appreciate it as a native product. Jazz became central to many discussions about musical nationalism. In the July 1917 issue of *The Seven Arts* Hiram Kelly Moderwell presented ragtime—that is, syncopated music, blues, spirituals—as the source of a genuine American music, indeed, the only original music produced in the United States.[39] Gilbert Seldes wrote about jazz in the same manner in *The Dial:*

> Jazz . . . is the symbol, or the byword, for a great many elements in the spirit of the time—as far as America is concerned it is actually our characteristic expression. . . . The fact that jazz is our current mode of expression, has reference to our time and the way we think and talk, is interesting. . . . Jazz, for us, isn't a last feverish excitement, a spasm of energy before death. It is the normal development of our resources, the expected, and wonderful, arrival of America at a point of creative intensity.[40]

Other writers perceived jazz as an embodiment of national qualities or characteristics. In *So This Is Jazz* (1926), Henry O. Osgood explained: "The free, frank, sometimes vulgar spirit of the *bourgeoisie,* the plebs, abides in [jazz]."[41] For the music critic William James Henderson, jazz had an "infectious expression of exuberance" characteristic of America: "The people of the United States possess no genuine national music created by themselves, but have adopted a type which none the less expresses their ebullience, their nervous energy and their aversion to artistic solemnities."[42]

Similarly, Harlem Renaissance intellectuals presented jazz and related musical forms as expressive of America. James Weldon Johnson claimed in his preface to *The Book of American Negro Poetry* (1922) that Uncle Remus folk tales, spirituals or slave songs, the cakewalk, and ragtime "were the only things artistic [outside the skyscraper] that have yet sprung from Ameri-can soil and have been universally acknowledged as distinctive American products." "Ragtime," he added, "has not only influenced American music, it has influenced American life; indeed, it has satur-ated American life. It has become the popular medium for our na-tional expression musically. And who can say that it does not express the blare and jangle and the surge, too, of our national spirit?"[43] J. A. Rogers, while ad-mitting the black contributions to jazz, also highlighted its Americanism in his article "Jazz at Home," which appeared in the *New Negro* anthology (1925):

> This makes it difficult to say whether jazz is more characteristic of the Negro or of contemporary America. As was shown, it is of Negro origin plus the influence of the American environment. It is Negro-American. Jazz proper, however, is in idiom—rhythmic, musical and pantomimic—thoroughly American Negro. . . . Once achieved, it is common property, and jazz has absorbed the national spirit, that tremendous spirit of go, the nervousness, lack of conventionality and boisterous good-nature characteristic of the American, white or black.[44]

For the critic Robert Coady jazz was African Americans' gift to American culture: "The American Negro has contributed to our young culture many of its most valuable qualities. He has given us . . . the best of our music."[45] William James Henderson's survey of American music in *The American Spirit in Art* (1927) noted the African American roots of jazz: "One of the most curious aspects of American history is to be found in the fact that the race whose individuals were brought to American shores as slaves and whose descendants have never been granted equality by their white neighbors, have given us our only distinctive native music."[46] While Coady and Henderson speak of jazz as a gift to American culture, this music clearly was taken by America, as much as given to it. Some African American writers, musicians, and critics were willing to "give" jazz to the larger culture—to make it "common property," as Rogers phrased it—as a way to validate their own achievements and make a place for themselves in American society; at the same time, white Americans appropriated jazz as they sought a native art and culture to help define their national identity.

Visual artists turned to this "common property," made it their own, and made it into their own version of America. Early twentieth-century art journals and little magazines advocated this appropriation: they identified jazz, ragtime, and other popular arts as the material that would provide the foundation for a modern American art. In *Broom,* Matthew Josephson named jazz as a possible source for a new indigenous art.[47] Coady, writing in *The Soil,* identified the fertile "soil" for an American art in the materials of contemporary culture: machinery, skyscrapers, and African American musical forms—"Bert Williams, Rag-time, the Buck and Wing and the Clog. Syncopation and the Cake-Walk . . . the Minstrels."[48]

Two American-born painters, Arthur Dove (1880–1946) and Stuart Davis (1892–1964), made jazz paintings in a conscious effort to contribute to the formation of a national cultural identity. Both artists were committed to modernism, but struggled with the problem of Americanizing the style. Jazz offered them both a formal model—an American model of abstraction—and a subject considered to embody that vague entity, the American spirit. When identified as American, jazz often lost its African and African American associations in commercial music and visual representations. Dove's and Davis's efforts to paint jazz participated in this music's transformation—its de-Africanization, its sanitization. Their jazz paintings resonated with the meanings of jazz circulating in the culture: speedy, restless, chaotic, industrial, mechanical, urban.

## The Jazz Paintings of Arthur Dove

Arthur Dove appreciated a wide range of music from Bach to Bing Crosby and frequently mentioned the popular musical performers Duke Ellington, Ella Fitzgerald, George Gershwin, Benny Goodman, Glenn Miller, and Paul Whiteman in his diaries.[49] Music, from singing and dancing to playing the mandolin, piano, and drums in impromptu bands, informed his life; like many of his contemporaries, he enjoyed the new sound technology of the radio and phonograph. As part of his day-to-day routine, music also shaped Dove's writings about art, and his paintings. His essays refer to music as a model for the visual arts and some fifteen paintings and sketches, produced throughout his career, have music or the names of songs in their titles: *Music* (1913), *Sentimental Music* (1913–17), *Chinese Music* (1923), *Factory Music* (1923), *George Gershwin— Rhapsody in Blue, Part I* (1927), *George Gershwin— Rhapsody in Blue, Part II* (1927), *I'll Build a Stairway to Paradise—George Gershwin* (1927), *An Orange Grove in California—Irving Berlin* (1927), *Improvision* (1927), *Rhythm Rag* (1927), *Primitive Jazz* (1929), *The Moon Was Laughing at Me* (1936), *Me and the Moon* (1937), *Swing Music (Louis Armstrong)* (1938), *Primitive Music* (1943–44). Several lost sketches had titles taken from the music of Duke Ellington, Bing Crosby, and Gershwin.[50]

While some of these paintings treat music in general as a theme, most have jazz and popular music as their specific source. Dove's use of this music, particularly in his six paintings from 1927, must be understood in the context of his goal—and the Stieglitz circle's concern—to identify his art as American. Critics and scholars have often presented Dove's nature-related paintings, such as *Thunderstorm* (1921) or *Waterfall* (1925), as evidence of his commitment to cultural nationalism.[51] These landscapes are interpreted as a continuation of an American Romantic tradition initiated by the nineteenth-century writers Emerson and Whitman. His music paintings, however, are much more self-consciously nationalist, visualizing the dynamism that Dove saw as typifying modern America. By painting jazz Dove not only stamped his art as native but did so using a modern style. He rejected the descriptive realism of American Scene painting and fashioned instead a form of abstraction rooted in native, nationalist sources.

That Dove should be interested in painting music and should see music as a model for a modern visual

Figure 52

Arthur Dove, *Music,* 1913. Oil on cardboard, 15½ × 11½ in. (39.4 × 29.2 cm). Location unknown.

**Figure 53**

Arthur Dove, *Sentimental Music,* 1913–17. Pastel on rough paper, 21¼ × 17⅞ in. (54 × 45.4 cm). New York, Metropolitan Museum of Art (Alfred Stieglitz Collection, 1949, 49.70.77. All rights reserved).

art is not surprising.[52] His earliest music paintings, *Music* and *Sentimental Music* (figs. 52, 53), responded to the synaesthetic theories popular among the New York avant garde at the time and in particular argue Francis Picabia's influence. After his arrival in New York in January 1913, Picabia visited Stieglitz's Gallery 291 almost daily.[53] He gained notoriety for his abstract paintings at the Armory Show and his opinions on modern art, printed in the popular press. Picabia's reliance on the musical analogy to explain abstraction and his own examples of abstract painted jazz, exhibited at Gallery 291 in 1913 (figs. 29, 30), seem to have made a strong impression on Dove.

Dove must have known Picabia's theories and paintings, since both artists were in the Stieglitz circle at this time and Picabia's ideas were widely published in newspapers and in *Camera Work*. The critic Samuel Swift of the *New York Sun* recorded Dove's impressions of Picabia's Gallery 291 show and contended that Dove could understand the French painter's art because he used similar means of expression.[54] *Music* and *Sentimental Music* display some formal parallels with Picabia's paintings. The former has an affinity with *Dances at the Spring* (fig. 28), exhibited at the Armory Show: both share a color scheme of ocher and brown, modulated hues, simplified natural forms, angular shapes, and repeated arcs.[55] *Sentimental Music* and *Negro Song* have a similar compositional structure, with central elongated, organic, vertically oriented forms. The two works were perhaps in one reviewer's mind when he or she made a comparison between Dove and Picabia: "These artists found that they had worked out similar form and colors to express similar ideas. Both, for instance, had chosen the same shade of purple to express symbolically a certain negro quality."[56] *Negro Song* and *Negro Song II* record Picabia's responses to the sounds of jazz in a Harlem restaurant. The painter used gray and purple in *Negro Song II* and pink and gray in *Negro Song,* colors echoed in the pink and purplish-gray palette of *Sentimental Music*. Dove's awareness of Picabia's art and ideas in all likelihood encouraged him not only to produce his own music paintings but also to paint equivalents of American popular music.

Painting music, especially popular music, continued to intrigue Dove throughout his career. Two works from the early 1920s indicate that he was looking to specific musical genres and sounds from the modern environment. In *Chinese Music* (fig. 54), as in his music paintings of the 1910s, repeated organic forms imply the dynamism of music. Modulated green, blue, and red, mixed with metallic paint, create a pulsating, shimmering surface; a swirl on the right expands from a small circle to a large sawtooth form, suggesting a sound wave. For Dove, these forms and the red, gold, and metallic green in *Chinese Music* evoked Oriental music, which, in the 1910s and 1920s, was enjoying a vogue. Arthur Jerome Eddy wrote about Chinese music in *Cubists and Post-Impressionists* (1914): "The great majority of people on first hearing Chinese music exclaim, 'What a horrid din!' and turn away."[57] Dove's *Chinese Music,* with its metallic paint and machinelike forms, offers a visual equivalent of this sentiment. The painting may be a response to a specific song; several contemporary fox-trots and jazz-inspired pieces had Oriental themes: among them, "Chinese Fox Trot" and "Ching-a-Ling's Jazz Bazaar."[58]

Dove must have explored a similar din and dissonance in *Factory Music,* exhibited in 1925 at Anderson Galleries, but now lost.[59] The title of this work reveals his interest in American industry—a subject often discussed in the cultural journals *The Soil* and *Broom,* and a popular theme in the New York avant garde, as were machine music and noise music, the specific theme of the work. *Factory Music* clearly shows Dove's turn to contemporary subject matter. The natural themes that typified his early work gave way to paintings and collages of the industrial and consumer cul-

ture, such as *Gear* (1922) and *Ten-Cent Store* (1924). This change ran somewhat counter to the prevailing taste of the critics closest to the Stieglitz circle, such as the cultural nationalists of *The Seven Arts* and *The Dial,* Paul Rosenfeld, Van Wyck Brooks, and Waldo Frank. They encouraged artists to respond with genuine emotion to the contemporary scene and to develop an art from the life around them, but they also demanded that artists maintain the established traditions of American art (which they themselves often defined); premier among these was the great American landscape tradition.[60]

Many of Dove's 1920s paintings seem to draw on a different thread of cultural nationalism, that defined by the magazines *The Soil* and *Broom* and echoing the urban tone of French Cubist and New York Dada collage. Like Stuart Davis, Charles Demuth, and Gerald Murphy, he appropriated objects and images related to American consumerism in his collages: *Huntington Harbor* (1924) incorporates clippings from *Yachting* magazine and a sign for the Long Island Railroad; *Long Island* (1925) contains a magazine illustration of an automobile; a Woolworth price card figures in *Ten-Cent Store;* and the American consumer, *Miss Woolworth* (1924), is built from mass-produced items available at the department store—artificial flowers, stockings, a mask, insoles, a purse, garden gloves, a watch, a ring brooch, and a necklace.

The din of *Chinese Music* and the machine noise of *Factory Music* came out of this same impulse, which presented jazz as another consumer product. Jazz was the subject of six paintings that Dove exhibited at Stieglitz's Intimate Gallery from December 12, 1927 to January 11, 1928.[61] Dove often listened to music on the phonograph and radio while living on board the yawl *Mona,* docked off Halesite, Long Island, and the Dove diaries indicate that the painter and his wife, Helen Torr (nicknamed Reds), often went to movies, vaudeville shows, and concerts that included popular-music

Figure 54

Arthur Dove, *Chinese Music,* 1923. Oil on wood, 21⅝ × 18⅛ in. (54.9 × 46 cm). Philadelphia Museum of Art (Alfred Stieglitz Collection).

Figure 55

Arthur Dove, *George Gershwin—Rhapsody in Blue, Part I,* 1927. Oil and metallic paint with clock spring on aluminum, 11¾ × 9¾ in. (29.8 × 24.8 cm). Private collection.

performances. In December 1925 he attended a Paul Whiteman concert in New York; this event seems to have sparked his enthusiasm for jazz, for he purchased five jazz albums during the summer of 1926. It was this consumer product—the commercial jazz of Whiteman's recordings—that served as the basis of Dove's work the following December.[62]

George Gershwin's music, performed by the Paul Whiteman Orchestra, inspired three of the six 1927 music paintings—*George Gershwin—Rhapsody in Blue, Part I, George Gershwin—Rhapsody in Blue, Part II,* and *I'll Build a Stairway to Paradise—Gershwin.* Along with his brother, Ira, Gershwin produced numerous popular songs for Broadway shows that advanced the notion of a national music in which art music and popular music—folk songs, the blues, jazz—were combined. In November 1923 Whiteman asked Gershwin to write an extended jazz piece for a "highbrow" concert, and the composer responded in early 1924 with *Rhapsody in Blue.* Acclaimed as the hit of the 1924 concert, which was called *An Experiment in Modern Music,* this work was first recorded in June of that year by Whiteman and his band, with Gershwin at the piano. In the early 78 rpm phonograph records *Rhapsody in Blue* was divided into two parts, with each section filling one side of the album: Part I contained the moderately paced opening allegro and Part II had an abridged slow middle section and brisk finale.[63] Dove must have owned one of these recordings, for he painted his *Rhapsody in Blue* in two parts.

As we know, modernist artists explored many ways to create visual equivalents of music. Dove explained that he wanted to show his audience the connection between abstraction and experience in his music paintings: "They have waxed enthusiastic over a 'thing' of mine being done from Gershwin's 'Rhapsody in Blue' not as yet completed, but I feel it will make people see that the so called 'abstractions' are not abstract at all. . . . It is illustration."[64] By "illustration," he undoubtedly wished to imply something close to the concept of equivalents—a concept frequently discussed in the Stieglitz circle. An expression of this aesthetic can be seen in Stieglitz's own photographic cloud studies (which Dove saw in 1924), called *music, songs of the sky,* and *equivalents* to suggest that they were meant to convey the artist's feelings.[65] Similarly, in *George Gershwin—Rhapsody in Blue, Part I* (fig. 55), Dove "illustrated," or created an "equivalent," of Gershwin's composition; he used an abstract visual language to suggest his emotional response to the music. Since we know the musical sources, we can also read back and forth from the recording to the image, seeing parallels between musical passages and visual forms. In these 1927 works Dove developed a rather literal lexicon for visualizing musical sounds: line describes melody and tempo, color the instrumentation, hue and line density the loudness or softness of sounds.

Dove's 1927 catalog essay provides clues to a reading of his music paintings. As he explained in this document, line was an equivalent of movement (a musical quality), color of sound: "The line was a moving point reducing the moving volume to one dimension. From then on it is expressed in terms of color as music is in terms of sound."[66] In *Rhapsody in Blue, Part I,* line and color correspond to the music; for example, the spiral of the central clock spring matches the rising notes of the opening clarinet. In his works of the 1920s Dove experimented often with the spiral, a form that he associated with the passage of time.[67] This spiral, then, can be read as representing the musical qualities of movement and time. The oscillating black line to the left of the clock spring suggests the melody in the early measures and the fluttering clarinet. Much of the 1920s recording of the first part of *Rhapsody in Blue* contains piano passages in which Gershwin chases notes up and down the keyboard; the energetic lines on the left and right edges of the collage suggest the mood of these sections. Color seems to correspond to the mixed instrumentation. The yellow-red circle

perhaps pictures the drum beats and cymbal clashes that punctuate the *Rhapsody's* opening, while blue tints and shades suggest the "blue notes" of Gershwin's composition and, of course, the colorful title of the piece. Two attached clock springs and the metallic paint, which link this work to *Chinese Music, Factory Music,* and the 1920s collages, represent the shrill, steely qualities of Gershwin's *Rhapsody,* particularly the two opening clarinet *glissandi.*

Again using line and color as figures for the parts of music, Dove envisioned the second half of Gershwin's work—the slow section and brisk finale—in *George Gershwin—Rhapsody in Blue, Part II* (plate 6). Here line appears to imply pitch intensity and melodic progression. Thin curves suggest the soft sound of the *Rhapsody's* middle section, while the darker lines to the left are visual analogs of the crescendo at the composition's end. The oval frame and downward- and upward-sweeping lines create a whirling motion that communicates the music's energy. Broken black lines perhaps indicate the dominant piano in the second part of the recording, while metallic paint and fragmented lines evoke the piano runs, brass, and cymbals of the pulse-quickening finale.

A Gershwin piece inspired another of Dove's 1927 music paintings, *George Gershwin—I'll Build a Stairway to Paradise* (fig. 56). The first-act finale and hit song of the revue *George White's Scandals of 1922,* "I'll Build a Stairway to Paradise" was also featured in a November 1923 concert at New York's Aeolian Hall with the soprano Eva Gauthier and Gershwin at the piano. Like *Rhapsody in Blue,* this song in its concert-hall performance marked the growing acceptance of jazz on the concert stage and its presumed elevation, or "improvement."[68] While Dove may have been familiar with these events, he certainly knew the tune from a phonograph record, which he played over and over again while making his painting.[69] The original 1922 Whiteman recording of "I'll Build a Stairway to Paradise" was an animated performance that included banjos, cymbals, and brass and an improvised solo by a trumpet with a kazoo mute. Dove created a visual counterpart to this bustling, brassy music. The ascending composition and short, layered brushstrokes of the painting *Stairway to Paradise* suggest the stairway in the lyrics as well as the rising chords in the music. Dark blues and reds at the bottom gradually lighten to silvery hues at the top, while the central silver cylinder explodes, showering festive streamers. These streamer lines and curls follow the recurrent trills of the melody. Fluctuating lines and shapes, dabs of color, textured brushstrokes, and metallic paint all communicate the energy of the song.

In *An Orange Grove in California—Irving Berlin* (fig. 57), Dove responded to another popular composer of the period. Originally written for *The Music Box Revue of 1923,* Berlin's song was also performed at *An Experiment in Modern Music* in February 1924, along with Gershwin's *Rhapsody in Blue.*[70] In Whiteman's recording, which Dove must have owned,[71] a jazz band of banjos, percussion, and brass performed the verses with choruses played by solo instruments—the first chorus a trumpet, the second a trombone with a megaphone mute. As in the other jazz paintings, Dove translates sounds from a phonograph recording directly into line and color. Reflecting the song's title, orange dominates the work. Sparkling silver tones suggest the music's shrill sounds, while splashes of black paint, corkscrews, and wriggles dancing on the surface echo its lively rhythm. Zigzags and ripples—some thinly painted, some thickly—describe the falling notes of the melody, as played with varying force by instruments ranging from clarinets to trumpets.

Two other paintings from the 1927 series have musical titles: *Rhythm Rag,* now lost, was inspired by a Whiteman recording of the same name; *Improvision* (fig. 58) refers more generally to jazz and its characteristic improvisation.[72] In the latter, crisscrossed lines in the lower right center recall musical notations such as staves and sharps, while the nervous calligraphy evokes

Figure 56

Arthur Dove, *George Gershwin—I'll Build a Stairway to Paradise,* 1927. Oil and metallic paint on board, 20 × 15 in. (50.8 × 38.1 cm). Boston, Museum of Fine Arts (gift of the William H. Lane Foundation).

Figure 57

Arthur Dove, *An Orange Grove in California—Irving Berlin,* 1927. Oil on card-board, 20 × 15 in. (50.8 × 38.1 cm). Madrid, © Fundacion Coleccion Thyssen–Bornemisza (all rights reserved).

Figure 58

Arthur Dove, *Improvision,* 1927. Oil on pressed board, 15½ × 14½ in. (39.4 × 36.8 cm). Lucile and Donald Graham Collection.

Figure 59

Wassily Kandinsky, *The Garden of Love (Improvisation Number 27),* 1912. Oil on canvas, 47⅜ × 55¼ in. (120.3 × 140.3 cm). New York, Metropolitan Museum of Art (Alfred Stieglitz Collection, 1949, 49.70.1. All rights reserved. © 1997 Artists Rights Society [ARS], New York/ADAGP, Paris).

jazz's spontaneity and energy. The calligraphic style of *Improvision* and the other 1927 music paintings was inspired not only by jazz but by the paintings of the Russian artist Wassily Kandinsky. When Dove decided to "illustrate" the improvisatory music of jazz, he looked to Kandinsky's famous *Improvisations* as models. Splashes of vibrant color, energetic line, and cross-hatched marks recall forms in Kandinsky's *The Garden of Love (Improvisation Number 27)* (fig. 59), which Stieglitz had bought in 1913. The painting would thus have been available for Dove's study.[73] Dove's catalog essay for his 1927–28 exhibition makes clear the debt to Kandinsky:

The line is the result of reducing dimension from the solid to the plane then to the point. A moving point could follow a waterfall and dance. . . . I should like to take wind and water and sand as a motif and work with them, but it has to be simplified in most cases to color and force lines and substances, just as music has done with sound. . . . The line was a moving point reducing the moving volume to one dimension. From then on it is expressed in terms of color as music is in terms of sound. As the point moves it becomes a line, as the line moves, it becomes a plane, as the plane moves, it becomes a solid, as the solid moves, it becomes life and as life moves, it become the present.[74]

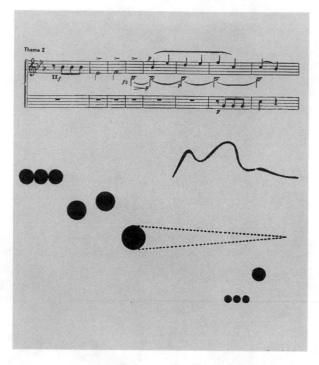

Figure 60

Wassily Kandinsky, *Theme 2 Translated into Points,* 1926 (diagram published in the 1947 English edition of *Point and Line to Plane,* repr. New York: Dover, 1979, 45. © 1997 Artists Rights Society [ARS], New York/ADAGP, Paris).

These point-and-line theories, especially the description of music as color and line and the statement that a line may "dance," echo Kandinsky's text *Point and Line to Plane* (1926). In this treatise musical scores are translated into line and music is characterized in linear terms (fig. 60), as Dove did in his essay and his own jazz paintings.

While stylistically indebted to European modernism, these jazz paintings nevertheless represent an effort by Dove to define a national identity through art, without relying on the mechanical trick of painting literal American scenes or subjects. Isolationism and xenophobia marked 1920s American culture. The American painters Georgia O'Keeffe and Charles Sheeler were painting New York skyscrapers to make a point, and critics were stamping any artist who worked with such native themes American. In Dove's estimation a native expression could not be established through subject matter alone; being an American artist and producing a native art did not simply require that an artist paint an American subject. While many of his contemporaries turned to descriptive, realistic scenes of American life, he remained committed to abstraction as a means of molding an indigenous art. He wrote:

What constitutes American painting?

When a man paints the El, a 1740 house or a miner's shack, he is likely to be called by his critics, American. These things may be in America, but it's what is in the artist that counts. What do we call "American" outside of painting? Inventiveness, restlessness, speed, change.

Well, then, a painter may put all these qualities in a still life or an abstraction, and be going more native than another who sits quietly copying a skyscraper.[75]

The 1927 jazz paintings can be understood as Dove's version of "going native." If speed was a quality that typified America, the agitated line in *An Orange Grove in California* and other works may be read as conveying a nationalist temper. Dove observed: "The music things were done to speed the line up to the pace at which we live to-day."[76] An artist could communicate dynamism through line, as Dove later explained to the art critic Samuel Kootz: "The choice of form was reduced from the plane to the line. . . . The line was the only thing that had speed enough."[77] These jazz paintings illustrate an American subject, though not a concrete one: the abstract quality of speed that Dove saw as modern and native. Just as a musician could convey an American flavor through the abstraction of organized sound, so too could a painter, through the jazz of paint.

The art critic Edwin Alden Jewell of the *New York Times* also detected a native flavor in Dove's 1927 music paintings. Stieglitz presented *An Orange Grove in California—Irving Berlin* to Jewell, who admired it so much that he used it as the frontispiece for his book, *Americans* (1930), in which he attempted to define the characteristics of an indigenous art.[78] The critic had toyed with the idea of painting the American flag as the frontispiece, but used Dove's painting instead; he seems to have understood the two images as interchangeable national emblems. Jewell's definition of an American essence in art recalls Dove's, praising the abstract and voicing a rather romantic notion of the artist that is typical of the period:

> What is America? "Does reproducing the physical aspect of the American landscape make an American art?" Surely not. And surely "subject" is a most tricky criterion when it comes to trying to decide about art's nationality. Since I suppose we are mostly agreed that it is the precious flame burning in the heart or mind of the artist that counts, what concretely is painted (subject) must be esteemed of secondary importance.[79]

Although both Jewell and Dove considered subject matter secondary, it was not without value in Dove's Americanist enterprise. That the painter and his critic saw an Americanness in his art is due not only to its abstract qualities but to its jazz theme. The dilemma for many American modernists was that, because they embraced European modernist styles, they were perceived as un-American. For Dove, using jazz as a subject helped to temper his foreign-inspired style. Gershwin's *Rhapsody in Blue,* one of Dove's subjects, was a highly publicized jazz composition with overt and clearly understood nationalist associations. By definition, a rhapsody is a fantastic, often loosely formed composition; by tradition, it often has a heroic or national character, as do Franz Liszt's *Hungarian Rhapsodies* (1851–86) and Antonín Dvořák's *Slavonic Rhapsodies* (1878). Following such models, Gershwin had first intended to call his work *American Rhapsody,* but changed the title when his brother suggested the present one after seeing James McNeill Whistler's paintings, with their musical titles and atmospheric colors.[80] Despite this name change, for the composer *Rhapsody in Blue* expressed American inclusiveness and modernity, the urban scene and its multiethnic population:

> It was on the train [to Boston], with its steely rhythms, its rattle-ty bang that is so often so stimulating to a composer. . . . And there I suddenly heard— and even saw on paper—the complete construction of the rhapsody, from beginning to end. . . . I heard it as a sort of musical kaleidoscope of America—of our vast melting pot, of our unduplicated national pep, of our blues, our metropolitan madness.[81]

As a consumer product, jazz was packaged as American; it was this commercial jazz that Dove knew best and that remained a source for his art into the 1930s and 1940s. He continued to attend concerts of the Whiteman Orchestra[82] and others, and in later years especially admired Ella Fitzgerald, Glenn Miller, and Benny Goodman. But, like many Americans of his era, Dove became acquainted with jazz primarily in its more sedate, white forms, through the phonograph, radio, and film. He looked to jazz recordings as a source for his paintings in the late twenties and to the radio and motion pictures in the following decade. Not only did jazz become the subject matter of his art, but the experience of listening to it in mechanical reproduction provided him with models for thinking about and explaining abstraction. It also continued to help him formulate a nationalist modernism.[83]

Like the phonograph, radio and motion pictures disseminated popular music widely, especially jazz and swing. More than the phonograph, radio was responsible for the promotion and growth of jazz in the 1920s and 1930s. Broadcasts rarely used phonograph recordings and relied on live concerts and performances from dance bands in ballrooms, restaurants, and nightclubs, such as the Cotton Club. In 1938, music filled 53 percent of radio programs, with *The Chesterfield Program, The Raleigh-Kool Program,* and *The Lucky Strike Hit Parade* showcasing the Big Band swing sounds of Goodman, Miller, and Tommy Dorsey.[84] After the introduction of sound in *The Jazz Singer* (1927), motion pictures offered another medium for bringing jazz to the public. One study estimates that 63 shorts, 80 full-length features, 5 cartoons, and 2 newsreels featured jazz in American movie theaters between 1917 and 1940.[85]

Radio inspired at least two of Dove's paintings, *The Moon Was Laughing at Me* and *Me and the Moon* (figs. 61, 62). According to his wife, Dove was working on *The Moon Was Laughing at Me* in December 1936 and on his second radio painting, which she referred to as "'From the Radio,' song with moon in it," the following February.[86] The title *The Moon Was Laughing at Me* is written on the reverse of the first, along with the word *radio; Me and the Moon* can be identified as the second radio painting because its title, like that of *The Moon Was Laughing at Me,* was in quotation marks, indicating that it was a song title, in an American Place exhibition catalog.[87] These two works undoubtedly record Dove's impression of two popular 1936

songs, "Me and the Moon" and "The Moon Is Grinning at Me."[88]

The experience of listening to music on the radio shaped Dove's abstract, expressive art. On the phonograph and radio music was divorced from its original source—the performer—and was reproduced and transmitted by invisible forces. From this mechanically reproduced music Dove painted abstractions and pseudo-landscapes, letting sounds stimulate his visual imagination. In the two radio works he pictured the effect of music coming over the radio much as one might visualize a person from his or her voice on the telephone. He explained this: "How do you feel about a person when you're talking over the phone? If you know them, or if you don't know them, do you get something, do you put that into words of your own, from what they say, or from what you think? Or if it were music over the radio, have you ever tried to think how it would look?"[89] Abandoning the calligraphic style of the 1927 music series in favor of a geometric, biomorphic manner,[90] he organized color and form to convey the moods and images that these songs formed in his mind. In both *The Moon Was Laughing at Me* and *Me and the Moon* dark hues set a nocturnal mood: yellow illuminates the surface, hinting at the presence of the moon or moonlight, and biomorphic forms and radiant lunar circles evoke a landscape scene. Dove's focus is on the impalpable and invisible; in his working method he relied on the ear to conjure up images for the eye, so that the paintings could stimulate the reverse effect in the viewer.

Music performance in film also inspired him. In October 1937 Dove and Reds saw the movie *Artists and Models,* which featured the trumpet player Louis Armstrong and his band in two scenes.[91] The following March, the painter created *Swing Music (Louis Armstrong)* (plate 7), either from his memory of the music in this film or from a phonograph recording. The title may refer to Armstrong's 1937 recording "Public Melody No. 1," from *Artists and Models,* or to

Figure 61

Arthur Dove, *The Moon Was Laughing at Me,* 1937. Wax emulsion on canvas, 6¼ × 8¼ in. (15.9 × 21 cm). Washington, D.C., Phillips Collection (bequest of Elmira Bier, 1976).

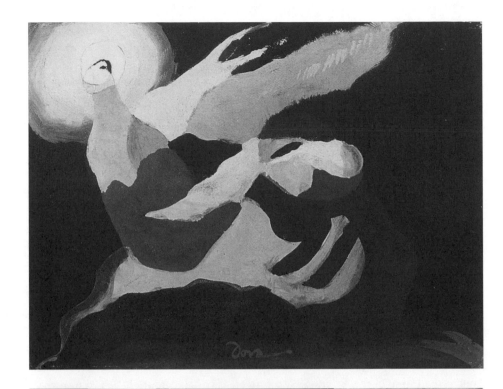

Figure 62

Arthur Dove, *Me and the Moon,* 1937. Wax emulsion on canvas, 18 × 26 in. (45.7 × 66 cm). Washington, D.C., Phillips Collection (acquired 1939).

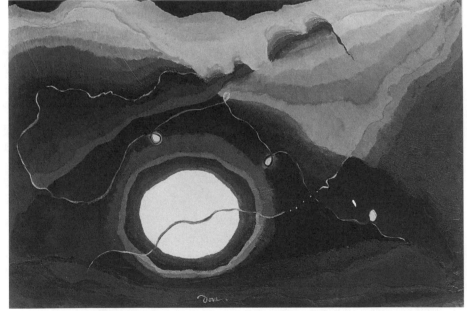

the 1936 Armstrong hit, "Swing That Music," recorded as a companion to the composer's autobiography of the same year and title.[92] Reproduced in this volume was a photograph of Armstrong on stage with a curtain backdrop decorated with an illustration of trumpet music, represented by musical notes and abstract shapes and lines emanating from a horn (fig. 63). Dove's *Swing Music* "illustrates" Armstrong's music in a similar fashion. Shapes expand like sound waves from a central point in the right center, and zigzags created by the edges of the shapes imply the melody's flow. An amorphous red form at left center and red forms throughout mark the trumpet's blare. Dove's use of red was not accidental, since trumpet sounds and this color were often paired: Kandinsky associated red with the trumpet in *Concerning the Spiritual in Art,*[93] as did such period songs as Richard Rodgers's "Red Hot Trumpet" (1929).

Dove suggests the presence of the musician as well as the music in this painting. At top right, a black shape seems to form a facial profile of Armstrong himself.[94] Armstrong's career paralleled the rise of jazz: he received his early musical training at the Waif's Home for Boys in New Orleans and eventually earned a spot as cornet player in Kid Ory's Jazz Orchestra, performing in New Orleans and along the Mississippi River. In the early twenties he gained wider recognition performing and recording with King Oliver's Creole Jazz Band in Chicago and then with Fletcher Henderson's band in New York. In 1925 he formed his own ensemble, Armstrong and His Hot Five, and this group's 1928 "West End Blues" established Armstrong's solo trumpet playing, with its vibrato, shakes, and rips, as a model for jazz soloists.

One jazz historian identified a distinguishing feature of Armstrong's style as his "incomparable sense of swing, that is, the sureness with which notes are placed in the time continuum and the remarkably

varied attack and release properties of his phrasing."[95] The property of swing attributed to Armstrong has been characterized as the inner drive, or "forward momentum," of his music; it has been argued that any single note from a phrase of his music possesses a forward thrust.[96] Popular songs of the 1930s such as Duke Ellington's "It Don't Mean a Thing If It Ain't Got That Swing" (1932) and Cole Porter's "Swing That Swing" (1935) also referred to swing, as did stage shows such as Eubie Blake's *Swing It* (1937). *Swing* described the Big Band jazz of the 1930s. Swing orchestras grew in size to include three or four trumpets, trombones, reed and rhythm sections, sometimes strings, and often vocalists; in such symphonic ensembles performances were less improvised and more orchestrated than in earlier jazz bands. Swing music was a commercial jazz that appealed to a wide audience and was promoted on phonograph recordings, radio, and in the movies, as well as through concert tours. It helped to revive the popular music market, which had been in decline during the early Depression years.

A 1938 *Life* magazine spread, "Swing: The Hottest and Best Kind of Jazz Reaches Its Golden Age," photographed the bands of Benny Goodman, Tommy Dorsey, Bob Crosby, Red Norvo, Artie Shaw, Duke Ellington, Count Basie, and Louis Armstrong. It outlined the features of their music: "But all definitions agree that Swing is based on: 1) a driving but fluid and unmechanical rhythm over which 2) soloists improvise as they play. Whatever the definition, everybody admits that of all jazz Swing is musically the most vital and interesting."[97] Armstrong offered his own definition of swing in his autobiography. He distinguished between "sweet" jazz and "hot" swing music, comparing the "sweet" jazz musician to writers of popular literature, who follow a standard formula, and the swing musician to great writers, who ignore popular taste and let only their own feelings inspire

Figure 63

Louis Armstrong and his
orchestra, Boston, 1936
(reproduced in Louis
Armstrong, *Swing That
Music,* New York:
Longmans, Green, 1936).

*Photograph by Richard Merrill*

LOUIS ARMSTRONG AND HIS ORCHESTRA, BOSTON, 1936

them.[98] For Armstrong, emotion and improvisation
characterized the swing musician: "Any average player,
if he's worth anything at all, can follow through a
score, as it's written there in front of him on his
instrument rack. But it takes a swing player, and a real
good one, to be able to leave that score and to know,
or 'feel,' just when to leave it and when to get back
on it." For Armstrong, this music was an indigenous
product: it was "growing into a finer and broader and
richer music, a music that is truly American. . . . Until
swing music came, America had no music it could
really call its own."[99]

For Armstrong, then, swing music was improvisatory, emotional, and American. For Dove, committed
to making an art that was nonrepresentational, full of
feeling, and American, swing and jazz served as the
perfect model: as music it was abstract; as jazz it was
both abstract and native. But what did it mean to
describe this music as American?

*Commercial Jazz and American Identity*

Jazz was used to label diverse types of early twentieth-
century music, some of which do not seem to qualify
as jazz to our late twentieth-century ears. Dove selected music that represented different forms of jazz as
practiced and understood in the 1920s and 1930s—the
jazzed-up classical style of Gershwin's *Rhapsody in
Blue,* the sweet jazz and pepped-up popular music of
Whiteman's orchestra, and Armstrong's swing, with its
raucous sounds presented on a symphonic scale. In
search of a native expression, both black and white
composers combined jazz with art-music forms,
thereby "elevating" it from lowbrow to highbrow, black
to white, African American to American, as Gershwin
did. This sanitizing transformation involved a shift of
venue from the dance hall to the concert hall, as the
music was "improved" from its popular or folk state—a
process premised upon a notion of black folk music

as unsophisticated and white art music as refined. In making this move to the concert stage and the popularization of the mass media, Whiteman disconnected jazz from African American sources and largely purged it of its dangerous, suggestive sensuality—that is, the "primitive" qualities that were equated with blackness. More than jazzed-up classical music and sweet jazz, swing preserved the strident sounds and sultriness of early jazz, but this too was edited and censored for popular consumption.

All of these jazz forms were perceived and constructed as American—but a particular brand of American. We can interpret them as the result of a whitening process, but the equation of this African American music with American music as a whole was also an infusion of blackness and black cultural practices into mainstream American life. The historian Eric Lott has argued, in his study of blackface minstrelsy, that this blackening of the national culture occurred even in the nineteenth century.[100] Yet early twentieth-century commercial-music practices and visual representations of jazz often masked this tendency and produced instead a music, images of music, and a notion of Americanness in which blackness was largely absent. In turning to these jazz forms as a marker of American cultural identity, Dove was influenced by, and participated in, this process.

Dove was undoubtedly familiar with the debates about the sanitizing of jazz. In the July 1917 issue of *The Seven Arts* Hiram Kelly Moderwell had criticized professional American musicians for not recognizing ragtime's potential as the source of a new national music. However, he saw value in ragtime—as well as other popular music forms—only insofar as they provided the foundation for a "great" classical music, in the same way, for example, that folk music served contemporary Russian composers:

> Here is the only original and characteristic music America has produced thus far. Whether it can be made the basis for a national school of composition as great as the Russian I do not know. But I know that there will be no great American music so long as American musicians despise our ragtime. . . . When an Aeolian Hall public applauds this programme of ragtime, then I shall expect to hear of great American symphonies.[101]

Moderwell's expectations were fulfilled by the concert *An Experiment in Modern Music,* performed at Aeolian Hall in New York on February 12, 1924. This event brought jazz and the notion of its ennoblement to public attention. Not only was jazz performed in a space typically reserved for art music, but the structure of the program asserted an evolution from a "crude" state to its present sophisticated form, as Paul Whiteman, the concert's organizer, commented: "Beginning with the earliest jazz composition, 'Livery Stable Blues,' we played twenty-six selections designed to exhibit legitimate scoring as contrasted with the former hit and miss effects which were also called jazz."[102] The concert started with this piece, which Whiteman considered the "crude jazz of the past," and ended with Edward Elgar's *Pomp and Circumstance,* with progressive steps of "improvement" made along the way. The penultimate item was Gershwin's *Rhapsody in Blue*—a composition that combined the classical and popular and that moved jazz into a new genre.

Dove was familiar with the classical jazz performed at *An Experiment in Modern Music* and with other sanitized forms of jazz. As jazz, ragtime, and other popular musics were "elevated" to the concert hall and "improved" by their incorporation into art-music forms, they were associated more closely with Western art music and white musicians and were proportionally de-Africanized:

> In the United States, the types of jazz that were most easily and widely accepted initially were the filtered

and hybridized versions that created less cultural dissonance. . . . The degree to which blacks could be left out of this musical equation was stunning. In the mid-1920s the composer John Alden Carpenter praised jazz as "the first art innovation originating in America to be accepted seriously in Europe," and then predicted that "the musical historian of the year 2,000 A.D. will find the birthday of American music and that of Irving Berlin to have been the same."[103]

The music's popularity and its validations by European critics accounted to some extent for its appropriation by white America, as the African American writer James Weldon Johnson remarked at the time: "Nobody thought of questioning the Negro's title as creator of [the spiritual] until its beauty and value were demonstrated. The same thing, in a greater degree, has transpired with regard to the Negro as the originator of America's popular medium of expression; in fact, to such a degree, that it is now completely divorced from all ideas associated with the Negro."[104]

In the 1920s the term *jazz* was often used to describe popular music in general, like that of Paul Whiteman's band—livelier than earlier pop but only mildly syncopated and without swing or improvisation. It was this music that Dove, like many listeners, understood as jazz, particularly in the late 1920s:

> The white publicists and critics who first defined jazz for the mass public rarely praised the music as an art form, and in fact they usually ignored the central role of blacks in its creation. White Americans felt that the off-sounding word applied only to the frenetic, ragtime-like music of white bands which received the greatest publicity in the mainstream white market. This "jazz" was generally considered to be an interesting (and mildly licentious) diversion, created not by blacks but by what one writer called "the Semitic purveyors of Broadway hits." Black jazz, and the black origins of swinging syncopation and blues harmony, were rarely acknowledged in the white press. The

> white listeners who came to the South Side [in Chicago] and Harlem often shared the notion that the "jungle music" they heard was a debased black form of white popular music.[105]

Just as the form of this music was dissociated from African American sources, its history was also rewritten as it became identified as a cultural product of white America. White, sweet jazz musicians appropriated this music as their own. Georg Brunis, for instance, proposed barbershop singing and Jewish hymns as the sources of jazz and the blues.[106] Many critics and early jazz historians considered the white musicians the most noteworthy jazz performers and composers precisely because they de-Africanized the music. The critic Gilbert Seldes distinguished two opposing strains of jazz—the Negro and the intellectual—in his 1923 article, "Toujours Jazz." While he equated African American qualities with certain American characteristics[107] and mentioned the black jazz artists Noble Sissle, Eubie Blake, and W. C. Handy, he showcased the white musicians Berlin, Gershwin, and Whiteman, praising their synthesis of the instinctive "negro side" of jazz and the intellectual symphonic tradition:

> Nowhere is the failure of the negro to exploit his gifts more obvious than in the use he has made of the jazz orchestra; for although nearly every negro jazz band is better than nearly every white band, no negro band has yet come up to the level of the best white ones, and the leader of the best of all, by a little joke, is called Whiteman. . . . To-day I know of no second to Whiteman in the complete exploitation of jazz. . . . All the free, the instinctive, the wild in negro jazz which could be integrated into his music, he has kept; he has added to it, has worked his material, until it runs sweetly in his dynamo, without grinding or scraping. It becomes the machine which conceals machinery. He has arrived at one high point of jazz.[108]

Whiteman had done away with the sounds associated with jazz's brothel past and created a smoother, sweeter, more respectable music, appropriate for a concert hall. His status as a composer of legitimate music was validated when he was crowned the "King of Jazz" by a representative of the Metropolitan Opera in a staged photograph that appeared in his 1926 book, *Jazz* (fig. 64).

Whiteman himself served to elevate, whiten, and Americanize jazz through his public image.[109] *Jazz,* an autobiography of sorts, presented a very personal history of his music. Throughout, the King of Jazz misnames or only vaguely alludes to blacks and their music. For him, jazz is American music, and *American* means white, pure, mainstream. He describes his band members as descended largely from "good" immigrants from northern Europe, reflecting the widespread race segregation in jazz bands before 1936.[110] The ideal jazz band becomes a microcosm of the ideal America of assimilated white immigrants:

> Perhaps the most important item in jazz equipment is that each player shall be American. It is better to be native-born American and better still, if one's parents were born here, for then one has had the American environment for two generations and that helps a great deal in playing jazz. At least, the musician must be a naturalized citizen, which means a considerable residence and a knowledge of language and customs.[111]

One illustration in Whiteman's book, entitled *Jazz within the Law* (fig. 65), pictured his ideal jazz band: all-white musicians dressed in white suits drinking buttermilk, playing "civilized," lawful music (not the music of brothels or speakeasies). Such images, accompanied by the terms *naturalized* and *native-born*, engaged the nativist discourse of the period. American postwar isolationism and conservatism nourished an ardent and often dangerous nationalism. Through the Palmer raids, restrictive immigration laws, and the revival of the Ku

Klux Klan, nativist white groups attempted to preserve the power that many perceived as diminished or threatened by the new immigrants from southern and eastern Europe and the growing presence of blacks in the urban north. They excluded Jews and African Americans from their America and identified them with subversive politics and urban decline and as threats to the survival of the white race.[112]

Whiteman's construct of jazz in America is exclusionary as well. His 1930 film, *King of Jazz,* wrote African Americans out of jazz history and established his own brand of sweet, white jazz as canonical. This movie, Universal Pictures' first technicolor film, is a lavish Broadway-style revue with seven numbers, ranging from comedy sketches to song-and-dance sequences, performed by Whiteman and his band and Bing Crosby and the Rhythm Boys, among others. Short sequences (in which a colossal Paul Whiteman Scrapbook opens and pages are turned) introduce each skit or number and provide the unifying framework of the film. After Whiteman appears at the beginning, a narrator asks how he became the King of Jazz. The answer is a short animated cartoon sequence in which Whiteman is cast as a musical colonist: dressed as a hunter, he goes to Africa, where he tames a lion, the "king of the jungle," by singing the black spiritual "Daniel in the Lion's Den," acting "black," and using music to soothe the savage beast. He then takes the lion's place as monarch and a monkey drops a coconut on his head, "crowning" him. This cartoon presents the King of Jazz as explorer and colonizer in darkest Africa—the white man who takes control and possession of jazz at its primitive source and civilizes it. Whiteman becomes the link with African music, its discoverer, translator, and redeemer. While the film is particularly crude, it is by no means out of step with a common sentiment about jazz and race in 1930s America.

*King of Jazz* whitens jazz relentlessly. Whiteman's all-white band and all-white female chorus line are

Figure 64

Jeanne Gordon of the
Metropolitan Opera
crowning the King of Jazz,
1926 (reproduced in Paul
Whiteman, *Jazz,* New
York: J. H. Sears, 1926).

Figure 65

*Jazz within the Law,* Paul Whiteman's band (reproduced in his *Jazz,* New York: J. H. Sears, 1926).

the movie's central actors. Blacks are essentially absent from the skits and stories; there are only two black characters in the entire film and they are presented as comical, childlike, and primitive in the Hollywood tradition. These stereotypes frame the history of jazz in popular culture. In one sequence in *King of Jazz* Whiteman instructs the audience that jazz combines the most primitive and the most modern musical elements. This music, he explains, was "born in the African jungle to the beating of the voodoo drum," demonstrated in the movie by a single black figure dancing on a drumhead. (This dancer seems to be wearing full-body black makeup.) Thus, Whiteman states that the roots of jazz are in African music, which he defines as undeveloped and unsophisticated, based mainly on simple rhythm. The movie then contrasts

this primitive phase of jazz with Gershwin's *Rhapsody in Blue* (the only piece of music for which Whiteman's band is today known). Its complex melodies, rhythms, and instrumentation (including blue pianos) are emphasized and its performance is staged with musicians in top hats and tuxedos, chorus girls in evening gowns, and backdrops with skyscraper designs—all classic Hollywood signifiers of modern, urban, upper-class, civilized sophistication.

Nevertheless, while this movie consciously whitens jazz, at the same time it also unconsciously participates in the blackening of white culture and American identity, as the mainstream absorbs the powerful style and voice of the marginalized culture. The colonizer is shaped by the colonized. Whiteman appropriates and converts black jazz, yet he himself must masquerade as black to gain access to this music by singing a spiritual in the African jungle. African Americans are excluded from the movie's version of the melting pot, but their invisible presence remains audible: in the finale the song "Stars and Stripes Forever" is ornamented with excerpts from a spiritual. The movie makes the argument that black music transformed white, Western, European music in the early twentieth century. Indeed, in Germany black jazz performers from the Chocolate Kiddies to Duke Ellington were widely admired and imitated,[113] and composers throughout Europe used jazz to reinvent traditional musical forms, as Ernst Krenek did in his 1927 opera *Jonny spielt auf* (*Johnny Strikes Up the Band*). American composers such as Gershwin and Aaron Copland incorporated jazz into their works to Americanize their otherwise European-derived styles.[114] While blacks and their music were often expelled from constructs of America, they nonetheless influenced notions of a national music and identity. White performers paid tribute to black jazz musicians in their mimicry, however masked or unintentional that homage might be.[115] Black presence is not seen, but only heard in the music; blacks become dematerialized and abstracted through this representation.

*King of Jazz* defines jazz and Americanism through other ethnic exclusions and transformations as well. Along with blacks, Jews are explicitly barred from the melting pot in the film; they are Americanized not by the crucible of America but by a figurative conversion through language instruction. In a scene of a group singalong to the tune of "Nellie," the chorus is first written in subtitles on the screen in Yiddish, and no one in the film sings; then the English lyrics appear and the cast sings enthusiastically.

The film's finale features a gigantic, literal melting pot, revealed when Whiteman's scrapbook opens and the narrator announces: "America is a melting pot of music wherein the melodies of all nations are fused into one great new rhythm—JAZZ!" Representatives

from diverse ethnic groups, dressed in stereotypical national costumes—Italian accordionists, Scots bagpipers, Russian dancers, Irish harp players and tenors, Spanish flamenco dancers (but no blacks or Jews)—walk into a colossal cauldron (fig. 66). Master chef Whiteman stirs these ethnic types together in the pot to make white, accentless, English-speaking Americans: cowgirls in golden costumes and cowboys holding saxophones; these parade out of the crucible as the orchestra celebrates the meltdown by playing "Stars and Stripes Forever."[116] This construct of America demands the perfect assimilation of immigrants and proposes jazz as the product that will emerge from the breakdown of ethnic difference.

This whitening of jazz occurred in other commercial forms of music. As black jazz musicians left the South, their music became enmeshed in the dominant white culture of the North. As early as 1915 black riverboat jazz bands began adapting their work to the tastes of white audiences. For example, performers on the Streckfus cruise line, which operated out of New Orleans, were trained to play dance music—fox-trots, waltzes, one-steps—for the largely white clientele. Jazz became a commodity and promoters controlled their product to make it profitable, often diluting the music in the studio by simplifying melodies and eliminating improvisation.[117]

The new music industries of recording, radio, publishing, touring, and nightclubs helped to commodify jazz as well. The primary interest was in creating marketable products. While hot jazz played on some commercial radio stations, sweet or smooth jazz dominated programming in the 1930s. But the Depression threatened the growing prosperity of jazz musicians and altered their music. Facing declining record sales and the repeal of Prohibition in 1933, which closed many speakeasies and other jazz locales, many musicians moved to New York and entered the commercial dance-band market to survive. This meeting of jazz and mass marketing produced the Big Band era of

Figure 66

Still from the film *King of Jazz,* 1930. Williamstown, Mass., Williams College, Chapin Library of Rare Books.

1935–47. The mellow, smooth jazz of the Benny Goodman, Tommy Dorsey, and Bob Crosby bands was upbeat and soothing to anxious audiences in search of a cheap good time. It helped to revive the record and touring industries in the late 1930s.[118]

Not all swing jazz was white, and not all of it was equally bland, but the music that enjoyed immense success—that overwhelmed competing sounds and styles—was that which became associated with classical music—high-art music, white cultural forms—and dissociated from earlier black jazz. In Armstrong's autobiography, *Swing That Music,* we can see the careful way the great swing musician negotiates his own African American identity with editors' and the white public's expectations of a black musician. He narrates the evolution of jazz from the raucous New Orleans sound to refined swing, with his own music exemplifying its progress. In his terms, jazz goes from "rigid," "awk-

ward," "unpolished," and "barbaric" "tribal and revival chants" to "refined," "sympathetic," "closely integrated," "softened," and "tempered" strains. This version of the jazz story validated Armstrong as a musician through the authority of white voices: the white band leader Rudy Vallee provided an introduction, the British musician and arranger Horace Gerlach an explanatory conclusion, and the photographs in the text were largely of Armstrong's white colleagues and predecessors.[119] Swing was presented as elevated and refined, a parallel to white cultural products.

For Arthur Dove, as for most white New Yorkers, jazz was thus not the exuberant sounds of the King Oliver Creole Jazz Band but rather the relatively tamer music of the Paul Whiteman Orchestra, the compositions of George Gershwin, and the swing sounds of Armstrong.[120] Dove did not go slumming in Harlem to see black jazz bands but formed his view of jazz

Figure 67

Miguel Covarrubias,
*Rhapsody in Blue,* 1931.
Lithograph. Private collec-
tion (reproduced in Alain
Locke, *The Negro in Art,*
1936, repr. New York:
Hacker Art Books, 1968,
189).

and popular music by reading (white) art and cultural
journals and listening to recordings and broadcasts. He
painted Gershwin's symphonic jazz, Whiteman's sweet
jazz, and Armstrong's swing—all commercial products.
Unlike Miguel Covarrubias's 1931 lithograph *Rhapsody
in Blue* (fig. 67), in which the title of the Gershwin
composition is used to describe a black blues singer
and jazz band, Dove's jazz abstractions, in which
sounds are transformed into color, line, and form, have
the effect of disassociating the music from its origins
and producers and emphasizing its abstract, universal
qualities. His images of jazz, like his experience of it,
were distanced from the performers and far indeed
from the experience of its originators. As in the invisible strains of the spiritual that plays at the end of *King
of Jazz,* black America is filtered through the abstract
language of Dove's paintings, so that the black influ-

ence on American music and identity is masked.[121]
Like the music that served as his immediate source,
Dove's images of jazz are sanitized and decorative, producing a notion of American identity dependent on
the commercial culture. Dove used jazz to illustrate
modernity and speed, because he saw these qualities as
intrinsically American and worthy of celebration.

*Stuart Davis's Americanized, Sanitized Jazz Paintings*

As it did for Dove, jazz provided a model for Stuart
Davis in his efforts to Americanize modernist art.
Davis's experiences and knowledge of jazz were more
varied than Dove's. He had direct contact with jazz
musicians, frequenting jazz bars in Newark in the
1910s, and Armstrong even played at the opening for

his 1943 solo exhibition at the Downtown Gallery in New York, an event that Duke Ellington, W. C. Handy, and Pete Johnson also attended.[122] He exchanged painting and music lessons with the jazz drummer George Wettling.[123] Commercial jazz also shaped Davis's ideas. His paintings show these different experiences and his own changing views of jazz. He described the external world of early jazz in his 1910s Realist paintings and drawings of black musicians in Newark's barrel houses. In these works he represented African American music as a contemporary, vital subject matter, part of the antiacademic rebellion of the New York Realists. In contrast, he identified jazz with abstract qualities—modernity, simultaneity, dynamism—in his later work, separating it from black culture specifically and equating it more broadly with urban America. Like contemporary musicians, he unwittingly sanitized and commodified jazz in his art, using bright colors and sharp, clean, machinelike forms, painting jazz lingo much as he did the typography of advertisements and billboards and packaging this art as an American product.

Davis experienced popular music as part of the modern, urban landscape during his early career. His father, Edward Wyatt Davis, as art director of the *Philadelphia Press* in the 1890s, had employed the Ashcan Realists John Sloan, George Luks, William Glackens, and Everett Shinn, so it is not surprising that Davis found his way into Robert Henri's School of Art in New York in 1909, studying with him until 1912. Henri fostered Davis's commitment to self-expression, experimentation, and cultural nationalism and urged the young painter to explore New York and immerse himself in the life around him, as Davis later recalled:

> We were encouraged to make sketches of everyday life in the streets, the theater, the restaurant, and everywhere else. These were transformed into paintings in the school studios. . . . Coleman, Henry

Glintenkamp and myself toured extensively in the metropolitan environs. Chinatown; the Bowery; the burlesque shows; the Brooklyn Bridge; McSorley's Saloon on East 7th Street; the Music Halls of Hoboken; the Negro Saloons; riding on the canal boats under the Public Market.[124]

The new urban entertainment centers figured prominently in Davis's artistic explorations of the city. These were important subjects for many of the New York Realists, as part of their vision of the dramatic urban "spectacle," shaped by the popular press and the consumer culture.[125] Sensationalist newspapers such as the New York *World* presented urban violence and the lives of the poor as picturesque and theatrical—visual codes that the artist-reporter Everett Shinn, for example, adopted in *Fire on Twenty-Fourth Street, New York City* (1907) and other drawings. Such images provided vicarious thrills for middle-class viewers, although Shinn used the visual device of empty foreground space to establish a sense of safe distance between the viewer and the painting's grim subject. Like sensational newspapers, the vaudeville stage too was a place of spectacle and entertainment that depended upon scandal for its effect.

The city and popular entertainment as spectacle appear in Davis's early works. The painter envisioned the theater as a dramatic and mysterious world in *Babette* (1912)—a world similar to that of the early jazz saloons. Sometime in 1912 Davis moved to Hoboken, New Jersey, where he shared a studio in the Terminal Building on Hudson Street with a fellow painter, Henry Glintenkamp. He later recalled his discovery of African American music on prowls through the streets and saloons of the area:

> [Glenn] Coleman and I were particularly hep to the jive, for that period, and spent much time listening to the Negro piano players in Newark dives. About the only thing then available on phonograph records was the Anvil Chorus. Our musical souls craved some-

thing a bit more on the solid side and it was necessary to go to the source to dig it. These saloons
catered to the poorest Negroes, and outside of beer, a
favorite drink was a glass of gin with a cherry in it
which sold for five cents. The pianists were unpaid,
playing for love of art alone. . . . But the big point
with us was that in all of these places you could hear
the blues, or tin-pan alley tune[s] turned into real
music, for the cost of a five cent beer.[126]

In this narrative Davis presents himself and his companion as insiders who understand the music ("hep to
the jive"), reject commercial records, and seek out the
real thing. For him, this jazz is "solid" and its musicians exemplary artists, natural and untainted by consumerism. Coleman too considered the music authentic, writing of one black pianist's performance: "I can
hear the tom-toms when this chap plays, . . . He's a
primitive expressing himself as best he knows how—
but this expression is real and deep. You may talk
about your Beethoven symphonies, but there's
as much real expression in the music of this boy as
can be found in any symphony orchestra. One
expresses the primitive, the other the over-sensitized.
This is a good protest against over-complicated
orchestra forms."[127]

Artists in the Henri and Stieglitz circles rejected
middle-class mores on the one hand and routinized,
mechanized modern society on the other; they
sought the vital and real in American life and turned
to groups, people, and art forms that they perceived
as liberated, unrestrained, and authentic. Artists often
found these qualities in working-class, immigrant
communities and cultures. Frequently outsiders to
these groups, they viewed them through their own
cultural lenses: working-class ethnics and blacks were
the urban primitive, the Other within the city, living
in a modern culture but free from its social restrictions. These groups' cultural products—boxing,
vaudeville, ragtime—were romanticized as emblems
of liberation.

Davis's and Coleman's attraction to jazz saloons,
performers, and music can be understood as part of
this quest for the urban primitive. In his initial
encounters with African American music Davis played
the role of artist-anthropologist-reporter, traveling to
the foreign regions of New York and its environs. His
forays into Newark and Harlem bars paralleled John
Sloan's ventures into working-class neighborhoods
and George Bellows's and Joseph Stella's excursions to
Coney Island. Davis and Coleman framed their
adventure as part of the urban spectacle, replicating in
print an encounter that many whites would only
experience a decade later, slumming in Harlem. As
travel companions in Newark's black community they
reported on and documented their journey in sketches
that portrayed it as an exotic experience. Emanuel
Julius and Clement Wood accompanied the two
painters, with the reporter Julius giving them voice:
"We left New York one rainy night, spent about 19
cents for a ticket, and rode to Newark. For a provin-
cial, supercilious, overbearing New Yorker to go to
Newark for no other purpose than to see the Negro
tenderloin sights—and spend an entire night going
from barrel house to barrel house—must, in the mind
of many, be the most convincing proof of insanity,
when one considers that slumming . . . can be done
right here in Manhattan. But to Newark we went—
the four of us." Julius's language presents the trip as
one of extreme distance and disorientation; the sights
they saw were of the "lowest of the most oppressed"
people, their dirty houses, alleys, and dance halls and
their gritty pleasure spots: "We heard wonderful piano
thumping, the kind that could come from no other
than the fingers of a Negro. It was Ragtime with a
capital R."[128]

Davis represented these clubs as dark, mysterious
places in the paintings and prints based on this and
other wild nights in Newark. Like Shinn's paintings
of the city, these works are dramatic spectacles that
keep the viewer at a safe distance. The sparsely lit and

Figure 68

Stuart Davis, *Jackson's Band,*
1913. Pencil on paper, 20 ×
15⅞ in. (50.8 × 40.3 cm).
Collection of Earl Davis.
(© 1996 Estate of Stuart
Davis/Licensed by VAGA,
New York).

decorated space in *The Back Room* (fig. 44) appears
crude compared to contemporary vaudeville theaters.
A black drummer and piano player sit in the left corner while figures stand in varied postures and gaze at
the floor, band, and a couple who dance under the
light of a lamp. One person seems to move toward
the dancers at center, creating a sense of tension. The
figures' faces are sketchy and some appear masklike,
adding to this eerie mood. As viewers, we are both
connected to and disconnected from the scene. The
floor tilts downward and opens up to us, yet we feel
detached from the room, whose dark, indistinct
atmosphere seems impenetrable.[129] Similarly, *Jackson's
Band* (fig. 68) sketches an unfocused, fragmented
experience of a jazz-bar interior.[130] This drawing
describes the same saloon in *The Back Room*, with
identical barrels, piano player, and drum ("Jackson's
Band"). Here, however, our perspective and position
differ. The figures fill the paper's surface, allowing us
no access to the room. We have more direct contact
with the club's clientele, particularly the black man in
the foreground; he engages us with his gaze and
appears to be sitting across the table from us. This figure is sketched with some detail, in contrast to the
generalized features of the background figures.

In these Realist works Davis documents ragtime
and jazz in their setting: he describes their accouter-
ments—the barrel house, instruments, dancers—and
their exotic, mysterious environment. Davis as artist
and we as presumably middle-class viewers encounter
this music and its social spaces at one remove.
Ultimately, we are tourists and outsiders in the world
of jazz and other working-class entertainments—
vaudeville, burlesque, boxing.[131]

As jazz moved out of black saloons and bordellos,
it became less mysterious and tension-filled, less black
and more white, less African American and more
American. Davis's perceptions and uses of jazz in his
later art and writings also changed accordingly. While
both his early and late representations of jazz are

linked to a continued interest in the urban experience, the nature of that interest and experience changed; his early works show Davis as a Realist, his later jazz paintings as an abstractionist. European modernism now replaced Henri's aesthetic as the primary influence on his work. In 1913 the young painter saw the Armory Show in New York—an event that he later said was central to the formation of his art. He reacted favorably to the works of Van Gogh, Gauguin, and Matisse and became fascinated with the problems of abstract color relationships so evident in the works of the Post-Impressionists. From the 1910s through the 1920s Davis experimented with various modernist styles: he worked in a Post-Impressionist and Fauvist manner with Charles Demuth in Gloucester, Massachusetts in 1914–16, and by the next decade had evolved an abstract manner informed by a study of Synthetic Cubism.

Never, however, did Davis completely abandon visible reality in his art. Though he worked with geometry and color-space theory in his mature works, he was always attracted to the American environment as a source of inspiration. He said, "I'm not one of those who hold that painting comes out of nothing. It may be subjects I'm interested in at any time. Light, objects, buildings, people, sounds, the context of a phrase of writing, and always jazz music."[132] He insisted that contact with the American scene was essential in constructing a national identity in his art—an abstract art that was increasingly viewed as foreign and un-American in the 1920s and 1930s. At this time he wanted to create a modern native art and reacted strongly against American Scene painting, then a prevalent movement. He disliked the literalism, hostility to avant-garde styles, lack of social consciousness, and rightist politics of Thomas Hart Benton, but continued to place high value on American imagery and renounced pure abstraction: "In my own case, I have enjoyed the dynamic American scene for many years past, and all of my

pictures (including the ones I painted in Paris) are referential to it. They all have their originating impulse in the impact of the contemporary American environment."[133] Like Dove, Davis wanted to portray the spirit, not the external reality of his subject, and considered abstraction the appropriate means to represent modern America.

Also like Dove, Davis considered jazz an ideal subject, part of modern life, expressive of an indigenous spirit, and not amenable to illustration by traditional pictorial means. He viewed jazz as a musical trope for the American environment and its dynamism. His favorite composers, Armstrong, Cab Calloway, Earl Hines, George Wettling, and Fats Waller, conveyed jazz's free quality and sense of excitement, and he sought to communicate this same tempo in his art.[134] Davis wrote of his admiration for Armstrong: "Every artist has models of greatness in the arts which guide his development. Louis Armstrong has always been one of the most important for me. Not to illustrate his musical ideas, but as an example of direct expression which transforms Subject Matter into Art."[135] For Davis, jazz was comparable in its directness of expression to European modernism, as he states in the epigraph to this chapter. Jazz, in a sense, was American modernism.

Jazz became an integral part of Davis's work in the 1930s and early 1940s. According to the artist, the music at first affected him unconsciously:

Tell your friend that I have always liked hot music. There's something wrong with any American who doesn't. But I never realized that it was influencing my work until one day I put on a favorite record and listened to it while I was looking at a painting I had just finished. Then I got a funny feeling. If I looked, or if I listened, there was no shifting of attention. It seemed to amount to the same thing—like twins, a kinship. After that, for a long time, I played records while I painted.[136]

This comment raises the question of Davis's intentionality. Did he set out to construct parallels between jazz and his art, or was this, as he states, something he discovered by chance? Did he plan his paintings as one might compose or orchestrate a jazz piece, or did he improvise, as some jazz musicians do? Did he use jazz as an analogy for his art, a useful, accessible way to discuss his own abstraction, which was often criticized as elitist? Did he present his painting in jazz terms to shape audiences' perception of it, hoping that if he spoke or wrote about his abstractions as jazzlike, viewers would eventually begin to see his foreign-inspired modernism as American?

Seeing music as a model for abstraction, of course, was common in art writing and criticism, and Davis was not unique in comparing his art to music. He perceived the formal properties of the canvas and the process of making a painting as analogous to musical structure and composition. Like a musician, Davis thought that he could convey emotion through abstract forms. He wrote of the mural he painted for Studio B, WNYC, New York's public radio station (fig. 69): "I have taken elements relating to radio and composed them in a harmonious design of shape, color, and direction. The result is a visual decoration which creates a mood in the spectator, just as a piece of music creates a mood, instead of giving some kind of factual information or instruction."[137] He proposed a structure for painting composition similar to that of musical composition: "It is even possible to have a set formula for a good picture. The formula capable of adaptation to various associational ideas. As in

Figure 69

Stuart Davis, untitled mural for Studio B, WNYC, 1939. Oil on canvas, 84 × 132 in. (213.4 × 335.3 cm). Collection of the City of New York (courtesy of the Art Commission of the City of New York. © 1996 Estate of Stuart Davis/ Licensed by VAGA, New York)

music, the blues, a set form, are always good and one might say that they express everything that can be expressed."[138]

While Davis relied on musical language in general to help explain his nonrepresentational art, he used a particular musical form, jazz, to reach a wide audience and to emphasize the Americanness of his art. We cannot be certain if he looked to specific jazz compositions in creating individual works, as Dove did, but we know that he referred to jazz in his paintings in a number of ways: he "illustrated" its sounds; he equated jazz with the American scene and the modern city; he appropriated jazz lingo. And, like Dove's work, his jazz paintings and writings were tied to the commercial jazz of the period.

In the 1920s and 1930s Davis listened to radio and phonograph jazz, in contrast to his earlier direct encounters with the music: "It seems fantastic to think that today I can sit in my centrally-located and centrally-heated studio and hear [jazz] without taking a bus to Newark or Harlem. It is only necessary to lean slightly to the right and turn the radio dial, at the right time and place. Or if it isn't the right time you lean slightly to the left and turn on the phonograph to hear Wesley Wallace's 'Train 29.' "[139] Davis's diary entries in the late thirties note radio programs of interest, particularly jazz programs.[140] He painted radio jazz into his mural for the WNYC radio studio. Like Dove's 1936–37 radio paintings, Davis's 1939 radio-station mural visualizes the invisible process of sound transmission. In his working notes he wrote about his aims in this painting: he wanted to show "a series of formal relations which are identified with musical instruments, radio antenna, ether waves, operators panel, and electrical symbols, etc. These various elements are presented in an imaginative rather than a factual relationship."[141] Davis included images of the saxophone and clarinet—two instruments associated with jazz, especially 1930s swing. The bright colors and musical notations around the sax signify its music,

which is then transmitted to the central shape and travels through its wires, lines, and squiggles to be sent off through the white line—ether waves—into the radio on the right. Using signs, symbols, and abbreviated forms, Davis envisions the journey of swing sounds from the studio through the radio.

In this mural Davis brought together technology, jazz, and abstraction to construct a work both modern and American—a work that expressed national identity in modernist terms. He produced several works dedicated to the radio and its place in modern American society, including *Radio Tubes* (1931) and a mural for the Hall of Communications at the New York World's Fair (1939). The radio's technology helped both Davis and Dove think about abstraction. Davis wrote about "music through the radio" as part of the new American environment and commented in 1940: "An artist who has used the telegraph, telephone and radio doesn't feel the same way about light and color as one who has not."[142] These new machines transformed the way people saw the world. In his "Self-Interview," he identified the movies and radio as contributors to a vital American culture and as creators of a new reality: "[Movies and radio] allow us to experience hundreds of diverse scenes, sounds and ideas in a juxtaposition that has never before been possible. Regardless of their significance they force a new sense of reality and this must of course be reflected in art."[143] This new reality was best visualized through abstraction; Davis considered radio transmission the "essence of abstraction."[144]

Like Dove, Davis was enchanted by the Americanness of jazz. When asked in his "Self-Interview" which artists he thought best reflected the vital American spirit, he named Cab Calloway, Armstrong, and the three Doctors. With the artist Walter Quirt, he planned a Festival of Creative Swing Music and Modern Painting in 1941. According to Davis and Quirt, this festival (which was never funded) was intended to show "the relationship between the two art forms, to demonstrate the similarities in their origins, to show how both were authentic art expressions of contemporary society, and finally to show the genuine American character of their expression."[145] Several of Davis's paintings of the late 1930s and early 1940s assert this relationship among swing, modernism, and American cultural identity, in particular, *Swing Landscape* (1938) and *Hot Still Scape for Six Colors—Seventh Avenue Style* (1940; plate 5).

Jazz as metaphor for the dynamic American scene informed *Swing Landscape* (fig. 70), a mural planned for the Williamsburg Housing Project in New York. Here, Davis transformed the busy Gloucester, Massachusetts waterfront into a panorama of abstract patterns and vibrant colors, which he gave a jazzy title. Visual clues—blue for sky and sea; schematic renderings of buoys, rigging, masts, houses, chimneys—symbolize the harbor scene. Purely abstract reds, oranges, yellows, and hot pinks punctuate the blue to produce visual contrast and energy. The salient quality of swing, its driving forward momentum, is the keynote of *Swing Landscape*. Repeated hot colors convey this quality, as do the diagonals and curves that counterpoint the vertical masts at left and right center.

This quality of movement was equated with music and with "swinging" in other contemporary sources. Dove, for example, defined swing as a rhythm beyond space, a kind of fourth-dimensional experience:

> Just at present, I have come to the conclusion that one must have a flexible form or formation that is governed by some definite rhythmic sense beyond mere geometrical repetition, to express and put in space an idea so that those with sensitive instruments can pick it up, and further that means an expression has to have grown long enough to establish itself as an automatic force.
>
> The play or spread or swing of space can only be felt through this kind of consciousness.[146]

Dove spoke of creating a sense of rhythm not by repetition of form but through some other kind of visual movement; he used the term *swinging* to describe that quality of motion in his paintings of the 1930s. Like Davis's *Swing Landscape*, Dove's landscape *Swinging in the Park (there were colored people there)* (1930) used abstract patterns and schematic forms. Sweeping lines overlay the dominant organic shapes to suggest energy and a sense of movement or rhythm independent of

Figure 70

Stuart Davis, *Swing Landscape,* 1938. Oil on canvas, 86¾ × 172⅞ in. (220.3 × 439 cm). Bloomington, Indiana University Art Museum (© 1996 Estate of Stuart Davis/Licensed by VAGA, New York).

any literal description—"beyond space," in his phrase. Critics saw this painting as expressing pure movement and, thus, musicality. Edwin Alden Jewell used *Swinging in the Park* to illustrate a 1937 article, "Concerning That Plea for Motion." Music, Jewell thought, could not be pictured without this sense of movement: "That rhythm can be visualized; that motion, color, form and sound are interchangeable elements from a common source are facts undeniable as that the world we live upon is round." Movement in a painting could be created as the play of forces in the design—the "pulsing sum of a picture's plastic elements," "the journey of the line" as a kind of tempo, the interaction of masses and forms.[147]

While Dove depended largely on line to create a swinging rhythm, Davis worked with shape and color to build a similar effect in *Swing Landscape* and *Hot Still Scape for Six Colors—Seventh Avenue Style* (plate 5). In the latter he blended still-life and landscape elements from a modern city-dweller's experience: "Fruit and flowers; kitchen utensils; Fall skies; horizons; taxicabs; radio; art exhibitions and reproductions; fast travel; Americana; movies; electric signs; dynamics of city sights and sounds." Davis used musical analogies to describe *Hot Still Scape* and its representation of the simultaneity of modern urban experience. The jazz term *hot* in the title characterized urban dynamism: "[It] is called *Hot* because of its dynamic mood, as opposed to a serene or pastoral mood." The six colors—white, yellow, blue, orange, red, black—replicated this energy as well as the multiplicity and fragmentary perception of objects in the city: "[The colors] are used as the instruments in a musical composition might be, where the tone-color variety results from the simultaneous juxtaposition of different instrument groups."[148] Davis likened color to musical instruments playing with and against one another. In music the timbre, or tone quality of an instrument, is described as its color; in fact, the German word for timbre is *klangfarbe,* or tone color.[149] Different instrument

groups are played at the same time for contrast. For Davis, musical instrumentation was analogous to the simultaneity that he created visually in *Hot Still Scape.*

The six colors in this painting perhaps refer directly to swing-band instrumentation—the red-hot trumpet, for example. Although the term *hot* was widely used to describe jazz, and especially swing, and referred to the improvisational energy of the music, swing was on the whole much less improvised, or hot, than earlier jazz. Swing ensembles performed structured, orchestrated compositions with some ornamental improvised passages. *Hot Still Scape* parallels this form. One of the things that Davis admired in jazz, and particularly in the music of Earl Hines, was the use of intervals or spaces between sounds.[150] He thought that this same effect could be used in painting; what was left out reinforced the solid forms of objects. For Davis, the spaces between objects were as important as the objects themselves, as is evident in *Hot Still Scape.* Davis planned this work with care: he used the planar structure from his earlier *Eggbeater No. 2* (1927–28) as the underlying framework, and selected and organized colors using his color-space system.[151] He laid down a frame of red on three sides and yellow on one. Jumbled fragments, objects, and signs meet in the center on interlocking planes. Along with the colors, the interplay of these planes, objects, and empty spaces creates movement and energy. High-intensity reds, yellows, and oranges play against the cool blue and black and white. These hot colors help to animate dynamic shapes—the staccato daubs, curves and squiggles, diagonal planes, arrows, and sequentially placed balls.

The words *hot* and *swing* in *Swing Landscape* and *Hot Still Scape* underscore the importance that contemporary commercial jazz had in shaping Davis's art. This music influenced other paintings by Davis during this time. The language of jazz culture entered his iconography; he brought his earlier interest in advertising and lettering to his jazz paintings, incorporating the jargon phrases and song titles that served as ads on the radio in his canvases. The visual culture of consumerism had long attracted Davis and figured in his art. His early Realist works had often included the shop signs and billboards that marked the urban landscape, as in *Bleecker Street* (1913); a decade later the new products of the consumer culture became his subject matter, in such paintings as *Bull Durham* (1922) and *Lucky Strike* (1921). Davis's interest in the language of consumerism—advertising, typography, graphics—is also evident in his mural for Gar Spark's Nut Shop in Newark, New Jersey (1921), a large-scale wall painting composed entirely of lettering.[152]

Davis combined his interest in advertising and jazz in *American Painting* and *New York under Gaslight* (figs. 71, 72). He produced the former work for the first biennial exhibition at New York's Whitney Museum of American Art; like other artists in the show, he sought in his entry to define a native art for the 1930s.[153] Davis referred in the painting to swing by quoting the lyric from a popular Duke Ellington song, "It don't mean a thing, if it ain't got that swing." He used this as one of several signs of modern America; the others were a Wedell–Williams racing plane, a top-hatted socialite, a skyscraper, and a hand with a pistol.[154] His use of cartoonlike forms is indebted to another Americanism: graphic arts and advertising. His representation of jazz is reduced to a song title, the vehicle through which the music was identified and sold to contemporary audiences. Jazz is paired with a skyscraper in a familiar association with modern architecture and the city. Davis once again linked jazz, the city, and the consumer culture in *New York under Gaslight,* a cityscape that includes buildings around the Brooklyn Bridge and nearby Canal Street, as well as Davis's own studio at 43 Seventh Avenue. The jazzy phrase "Dig This Fine Art Jive" is one of a number of signs in this urban landscape—signs that include *room for rent, dentist, Garcia cigar store,* and a billboard ad for gin.

In Davis's late paintings and writings, then, jazz is equated with the spirit of the urban city and modernity and presented as a marker of the consumer culture. As an American product it takes on specific meanings in his art. While in an essay entitled "The Cube Root" (1943) he described jazz as "Negro music,"[155] in *Hot Still Scape* and his other late representations of jazz blacks were as invisible as in Dove's music paintings. The change in Davis's imagery from scenes of black jazz clubs to the abstractions of the 1930s and 1940s coincidentally parallels a similar whitening process in jazz itself. He constructed a "new realism" that made use of American cultural artifacts, among them jazz; his intent was apparently to appeal to a wide popular audience.

Davis wrote about jazz as an art of freedom: "Real jazz, that is to say Jazz as an Art, is characterized by complete freedom in its expression."[156] In the late 1930s and 1940s this characterization took on political associations for him and his viewers, and jazz became emblematic of American democracy.[157] In the context of the Depression and as fascism arose in Europe, he grew increasingly committed to a socially active art, although he refrained from making his paintings overtly propagandistic. Rather, his formula for a political art relied upon abstraction. The jazz-inspired *Hot Still Scape* had an alternate title that clearly linked jazz, the city, and democracy: *Art of an Urban Democracy, 7th Avenue.* For Davis, the democratic "free exchange of ideas" depended upon new communications technologies, which he celebrated in his *History of Communications* mural for the 1939 New York World's Fair.[158] He paired jazz with the new machines in his mural for WNYC (fig. 69) and *Hot Still Scape,* declaring both to be instruments of American democracy. In the politically charged decades between the world wars modernism was attacked as foreign and Americanism highly valued, and visual artists of every stripe sought to identify their work as native. Jazz as subject served the art of Dove and

Figure 71

Stuart Davis, *American
Painting,* 1932–51. Oil on
canvas, 40 × 50¼ in. (101.6
× 127.6 cm). Omaha,
Joslyn Art Museum (lent
by the University of
Nebraska at Omaha. ©
1996 Estate of Stuart
Davis/Licensed by VAGA,
New York).

Figure 72

Stuart Davis, *New York
under Gaslight,* 1941. Oil on
canvas, 32 × 45 in. (81.3 ×
114.3 cm). Jerusalem, Israel
Museum (Photograph ©
the Israel Museum. © 1996
Estate of Stuart Davis/
Licensed by VAGA, New
York).

Davis in this context. Both painters saw jazz as American, a music that embodied the spirit of the urban environment—restless, fast, dynamic, energetic. In seeing jazz this way they were responding to widespread debates about it, as well as to their own experiences of it. In the process of looking and listening, however, Dove and Davis, like many of their contemporaries, abstracted and distanced jazz in ways that did not always remain true to the music's roots, though they were fruitful visually. Modernist artists and musicians took possession of a sanitized commercial form of jazz as their own and used it to invent emblems of national identity in its many inflections—modern, urban, even democratic.

But how did African American modernists respond to jazz? How did they see this music, and what role did it play in the construction of their distinct racial and national identity? Did the modern, urban scene suggest liberation to African American artists, as it did to Davis and Dove?

But jazz to me is one of the inherent expressions of Negro life in America: the eternal tom-tom beating in the Negro soul—the tom-tom of revolt against weariness in a white world, a world of subway trains, and work, work, work; the tom-tom of joy and laughter, and pain swallowed in a smile.

Langston Hughes, 1926

In the field of popular music it is universally admitted that the Negro has made a distinct contribution to the art of the modern world through jazz, the blues, boogie-woogie, and the latest form of be-bop.

Aaron Douglas, n.d.

# 4. JAZZ AND AFRICAN AMERICAN IDENTITY
## AARON DOUGLAS'S *SONG OF THE TOWERS* (1934)

In their paintings of the 1920s and 1930s Dove and Davis participated in sanitizing and de-Africanizing jazz, as did the composer Gershwin and the band leader Whiteman. For them, jazz was more than a music: it embodied the qualities of modern America; it was American, and American meant energetic, democratic, and, by tacit assumption, white. Dove's and Davis's abstract paintings offered visual equivalents of jazz vitality; meanwhile, the history and originators of jazz were largely left out of the picture. In Dove's *Swing Music (Louis Armstrong)* (plate 7), the trumpeter appears as a mere ghostly silhouette, lost amid the swirls of color that signify sound; the musician merges with the music. Davis's *American Painting* (fig. 71) represents Duke Ellington's music as consumer product, reduced to the label, "It don't mean a thing if it ain't got that swing."[1] For African American artists, in contrast, the makers as well as the consumers of jazz take center stage; Aaron Douglas's *Aspects of Negro Life: Song of the Towers* (plate 8) is an exemplar of this difference.

For Douglas (1899–1979), representing jazz was part of constructing a racial and national identity in his art. His images of jazz and of African American identity can be read in terms of W. E. B. Du Bois's concept of "double-consciousness," which he set out in *The Souls of Black Folk* (1903). As Du Bois explained, black Americans experience a divided self because they remain culturally distinct from, yet also part of, the United States:

> The Negro is a sort of seventh son, born with a veil, and gifted with second-sight in this American world,—a world which yields him no true self-consciousness, but only lets him see himself through the revelation of the other world. It is a peculiar sensation, this double-consciousness, this sense of always looking at one's self through the eyes of others, of measuring one's soul by the tape of a world that looks on in amused contempt and pity. One ever feels his two-ness,—an American, a Negro; two souls, two thoughts, two unreconciled strivings; two warring ideals in one dark body, whose dogged strength alone keeps it from being torn asunder.
>
> The history of the American Negro is the history of this strife,—this longing to attain self-conscious manhood, to merge his double self into a better and truer self. In this merging he wishes neither of the older selves to be lost. He would not Africanize America . . . He would not bleach his Negro soul in a flood of white Americanism. . . . He simply wishes to make it possible for a man to be both a Negro and an American.[2]

Du Bois's terms *Negro* and *American* have usually been understood as referring to African American and American identities. Recently, critics have extended the boundaries of "double-consciousness" to include Pan-Africanism and a diasporic nationalism, with Du Bois's *Negro* also meaning *African*.[3] Either way, Du Bois's powerful image of the African American self as fragmented, split, desirous of a merging that would simultaneously permit the survival of multiple identi-

ties, remains a profoundly disturbing and influential expression of racial identity.

This notion of seeing oneself through multiple lenses, as both American and of African descent, shaped the New Negro movement and the Harlem Renaissance. Black artists and intellectuals did not desire to separate themselves from the so-called dominant culture (as did, for example, Marcus Garvey's Back to Africa movement), but sought to negotiate a position, an identity, as both Negro and American. This negotiation can be seen in Douglas's images of jazz, in particular *Song of the Towers*. Here the painter presents jazz iconically, as an emblem of an African heritage and African American culture, embodied in the figure of the saxophone player. The sax player refers to other types in black art, literature, music, and history, such as the preacher. Douglas simultaneously represented jazz as it had been defined in the wider popular culture—as an urban American music that signified liberation and self-expression. But for Douglas, jazz and the jazz musician also stood for the double-sided racial self, at once African American and American. He attempted to reconcile the striving of two souls in this figure—the New Negro, the merged self, both Negro and American. Like Marin, Stella, Dove, and Davis, Douglas employed music (represented by the musician) and the urban scene to construct cultural identity, but for him the enterprise was no mere exercise in modernism: it was a battle for coherence and for a place in the world.

## *The Harlem Renaissance and African American Identity*

Douglas's participation in the Harlem Renaissance molded his understanding of "double-consciousness." In 1925, after training at the University of Nebraska and then teaching in Kansas City high schools, he moved to New York, where he studied mural painting with the German artist Winold Reiss until 1927.

Influenced by this teacher as well as the 1925 *Survey Graphic* issue entitled "Harlem: Mecca of the New Negro," the young artist began to look to African art as a source for a racial expression; he abandoned his early academic style in favor of a flat, symbolic manner, Africanist in flavor.[4]

Douglas's work in this mode drew the attention of leaders of the New Negro movement, from James Weldon Johnson and Alain Locke to Charles S. Johnson and Du Bois.[5] These writers believed that blacks could advance in American society through artistic achievement, education, and the guidance of an elite they called the "Talented Tenth." As Johnson explained: "The status of the Negro in the United States is more a question of national mental attitude toward the race than of actual conditions. And nothing will do more to change that mental attitude and raise his status than a demonstration of intellectual parity by the Negro through the production of literature and art."[6] That is, social conditions could be improved if stereotypes were destroyed, and the arts were singled out as key instruments in this process. As a result, numerous institutions active in Harlem encouraged African American arts. The National Association for the Advancement of Colored People (NAACP) and the Urban League published the magazines *The Crisis* and *Opportunity* respectively, and promoted the black writers Claude McKay, Jean Toomer, Countée Cullen, and Langston Hughes. They also supported visual artists, as did the Harmon Foundation, which held national competitions exclusively for black artists.[7] In the 1920s these enterprises were centered in Harlem, where African American art and culture flowered.

Douglas benefited from the new patronage opportunities. He produced portraits and wall decorations for private homes in the mid-1920s and soon became the illustrator for Harlem Renaissance publications. He won competitions in *The Crisis* and *Opportunity,* published drawings in these journals as well as in *Fire!!*

and *Theatre Arts,* and did book illustrations for *The New Negro* (1925), James Weldon Johnson's *God's Trombones: Seven Negro Sermons in Verse* (1927), and Paul Morand's *Black Magic* (1929).[8] Douglas secured his place as a prominent black artist through public mural commissions, many at African American institutions. He painted wall decorations for the Club Ebony on 129th Street and Lenox Avenue in Harlem (1927) and works entitled *The Negro through the Ages* at Fisk University Library, Nashville, Tennessee (1930); *Harriet Tubman* at Bennett College for Women, Greensboro, North Carolina (1930); *Evolution of Negro Dance* at College Inn, the Sherman Hotel, Chicago (1930); *Aspects of Negro Life* at the Countée Cullen Branch of the New York Public Library (1934); and billiard-room murals at the 135th Street (Harlem) branch of the YMCA (1930s). These projects made him a leader in the efforts to advance African American art and culture in the United States.[9]

At this time many African American artists, writers, and intellectuals sought to form a new culture and identity and to bring about social change through a racial art. But this goal posed a dilemma. As Douglas wrote to the Harlem poet Langston Hughes, "Your problem Langston, my problem, no our problem is to conceive, develop, establish an art era. Not white painted black."[10] How could black artists create an art—poetry, painting, or music—distinct from white cultural products? How could they construct an African American art? Participants in the New Negro movement held conflicting opinions about the best way to achieve a racial art. Hughes criticized the demand of his white patrons that he write poetry consistent with the stereotype of the primitive black. Both Hughes and Douglas were among the young black writers and artists who, in November 1926, published the single issue of *Fire!!,* proclaiming their rejection of the artistic standards of the NAACP and Urban League and advocating a black art under black patronage as the only possible way to accomplish a true racial expression. But could black-only patronage insure racial authenticity? Wouldn't "double-consciousness" shape the form and content of such an art?

While Douglas did not produce a white art painted black, he did create an art that merged white and black, with both European and African roots. He formulated a racial art by mining the past as well as the present. African or Africanist art and the contemporary African American scene shaped his style: he held the view that African art, in both its original form and modernist translations, was the source for a specifically racial aesthetic. His art certainly drew on those styles then dominant in the mainstream New York art world, modernism (itself much affected by African art) and American Scene painting.[11] But Douglas and his colleagues framed these styles in racial terms.

Alain Locke, the foremost writer on black art at the time, called on contemporary artists to construct a new artistic and racial identity by reestablishing broken ties with the African cultural past and by painting the African American scene.[12] He saw that African American painters and sculptors faced a crisis; in contrast to writers, musicians, and dancers, they had lost touch with African folk-art traditions and thus had no foundation upon which to build a racial art in America. In Locke's estimation, black visual artists had developed slowly in the wake of the social degradation of slavery, and those, such as Henry Ossawa Tanner, who had won acclaim in the white world had only imitated European academic models. African American painters and sculptors had a great need to recover ancient skills—and indeed a sense of their own cultural history—by turning to the ancestral arts and emulating the abstract, controlled, conventionalized patterns found in African masks, sculpture, and fetishes. Since Picasso and other European modernists had already "validated" and appropriated these arts, Locke encouraged black artists to look to modernism, abstract in form and based on African art.

For Locke, moreover, developing a racial subject matter was as important as developing an African American form:

> There is a double duty and function to Negro art,— and by that we mean the proper development of the Negro subject as an artistic theme—the role of interpreting the Negro in the American scene to America at large is important, but more important still is the interpretation of the Negro to himself. Frankness compels the admission and constructive self-criticism dictates the wisdom of pointing out that the Negro's own conception of himself has been warped by prejudice and the common American stereotypes. To these there is no better or [more] effective antidote than a more representative Negro art of wider range and deeper penetration.[13]

On the African American artist's shoulders, then, fell the task of dismantling old stereotypes and creating a new type—the New Negro. Locke called upon African American artists to take advantage of a rising interest in the art world in exploring the American scene. Like white Americans, black artists had much to gain by coming home—rejecting European influences and painting their own unique environment. The representation of African American life was part of the "vigorous contemporary movement to be found native American art."[14] (In fact, the struggle of black artists to define themselves as distinct within a white American context was itself part of a broad concern of American artists to define themselves as distinct from Europe.)

For Locke, both the presence of African art as source and the representation of the African American scene were central to constructing a racial art and identity. He advocated a middle-of-the-road position between modernist, abstract design and Realist American Scene painting and directed black artists to build a racial art by looking to those sources and styles that had been accepted by white culture and institutions. Douglas achieved this negotiation between African and American, between modernism and American Scene, by using African formal elements and African American subject matter: he painted in a patterned, Africanist style and focused on present and past black life in the United States.

*Song of the Towers* was part of Douglas's federally funded 1934 mural series, *Aspects of Negro Life,* for the Countée Cullen Branch of the New York Public Library.[15] This work charted the history of American blacks from their African origins to present-day life in the urban North in four panels, *The Negro in an African Setting, From Slavery to Reconstruction, An Idyll of the Deep South,* and *Song of the Towers* (plate 8, figs. 73–75). Its style typified Douglas's manner in his public works (both illustrations and wall paintings)—a

style that he first developed in his drawings of the mid-1920s. He later discussed the evolution of this distinctive manner:

> I took the beginning steps toward this fairly complete visual statement as far back as 1925. At that time, pleas could be heard on all sides for a visual pattern comparable to, or rather suggestive of, the uniqueness found in the gestures and bodily movements of the Negro dance, and the sounds and vocal patterns as found in the Negro song. I finally undertook the task simply because there was no one else to do so.
>
> Under the guidance, inspiration, and encouragement of my teacher, Winold Reiss, I ventured forth. The results are these: Drawings for the *New Negro* . . . [and] Illustrations for the *Emperor Jones.*[16]

Figure 73

Aaron Douglas, *Aspects of Negro Life: The Negro in an African Setting,* 1934. Oil on canvas, 72 × 72 in. (182.9 × 182.9 cm). New York Public Library (Astor, Lenox and Tilden Foundations, Art and Artifacts Division, Schomburg Center for Research in Black Culture).

Figure 74

Aaron Douglas, *Aspects of Negro Life: From Slavery to Reconstruction,* 1934. Oil on canvas, 60 × 139 in. (152.4 × 353.1 cm). New York Public Library (Astor, Lenox and Tilden Foundations, Art and Artifacts Division, Schomburg Center for Research in Black Culture).

Figure 75

Aaron Douglas, *Aspects of Negro Life: An Idyll of the Deep South,* 1934. Oil on canvas, 60 × 139 in. (152.4 × 353.1 cm). New York Public Library (Astor, Lenox and Tilden Foundations, Art and Artifacts Division, Schomburg Center for Research in Black Culture).

In these works Douglas combined Reiss's abstract patterns with Art Deco rhythms and Egyptian mannerisms. Reiss's book decorations for *The New Negro* (fig. 76) combined flat organic and geometric patterns and stylized African masks to produce an Africanist style with a distinctive "moderne" flavor reminiscent of Art Deco. Emulating this manner in a drawing entitled *Invincible Music: The Spirit of Africa* (fig. 77), Douglas envisioned the African landscape geometrically, with ovals and zigzags signifying trees and foliage. The ancestral arts clearly shaped his treatment of the human figure: sharp facial features recall African masks, while the silhouetted, angular body draws on Egyptian art, whose source was at least partly in ancient Ethiopian (black) art. The December 1924 and May 1925 issues of *The Crisis* carried illustrated articles on Egyptian and Nubian art (fig. 78), and Douglas's own drawing of Tutankhamen's coffin mask graced the September 1926 cover.[17] Later, he wrote about Egyptian art as a black cultural product: "Our artistic contribution in ancient Egypt alone is enough to induce in us a great thrill of pride in our past as well as to inspire great hopes for the future."[18] This Egyptian manner also had a contemporary, popular

Figure 76

Winold Reiss, printed
book decorations, 1925
(reprinted with permission
of Scribner, a division of
Simon & Schuster, from
*The New Negro: Voices of the
Harlem Renaissance,* edited
by Alain Locke, New York:
Atheneum, 1992).

tang, for Art Deco artists and designers also adopted
Egyptian motifs (fig. 79), mixing the modern and
primitive to form a machine-age exoticism.[19] Abstract,
geometric, informed by African and Africanist art,
Douglas's style was endowed with a dual resonance,
both black and modern.

This manner became standard in Douglas's illustrations and mural paintings, including *Aspects of Negro
Life.* While perhaps more descriptive than the earlier
illustrations, these panels depend on a flat, ornamental
treatment of figures and landscape. The human forms
appear as two-dimensional cutouts, while trees, mountains, and city towers are all generalized. Angular figures and facial features recall Egyptian and African
prototypes, and ray lines, circular patterns, and decorative, exotic foliage bespeak the influence of Cubism
and Art Deco.[20]

While Douglas's style, with its affinity to modernism and Art Deco, addressed white audiences and
referred to Western art, his use of Egyptian and
Ethiopian art sources spoke directly to a black audience and especially to the pan-Africanism popular in
the New Negro movement. Such texts as Du Bois's
*Darkwater: Voices from Within the Veil* (1920) and *Dark
Princess* (1928) argued that blacks in Africa and the

diaspora were linked by a common past and future.[21]
Diasporic nationalism and Ethiopianism, offering
images of a black Christ, emerged in the years after
World War I in the separatist African church movement and gained strength as independence revolts
against colonial rule increased in Africa. Ethiopia figured strongly in pan-Africanism as a symbolic homeland for all blacks. And while many American blacks
were greatly interested in returning to Africa for resettlement, others sought a symbolic return to this "spiritual nation." Du Bois, for instance, talked about a
reunion with an "African ancestral spirit" as necessary
if blacks were to become a "thinking nation." African
American artists and intellectuals sought a "hidden
self" in their hidden past, an Africa of the spirit.[22] For
Douglas, an Africanist style was a conduit between this
common black past and the diasporic black nation.

Douglas constructed a racial art not only through
style but through the black as subject. He used this
stylistic turn to Africa to represent four moments or
periods in African American history in *Aspects of Negro
Life.* The first panel (fig. 73) describes the African
homeland as a spectacle of dance, beating drums, war-
riors, and a carved fetish—rituals and artifacts associated with the ancestral past; the next panel (fig. 74)

Figure 77

Aaron Douglas, *Invincible Music: The Spirit of Africa,* 1925 (reproduced in *Crisis* 31, no. 4, February 1926, 169).

Figure 78

Photograph of an Egyptian wall painting (reproduced in *Crisis* 29, no. 2, December 1924, 65, with the caption "A Black Princess").

sketches life for blacks in the post-Emancipation United States, mingling dancers and musicians, unchained slaves, tenant farmers in cotton fields, silhouettes of Ku Klux Klansmen, and a preacher pointing to a distant mountain; *An Idyll of the Deep South* (fig. 75) portrays slaves toiling in the southern cotton fields and listening to a banjo player's songs, while a lynching takes place at left; the final panel, *Song of the Towers* (plate 8), narrates more recent history—the black migration to northern industrial cities, the triumphs of the 1920s, and the Depression.

To reconstruct an African American past—telling and retelling narratives, celebrating heroes, and connecting the present culture with the African homeland—was essential for the formation of a racial identity in the Harlem Renaissance. There was a sense that blacks had lost their past and that their history had too often been defined through white narratives and perspectives. *The New Negro*, an influential anthology of essays, fiction, plays, poetry, and art published in New York (and based on the March 1925 issue on Harlem

of *Survey Graphic*), included a section called "The Negro Digs Up His Past" that contained articles on black figures from historical archives, folk literature, and the ancestral arts, as well as drawings and poems about black heritage. Reconstructing the past was key to vindicating and validating African Americans; identifying black achievements, heroes, and heroines was central to dismantling stereotypes. Douglas wrote about the importance of history to identity:

> Present day youth like those of my day is inclined to be impatient of the past. They feel the past as an obstacle, an impediment, and withall an intolerable burden. The attitude is, of course, a mistake. The past rather than constituting a burden on our backs or a stone around our necks can become, when properly understood, the hard inner core of life giving bounce and resilience to our efforts which would be otherwise flat and uninteresting.[23]

Visual artists and poets took an active role in this historical reconstruction. To define a racial aesthetic,

Figure 79

Jean Dunand, *Les Amants,*
n.d. Lacquer on wood
panel. Private collection
(© 1996 Artists Rights Society [ARS], New York/
SPADEM, Paris).

they looked not only to past art forms but to past
stories of heroes for their subject matter. Folk arts—
spirituals and folktales—served as a fertile source.
William H. Johnson based his painting *Swing Low,
Sweet Chariot* (1939) on black spirituals (that is, a his-
torical narrative and art); Palmer Hayden looked to a
folktale and song in his John Henry series (1944).
African American historical figures appeared in much
Harlem Renaissance art, not least in Douglas's *Harriet
Tubman* mural, Fisk University Library mural, and
*Aspects of Negro Life.*

This latter mural identified key moments in
African American history and created a continuity
between Africa and black culture in the United States.
With its focus on both fixed history and history in
the making, it embodied the New Negro movement's
preoccupations. *Aspects of Negro Life* was, however, also
part of the 1930s mural movement, which included
both black and white, urban and rural artists. This
decade witnessed the creation of numerous public
murals, many supported by the federal government
and using the past to reconstruct local, regional, and
national identity during the crisis of the Depression.
Douglas's own mural was federally funded, and he was
certainly aware of other contemporary mural projects.
For him, Thomas Hart Benton's murals and American
Scene paintings were of particular interest and influence.[24] Benton produced two noteworthy public
murals in New York at this time, *America Today* (1930)
for the New School of Social Research and *The Arts
of Life in America* (1932) for the Whitney Museum of
American Art. These two projects, which defined
national identity through diverse activities of
American life, past and present, served as appropriate
models for Douglas. Benton's murals presented indigenous music and black people as integral to American
culture. *The Arts of Life in America* included figures
drumming in a scene called *Indian Arts,* playing guitar
and fiddle in southern and western country scenes,
and popular bands and a black saxophone player in

*Arts of the City* (fig. 80). Alain Locke praised Benton for his representations of African Americans. While Benton's paintings of blacks—for example, *Minstrel Show* (1934)—often reinscribed old stereotypes, his portrayal in *America Today* of racial tensions in the South and heroic and muscular black workers was considered an advance in the representation of the race and a break from earlier typing.[25]

Douglas's *Aspects of Negro Life* relates to Benton's work, and American Scene painting generally, in several ways, most obviously its narrative quality. The series is more descriptive than Douglas's works of the 1920s, as David Driskell has noted: "When Douglas executed [these mural paintings], he had begun to reconsider the use of realism in his work, responding to the art community's growing interest in portraiture and genre scenes."[26] But Benton's and Douglas's murals are also connected by their use of music to establish racial and national identity—to construct place, people, and history.

*Jazz and African American Identity*

Music has always been an important marker of racial identity for African American writers and artists. Du Bois gave close attention to spirituals in *The Souls of Black Folk*. He introduced each chapter with two epigraphs, one drawn from canonical European literature, the other from what he called the "sorrow songs"; the text ends with a chapter devoted to analyzing spirituals and their importance in black culture.

Figure 80

Thomas Hart Benton, *The Arts of Life in America,* right panel, *Arts of the City,* 1932. Tempera with oil glaze on canvas, 96 × 264 in. (243.8 × 671 cm), variable. New Britain, Conn., New Britain Museum of American Art (Harriet Russell Stanley Fund. Photograph by Arthur Evans. © 1996 T. H. Benton & R. P. Benton Testamentary Trusts/ Licensed by VAGA, New York).

Recently, both Eric J. Sundquist and Paul Gilroy have argued that black music functions as "the central sign of black cultural value, integrity, and autonomy" in *The Souls of Black Folk*.[27] This influential text alerted blacks to the significance of the vernacular culture, especially music, produced under slavery; spirituals became a way to construct a "modern African American culture as an extension of slave culture" and a way to transcend it.[28] The value in spirituals for many black intellectuals lay in their Du Boisian duality—their blackness (connected to Africa) and their Americanness (transformed under slavery).[29]

Just as Du Bois used music as a marker of racial identity and its duality, so too did Douglas, who was clearly aware of the connections music made. Reiss had made a jazz drawing, *Interpretations of Harlem Jazz,* to accompany J. A. Rogers's essay, "Jazz at Home."[30] Three of Douglas's early illustrations in *Opportunity* were related to music.[31] *Aspects of Negro Life* charted a virtual history of African American music. Tribal music and dance characterized the first scene (fig. 73), as Douglas wrote: "Dominant in [*The Negro in an African Setting*] are the strongly rhythmic arts of music, the dance and sculpture—and so the drummers, the dancers, and the carved fetish represent the exhilaration and rhythmic pulsation of life in Africa."[32] A trumpeter plays a supporting role in the second scene, *From Slavery through Reconstruction* (fig. 74), while a banjo player in the third, *An Idyll of the Deep South* (fig. 75), and a jazz saxophonist in the fourth, *Song of the Towers* (plate 8), take center stage. Douglas used music to give meaning to African American experience and to represent its history and identity, yet he did so by relying on mainly white stereotypes of blacks and their relation to music. He described Africa and its music as primitive and rhythm as a natural property of the race: "Lynching," he said of the slavery panel, "was an ever present horror, ceaseless toil in the fields was the daily lot of the majority, but still the American Negroes laughed and

sang and danced."[33] This image of happy, music-playing blacks recalls numerous nineteenth-century visual representations, such as William Sidney Mount's *Banjo Player* (1850s) and popular illustrations of the "Old Plantation Songster" variety that served to define and limit the social role of blacks and ease white discomfort.[34]

To label *Aspects of Negro Life* as merely stereotypical, however, is too reductive. While relying on types, Douglas gave his figures powerful gestures and dominant poses entirely lacking in white models. The preacher in *From Slavery through Reconstruction* and saxophonist in *Song of the Towers* both represent knowledge and power, not naive, long-suffering innocence. They stand as images of the "self-conscious manhood" that Du Bois wrote about in *The Souls of Black Folk*. These panels reveal the problems black artists faced in creating new types, especially in relation to music. On one hand, music was a source of identity for African Americans. Through it many blacks succeeded economically, and both black and white Americans viewed African American music, from spirituals to jazz, as an exemplary cultural achievement. Music also served as a source of continuity with the hidden past of Africa. On the other hand, the reliance of African American identity on music perpetuated stereotypes of blacks as naturally musical, intuitive, sensual, emotional, preliterate, and primitive. Music was both repressive and liberating.

This complexity can be seen in *Song of the Towers* (plate 8), which represents the ups and downs, triumphs and trials of American blacks from the 1910s through the 1930s. According to the painter, the figures embodied the position of blacks at specific historical moments: "A great migration, away from the clutching hand of serfdom in the south to the urban and industrial life of America, began during the First World War. And with it there was born a new will to creative self-expression which quickly grew into the New Negro Movement of the 'twenties. At its peak, the Depression brought confusion, dejection and frustration."[35] Douglas offered the following interpretation of *Song of the Towers,* when he made a copy of it for the governor's residence in Madison, Wisconsin:

> I call this mural *Songs of the Towers.* As the song is the most powerful and pervasive creative expression of American Negro Life, it is a natural instrument for representing all of the other arts as well as a perfect vehicle for conveying all of our various moods and conditions of life. I use three different types in this picture; Songs of Deliverance, Songs of Joy and the Dance and Songs of Depression or the blues.
>
> Among the songs of deliverance we find such well known spirituals as "Run, Mourner, Run," "Steal Away," "Let My People Go," "Did My Lord Deliver Daniel," etc. The second group would include rag time, jazz, and all other popular tunes. The third group would be made up of sorrow songs and the blues.[36]

Douglas identified the figures in *Song of the Towers,* and their corresponding historical moments, with musical forms. The man on the right represents the Great Migration: suitcase in hand, he escapes the clutches of slavery and sharecropper tenancy in the South (indicated by what Douglas identified as conventionalized representations of cotton and fire) and mounts a large cog wheel moving toward the industrial North. This figure and the Great Migration have their parallel in the spirituals, or songs of deliverance. In the opposite corner a dark, silhouetted figure seems weighed down, overwhelmed by, and embedded in the machines of urban society. For Douglas, this figure, "barely visible in the descending gloom, sinks wearily into a reclining posture as a fleshless hand held above its head bars its emergence into the light thereby condemning it to the fate of sinking ever farther beneath the cog wheel and into the yawning, glittering chasm, the symbol for Harlem and all of our other ghettos."[37] The ominous, clutching hand returns to indicate new threats to blacks during the Depression, and the smokestacks—

four puffing stacks on the right, a trickle from a single stack on the left—describe the decline in industrial and economic productivity in the 1930s. Douglas sees this figure as best represented by the blues, songs of depression and loss. These figures repeat poses taken from earlier art works. The right figure echoes that in Douglas's woodcut *Flight,* from the Emperor Jones series (fig. 81)—an appropriate source for this figure, who is also in flight. The weary figure as an image of bleakness and despair replicates one in *Weary As I Can Be* (fig. 82).

These two figures stand in contrast to the jazz musician, whose posture among the skyscrapers and machines of Harlem is animated and triumphant.[38] According to Douglas, the saxophonist personified the 1920s, when blacks achieved prosperity, both economically and artistically.[39] He is paired with the Statue of Liberty in the brightest of the concentric circles. Douglas commented that the black love of freedom was symbolized by this monument and African American "devotion to the arts [was] represented by the uplifted horn." He continued: "The central figure seen waving a saxophone and with raised foot tapping out carefree rhythms of joy and exultation represents or symbolizes all aspects of the Negro's creative life, especially in the period called the Negro Renaissance. As the massive, waving towers momentarily separate, we catch a fleeting glimpse of the Statue of Liberty far away in the distance."[40] Here, the dancing black man is freed of associations with minstrel buffoonery. Even the architecture tilts outward, an opening of light and air in the otherwise claustrophobic city—an urban image very different from Stella's *New York Interpreted* (plate 4). For Douglas, this saxophonist embodied the modern African American, 1920s prosperity, and artistic expression; his musical parallel is in the songs of joy and dance, or jazz. But why should a saxophonist be a symbol of triumph, and why jazz? How did Douglas and his fellow members of the Harlem Renaissance view this music?

Figure 81

Aaron Douglas, *Flight,* from the Emperor Jones series, c. 1926. Woodcut, 8½ × 5½ in. (21.6 × 14 cm). Private collection (photo by Breger & Associates).

Figure 82

Aaron Douglas, *Weary As I Can Be* (illustration to a Langston Hughes poem, reproduced in *Opportunity* 4, no. 46, October 1926, 314). New York Public Library (Astor, Lenox and Tilden Foundations, Art and Artifacts Division, Schomburg Center for Research in Black Culture).

As the historian Clement Alexander Price has pointed out, some African American intellectuals questioned the value of jazz: "For blacks who envisioned assimilation as a reasonable solution to the troubles of the past, jazz, like other vernacular aspects of the culture, was of dubious aesthetic and social value. There were those among the New Negro leadership, if not the artists, who would just as soon leave jazz to the desperate lower class."[41] They derided hot jazz primarily because of its association with vice, a backward rural culture, and negative racial stereotypes. For others, however, jazz was an important art form.

In *The Negro and His Music* Alain Locke discussed jazz as a modern and American music but also considered it (along with other black musical forms, such as spirituals) within African American history and culture. He viewed jazz through the eyes of an elite, educated black man whose aesthetic values were shaped by white, Western culture; he relied on stereotypes in arguing for jazz's racial base and considered that folk or popular music should be "elevated."[42] *The Negro and His Music* depended on musical categories and hierarchies—folk, popular, classical; hot, sweet—and the assertion that music evolves and improves over time. Like their white colleagues, Harlem Renaissance artists and critics looked to folk arts as a source for high art.[43] Locke, a member of the Talented Tenth, took this position, seeing jazz as a folk music that needed to be improved. In his opinion musicians must become educated so that they could transform folk music into a classical form: "If Negro music is to fulfill its best possibilities, Negroes must become musical by nurture and not rest content with being musical by nature. They must build up two things essential for the highest musical success;—a class of trained musicians who know and love the folk music and are able to develop it into great classical music, and a class of trained music lovers who will support by appreciation the best in the Negro's musical heritage and not allow it to be prostituted by the vaudeville stage or Tin Pan

Alley."[44] Black musicians must take ownership and control of jazz and not let it be commercialized—a process that tarnished and cheapened the music and disconnected it from its folk roots.

Locke's history of African American music was clearly addressed to white audiences as much as black and was framed by Western aesthetic standards. He relied on white stereotypes in pointing out the importance of music for blacks: "The Negro is by instinct and experience a music-maker."[45] He established the value of African American music by examining its use in art music, such as Antonín Dvořák's symphony *From the New World* (1893). His study focused on sweet jazz, centered in New York, rather than the "cruder" jazz of New Orleans or Chicago, because this form had gained international appeal and found acceptance in some white cultural institutions. For Locke, it therefore had a more universal appeal—a criterion of great art.

While the standards of high culture shaped Locke's perceptions of jazz, he did challenge accepted ideas about it. In *The Negro and His Music* he presented the history of jazz as a history of black music, in contrast to the perspective of Paul Whiteman or the film *King of Jazz*. His narrative placed the music in the possession of blacks and challenged the claims of white musicians and jazz histories. For Locke, jazz was "distinctively Negro"[46] and based on earlier African American music, in particular spirituals and ragtime. While recognizing white jazz musicians, he emphasized the contributions of black jazz performers and composers, Fletcher Henderson, Earl Hines, Fats Waller, Louis Armstrong, and especially Duke Ellington. He questioned the importance of Paul Whiteman's and George Gershwin's 1924 concert at Aeolian Hall as the event marking the acceptance of jazz as high art, citing an earlier black jazz concert:

But by 1912, three Negro conductors led a syncopated orchestra (today we would say a jazz orchestra), of a hundred and twenty-five Negro musicians in a "Concert of Negro Music." The coming-out party was at Carnegie Hall, the audience, the musical elite of New York, the atmosphere and the comparison challenged that of any concert of "classical music," and the compositions conducted by their own composers or arrangers. . . . But all those who with shorter memory remind us of the epoch-making significance of Paul Whiteman's famous concert of "Classical Jazz" in 1924 or of a similar concert of the Vincent Lopez orchestra the same year, ought to remember the historically more significant concert of *The Clef Club* at Carnegie Hall, May, 1912. For that night the Cinderella of Negro folk music found royal favor and recognition and under the wand of Negro musicians put off her kitchen rags. At that time ragtime grew up to full musical rank and the golden age of jazz really began.[47]

Locke moderated his claim, or placated white musicians and white audiences, by acknowledging that Whiteman and Gershwin had done "tremendous pioneer services to Negro and American music."[48]

Informed by elite, Western standards, Locke's history nonetheless defined jazz as African American, a music created by blacks that had to be transformed by blacks into high art. Similar attitudes informed other Harlem Renaissance writings on jazz, most notably J. A. Rogers's "Jazz at Home," published in *The New Negro*.[49] While Rogers admitted the association of jazz with modern America and its "nerve-strung, strident, mechanized civilization," he noted that its home was in Harlem: "[Jazz] is one part American and three parts American Negro, . . . it is really at home in its humble native soil wherever the modern unsophisticated Negro feels happy and sings and dances to his mood. It follows that jazz is more at home in Harlem than in Paris. . . . Someone had to have it first: that was the Negro."[50] Arguing that jazz belonged more to blacks than to contemporary America at large, Rogers repeated that jazz was "Negro-American" and unique

to the experience of blacks in this country: "[Jazz] is of Negro origin plus the influence of the American environment. . . . The Caucasian never could have invented it."[51] Black performers were jazz's "best expositors" and inimitable because they possessed an innate rhythm.[52] In his minihistory of jazz Rogers, like Locke, featured black performers and music—citing W. C. Handy's "Memphis Blues" (1920) as the first jazz classic, for example—but also pointed out that jazz had become "common property" and had "absorbed" the national spirit. While pioneer jazz works were created by black artists, the style was now being "sublimated," that is, performed with none of the "vulgarities and crudities of the lowly origin," by both black and white orchestras, and was even transforming the work of such avant-garde composers as Erik Satie and Darius Milhaud.[53]

Jazz, "one part American and three parts American Negro," influenced the themes and language of black novels, poems, and paintings, which further strengthened the connections between jazz and racial identity and transformed and elevated the music itself. The poet Langston Hughes was perhaps the foremost Harlem Renaissance artist to use jazz, which for him expressed African American life and culture in sublime form. Hughes saw jazz as a product of the folk, whom he defined as racially pure and uncorrupted by white culture.[54] Their cultural products offered more sophisticated black artists material for their own work. The poet himself turned to folk music in his writing. *The Weary Blues,* a collection of poems published in 1926, included "Danse Africaine," "Jazzonia," and "Jazz Band in a Paris Cafe"; jazz provided the structure for "The Cat and the Saxophone," in which upper- and lowercase letters create a jazzlike syncopated rhythm.[55]

Like their literary colleagues, visual artists perceived jazz as an authentic black cultural expression. Feeling that they had lost their link to folk traditions in their own medium, they looked to music as the art form that had maintained the strongest ties with its racial past. Jazz clubs, musicians, and dancing became the subject matter for many painters: William H. Johnson's *Jitterbug* (n.d.), Palmer Hayden's *Bal Jeunesse* (c. 1927), and Archibald J. Motley's *Blues* (1929; fig. 47) are examples. Douglas too portrayed jazz in the context of the African American scene. His mural at Chicago's College Inn presented waiters, dancers, and jazz musicians in a background of urban night life, while his first large-scale mural decorations for the Club Ebony in Harlem included *Jungle* and *Jazz* panels, now lost.[56]

Like many of his modernist contemporaries, Douglas saw formal equivalents between his painting and music. His art expressed African American music visually: "I shall not attempt to describe my feelings as I first tried to objectify with paint and brush what I thought to be the visual emanations or expressions that came into view with the sounds produced by the old black song makers of antebellum days when they first began to put together snatches and bits from Protestant hymns, along with half remembered tribal chants, lullabies, and work songs."[57] He considered his flat, geometric style a "visual pattern comparable to, or rather suggestive of, the uniqueness found in the gestures and bodily movements of Negro dance and the sounds and vocal patterns as found in the Negro song."[58] But what was it about these forms that Douglas saw as musical, as African American? Was it the sense of movement and rhythm? Or, lacking a visual African American tradition to follow, did he simply cite African American music—an art form already packaged as racial—as a source to give his own art a similar identity?

Although it may be difficult to detect specific parallels in Douglas's painting to African American music, it is tempting to read the resonating circles, the swift shifts in movement, the high energy as corresponding to the rich tones of spirituals or jazz's dynamism. The painter used varied methods to visualize music in his art. *Rise shine for thy light has come!* represents music in a conventional fashion—that is, with notes on a staff—

and in a manner recalling Du Bois's transcriptions of spirituals in *The Souls of Black Folk,* as does his drawing *Music,* published in *The New Negro* (figs. 83, 84). In *Play de Blues* (fig. 85), streaming curves correspond to sounds rising from a piano. These same forms appear in *Invincible Music: The Spirit of Africa* and *Roll, Jordan, Roll* (figs. 77, 86) and can be interpreted as either landscape elements—a river—or musical sounds. Douglas adopted similar devices in *Song of the Towers* (plate 8). Wavy lines at upper left—a form that appears in Douglas's other music works—may represent Harlem's noises and songs. Like the other New York Public Library panels, this one seems to ring with sound: the circular pattern recalls sound waves emanating from a central point, rather like what Dove did in *Fog Horns* (fig. 87) and what Douglas himself did in *Music,* one of his mural panels at Fisk University.

In *Song of the Towers* the sax player is the focus of the painting: he stands at center, while the diagonal posture of the fleeing figure, the tilted arms of the weary one, the buildings' lines, and the concentric circles all draw the eye to him and his musical instrument. His identity is crucial to this work. The saxophonist relates to figures in the other panels in *Aspects of Negro Life:* the African dancer, the banjo player in the cotton field, and the preacher, all of whom are centrally located in their respective panels. Through this positioning the painter creates a sense of continuity in African American experience from ancient Africa to modern America. We read the dancer, banjo player, and preacher as the predecessors of the saxophonist, who by association is connected back through the work songs of slave times to the ancestral spirits and their tribal chants. This figure, in his changing guises, is the protagonist in the narrative of African American music and history, as constructed in *Aspects of Negro Life.*

The saxophonist in *Song of the Towers* can be read in other ways. He is not only the descendant of the African dancer but relates to meanings of the musician

Figure 83

Aaron Douglas, *Rise shine for thy light has come!*, c. 1930. Gouache on paper, 12 × 9 in. (30.5 × 22.9 cm). Washington, D.C., Howard University Gallery of Art.

circulating in the New Negro movement and the wider popular culture. Embodying images of the musician from the African past, African American culture, and modern Western culture, the jazz saxophonist becomes an incarnation of Du Bois's concept of the New Negro, who merges African, African American, and American identities.

### The Saxophonist and African American Identity

The African American scene shaped Douglas's art: he painted descriptive views of New York and Harlem life in the 1930s; earlier, watching dancers and listening to music at the Savoy Ballroom and other nightclubs, he infused his work with his impressions. Gradually he transformed these ordinary experiences into abstract, symbolic representations in his drawings and public murals. He came to see contemporary life through the lens of African American history, religion, and myth.

Douglas was not the only artist to turn to traditional narratives, especially religious stories, in constructing a new sense of self. William H. Johnson depicted Christ as a black man in *Jesus and the Three Marys* (c. 1939–40),[59] while James Weldon Johnson reimagined biblical narratives with black main actors in a poem cycle called *God's Trombones: Seven Negro Sermons in Verse* (1927). In this text Johnson joined past and present in poems based on childhood memories of black preachers and a recent experience of a Kansas City preacher, whom he considered an artist and a man of power:

[The preacher] strode the pulpit up and down in what was actually a very rhythmic dance, and he brought into play the full gamut of his wonderful voice, a voice . . . not of an organ or a trumpet, but rather of a trombone, the instrument possessing above all others the power to express the wide and varied range of emotions encompassed by the human voice. . . . He intoned, he moaned, he pleaded—he blared, he crashed, he thundered.[60]

**Figure 84**

Aaron Douglas, *Music,* 1925 (reprinted with permission of Scribner, a division of Simon & Schuster, from *The New Negro: Voices of the Harlem Renaissance,* edited by Alain Locke, New York: Atheneum, 1992).

Figure 85

Aaron Douglas, *Play de Blues* (illustration reproduced in *Opportunity* 4, no. 46, October 1926, 315). New York Public Library (Astor, Lenox and Tilden Foundations, Art and Artifacts Division, Schomburg Center for Research in Black Culture).

Figure 86

Aaron Douglas, *Roll, Jordan, Roll,* 1925 (illustration reproduced in *Opportunity* 3, no. 35, November 1925, 332).

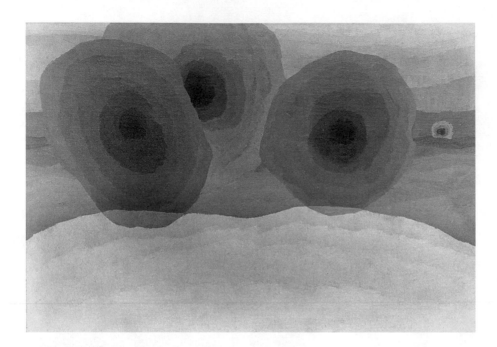

Figure 87

Arthur Dove, *Fog Horns,*
1929. Oil on canvas, 17¾ ×
25½ in. (45.1 × 64.8 cm).
Colorado Springs, Taylor
Museum for Southwestern
Studies of the Colorado
Springs Fine Arts Center.

Throughout *God's Trombones* Johnson translated sermons and biblical stories into images and a language relevant to African Americans. In "The Creation" God speaks in black vernacular: "I'm lonely—/I'll make me a world." Images referring to African American historical experience are adapted to frame religious figures: "This Great God,/Like a mammy bending over her baby." The parable of the Prodigal Son is set in an urban nightclub rife with danger: the modern city at night becomes sinful Babylon. Music is central to these stories: the preacher's expressive voice is like a trombone; in the dangerous speakeasy jazz accompanies dancers, gin, and gambling; the trumpeter Gabriel is the powerful figure who announces the world's end.

Douglas illustrated the narratives in *God's Trombones* in a sequence of drawings: *Lord, Listen—a Prayer, The Creation, The Prodigal Son, Go Down Death—A Funeral Sermon, Noah Built the Ark, The Crucifixion, Let My People Go, The Judgment Day;* these drawings as well as Johnson's verbal images informed *Song of the Towers.*

Like Johnson, Douglas cast blacks in these biblical stories: Christ in *The Crucifixion* and Gabriel in *The Judgment Day* (fig. 88). Such reenvisioning of religious stories gave a sense of identity and belonging to African Americans, enabling them to lay claim to the traditions of Christianity. Douglas himself commented on the power of such revisions of Judeo-Christian icons in his comments on William E. Scott's *The Flight into Egypt,* a cover design for *The Crisis* (December 1914): "We find them represented in a form noticeably Negro rather than Caucasian. . . . For me Mr. Scott's picture was the answer to the dream of a child who had never seen anything but the likeness of his detractors in childrens [*sic*] books, text books, Sunday school cards, everywhere."[61]

In Douglas's illustrations these black biblical figures possess power, presence, and strength. Heroic in scale, they stand in control: Noah masters the animals of the earth; Gabriel strides over the mountains and sea to command the rising of the dead. In *The Judgment Day*

Douglas presents the archangel Gabriel sounding the trumpet to awaken the dead, much as he appears in Johnson's verse:

> And Gabriel's going to ask him: Lord,
> How loud must I blow it?
> And God's a-going to tell him: Gabriel,
> Blow it calm and easy.
> Then putting one foot on the mountain top,
> And the other in the middle of the sea,
> Gabriel's going to stand and blow his horn,
> To wake the living nations.[62]

As both musician and religious figure, Gabriel is the predecessor of Douglas's saxophonist in *Song of the Towers.* The jazz player's striding pose recalls the angel's stance in *The Judgment Day,* while his upturned head and upraised arms signify prayer and deference to God—postures that Douglas used in his drawings *Lord, Listen—a Prayer* and *The Creation* (fig. 89), also in *God's Trombones.* Arms raised and gaze turned upward, bathed in light, he opposes the dark figures below. Light lifts him from the mundane to the mystical realm; the walls of the city open, like the Red Sea parting, to show the Promised Land. The musician played the role of religious figure and leader in many African American cultural traditions, and Douglas's musician would easily have been read as such by viewers visiting the Harlem branch of the New York Public Library.[63]

Gabriel as trumpeter was a common figure in black spirituals. The trumpet sounding on Judgment Day or in the battle of the righteous against the forces of wickedness is a recurrent image in these songs. In "De Angel Roll de Stone Away" and "In Dat Great Gittin' Up Morning" the trumpet sound is associated with power, liberation, and transcendence. As James Weldon Johnson explained in his introduction to *The Book of American Negro Spirituals* (1925), the lyrics of

Figure 88.

Aaron Douglas, *The Judgment Day,* 1927 (illustration reproduced in James Weldon Johnson, *God's Trombones: Seven Negro Sermons in Verse,* 1927. Copyright 1927 The Viking Press, Inc., renewed © 1955 by Grace Nail Johnson. Used by permission of Viking Penguin, a division of Penguin Books USA Inc.).

Figure 89

Aaron Douglas, *The Creation,* 1927 (illustration reproduced in *God's Trombones.* Copyright 1927 The Viking Press, Inc., renewed © 1955 by Grace Nail Johnson. Used by permission of Viking Penguin, a division of Penguin Books USA Inc.).

slave spirituals focused on the tribulations of the enslaved and exiled Jews in the Old Testament and the Crucifixion and Resurrection in the New—stories with which slaves particularly identified—and these songs were given renewed meaning in the twentieth century. Like the trumpeter of the spirituals and Johnson's *God's Trombones,* Douglas's saxophonist, modern-day urban Gabriel, sounded the music of liberation, the triumph of achievement over oppression. In his "Interpretation of *Songs of the Towers,*" Douglas mentions songs of deliverance, the well-known spirituals "Run, Mourner, Run," "Steal Away," "Let My People Go," and "Did My Lord Deliver Daniel." The figure on the left in *Song of the Towers,* in a pose signifying weariness, seems to refer to the spiritual "Weary Traveler": "Let us cheer the weary traveler,/Along the heavenly way./I'll take my gospel trumpet,/An' I'll begin to blow."[64] The painter perhaps deliberately re-created this scene from the spiritual: the weary traveler (the black migrant), discouraged and overwhelmed by the Depression, is cheered by the jazz saxophonist playing the gospel trumpet (the songs of joy).[65]

Other aspects of *Song of the Towers* assert the saxophonist's spiritual identity. Douglas placed his jazz musician among Harlem's towers and smokestacks. These same structures appeared in his study for *Aspects of Negro Life* (fig. 90), where they are set on a mountain top surrounded by light, in the realm of the divine.[66] In biblical narratives and spirituals the mountain was the dwelling place of God. For example the lyrics to the spiritual "Up on de Mountain" run: "Way up on de mountain, Lord! Mountain top, Lord! I heard God talkin' Lord!"[67] Langston Hughes imagined urban skyscrapers as heavenly spaces, describing New York as the "city of towers near to God, city of hopes and visions."[68] In *Song of the Towers* the mountain as divine space is envisioned in twentieth-century terms: Harlem and its musicians become the site and instruments of the fulfillment of an African American destiny.

Figure 90

Aaron Douglas, *Study for Aspects of Negro Life: From Slavery through Reconstruction,* 1934. Tempera on paper, 11 × 26 in. (28 × 66 cm). Private collection (photograph by Breger & Associates).

The jazz saxophonist also represented the African American artist, both past and present. Douglas portrayed his musician as James Weldon Johnson had described the anonymous authors of spirituals—that is, African American artists of the past—in his poem "O Black and Unknown Bards":

> O black and unknown bards of long ago,
> How came your lips to touch the sacred fire?
> How, in your darkness, did you come to know
> The power and beauty of the minstrel's lyre?
> Who first from midst his bonds lifted his eyes?
> Who first from out the still watch, lone and long,
> Feeling the ancient faith of prophets rise
>
> Within his dark-kept soul, burst into song? . . . O black
> slave singers, gone forgot, unfamed,
> You—you alone, of all the long, long line
> Of those who've sung untaught, unknown, unnamed,
> Have stretched out upward, seeking the divine.[69]

Poet, prophet, musician, gazing upward, bursting into song, in contact with the divine, celebratory, triumphant, and redemptive—surely this is Douglas's vision of the modern black artist.

Langston Hughes also represented the contemporary black creator as a figure standing on the mountain top: "We younger Negro artists who create now intend to express our individual dark-skinned selves without fear or shame. . . . We build our temples for tomorrow, strong as we know how, and we stand on top of the mountain, free within ourselves."[70] For Hughes, the symbolism of the mountain was not entirely positive: the mountain was the false desire of the race to emulate white culture and values, a barrier that black artists needed to surmount; artists of the 1920s were finally beginning to climb that mountain.[71] Hughes saw his own artistic efforts as connecting him to the jazzmen and blues singers of Harlem,[72] the strivers pictured by Douglas and described by him as embodying "the will to self-expression, the spontaneous creativeness of the late 1920s."[73]

In the 1930s the jazz saxophonist took on other meanings for African Americans. For Douglas, the saxophonist stood for the cultural achievements of the New Negro movement during the previous decade. He associated a liberated music with political liberty and the possibilities of democracy in *Song of the Towers.*[74] The New Negro movement equated artistic achievement with political freedom, advocating social advancement through the arts. Art became a symbol

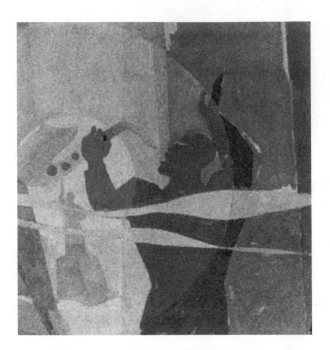

Figure 91

Aaron Douglas, *Aspects of Negro Life: Song of the Towers,* detail of plate 8.

and expression of liberation for African Americans, as the critic Paul Gilroy points out: "For the descendants of slaves, work signifies only servitude, misery, and subordination. Artistic expression, expanded beyond recognition from the grudging gifts offered by the masters as a token substitute for freedom from bondage, therefore becomes the means towards both individual self-fashioning and communal liberation."[75] As Davis saw, jazz could be associated with democracy as an element of American identity. Douglas makes this same connection in *Song of the Towers,* enclosing the saxophone (the instrument of jazz) and the Statue of Liberty together in the central circle (fig. 91). In fact, the pose of the saxophonist mimics that of Liberty.

Douglas offered an alternative and far less benign image of black liberation in his 1934 cover illustration for a planned magazine, *Spark: Organ of the Vanguard* (fig. 92). This drawing describes an unequivocal gesture of black power and freedom—the unchained arm and clenched fist that became so fierce and popular an emblem in the 1960s. The fist crashes through the surface of the picture plane, shattering scenes of violence and oppression—a lynching, soldiers with Nazi insignia, crowds in revolt, the spires of a grim metropolis; the beginning of the word *democracy* appears at lower right. We read the black saxophonist in *Song of the Towers* as a sanitized and more acceptable representation of the idea of black freedom, suitable, one would say, for a federally funded public mural.[76] Douglas chose the sax player as a figure unthreatening to white audiences, transforming him into a mythic figure from African American history and art.

For Douglas, the saxophonist expressed not only power, but the "anxiety and yearning from the soul of the Negro people."[77] According to the historian Burton W. Peretti, the music houses of Harlem, the nightclubs, and the Lafayette and Apollo theaters symbolized the black migrant's aspirations in the urban North: "Black community and culture were preserved

Figure 92

Aaron Douglas, cover illustration for *Spark: Organ of the Vanguard,* 1934. New York Public Library (Astor, Lenox and Tilden Foundations, Art and Artifacts Division, Schomburg Center for Research in Black Culture).

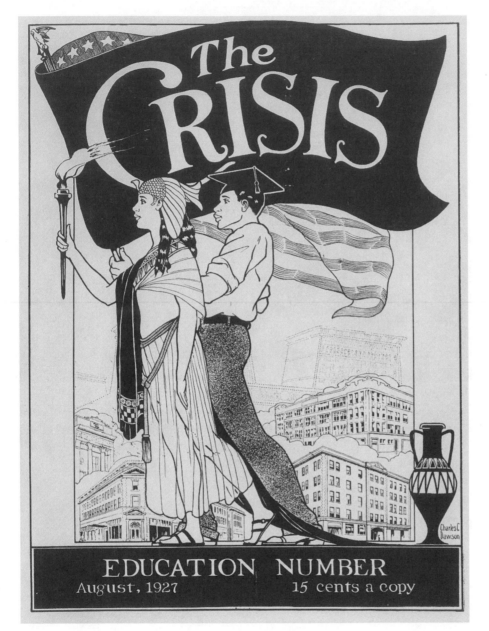

Figure 93

Charles C. Dawson, *Drawing with Five Negro Buildings,* 1927 (reproduced in *Crisis* 34, no. 6, August 1927, cover).

in elite-looking surroundings that presented visions of the good life embodied in music, dance, and elegant dress. The performers themselves realized what their eminence signified for migrants."[78] African American jazz soloists of the 1930s, often brilliantly successful, stood for the possible artistic and economic achievements of all blacks, even during the Depression. They kept alive hope for success and for black participation in the American dream and became popular heroes.

The virtuoso playing of jazz performers was identified with freedom and individuality. The saxophonist Coleman Hawkins was only one of many musicians who distanced themselves from Southern folk culture and cultivated a romantic, artistic identity in the manner of the nineteenth century.[79] These musicians embraced the qualities of the modernist artist—individuality, innovation, and of course liberty. The image of the jazz performer thus intersected with the construct of the modern Western artist.

Throughout the early twentieth century jazz continued to be seen as an art of freedom, spontaneity, and revolt, with an implied perception of the music as primitive. Both white and black writers on jazz employed stereotypes of blacks to establish the racial identity of this music (with blacks as more natural, primitive, liberated from social constraints), if from opposing motives. The jazz musician became the ideal modern, vanguard artist, with painters adopting the persona of the performer, as in Pablo Picasso's *Three Musicians* (1921) and Otto Dix's *To Beauty* (1922). Jazz and the jazz musician not only represented liberation within African American culture, but resonated in the culture at large, though not always for equally admirable reasons. The saxophonist thus had an identity beyond the African American community—a link Douglas emphatically forged in *Song of the Towers* by including the Statue of Liberty.

This monument, of course, had already served numerous symbolic functions by the 1930s, some of which seemed far removed from most African

Figure 94

George Grosz, *Jazzband,* 1928. Offset reproduction of a drawing, 7⅝ × 4⅝ in. (19.3 × 11.6 cm). (© 1996 Estate of George Grosz/ Licensed by VAGA, New York).

Figure 95

Thomas Hart Benton, *The Arts of Life in America, Arts of the City,* detail of figure 80.

Americans' experience. The Statue stood for many things: Franco-American friendship, freedom, the welcoming spirit, generosity, opportunity for immigrants, social stability, scientific progress, hope, the future, victory during the World War; ultimately, it was the emblem *par excellence* of American identity. Franklin Roosevelt emphasized the statue's value for immigrants at its 1936 rededication.[80] Although some blacks had willingly immigrated to the United States, most had found their arrival a less than liberating experience, and most had come long before the statue was erected. But Douglas was not alone in the New Negro movement in appropriating the Statue of Liberty. An illustrator recast Liberty as a young black woman with Egyptian features and dress on the August 1927 cover of *The Crisis* (fig. 93). By taking possession of the monument Douglas and his colleagues identified African Americans with other ethnic groups, other Americans of foreign heritage. They included blacks in the melting pot, a model of America from which they were often excluded, and offered white viewers a more complex notion of the American body politic.[81]

Douglas's iconography—both the Statue of Liberty and the jazz musician—was as much linked to national as to ethnic or racial identity. He appropriated preexisting signs to represent African American identity and include blacks in an imagined national community. His saxophonist in *Song of the Towers* took on meanings associated not only with African American history and culture but also with white representations of art and the artist. By the 1930s the jazz sax player often and widely signified modern America. He appeared as the American type not only in the American film *King of Jazz* but also in the German artist George Grosz's *Jazzband*[82] and Thomas Hart Benton's 1932 urban mural, *Arts of the City* (figs. 94, 95).

Jazz was, as we have seen, the quintessential music of the modern American city. Like Benton, Douglas located this music and its performer amid towering

Figure 96

Aaron Douglas, *Charleston,*
1929 (illustration repro-
duced in Paul Morand,
*Black Magic,* trans. Hamish
Miles. Copyright 1929,
renewed © 1957 by The
Viking Press, Inc., on
English translation from
French and illustrations.
Used by permission of
Viking Penguin, a division
of Penguin Books USA,
Inc.

skyscrapers, powerful machinery, and smokestacks. For Douglas, different musics represented different African American experiences and different moments in their history: drums/Africa; the banjo/slavery; jazz/the modern city and success.[83] While some of Douglas's sketches of jazz nightclubs, such as *Charleston* (fig. 96), portrayed the destructive, dangerous side of this music and the city, *Song of the Towers* envisioned black urban America as a source of optimism, with jazz at its center: here, jazz and the saxophonist symbolize hope. Douglas's jazzy metropolis, however, is not as enthusiastically upbeat as Davis's in *Hot Still Scape for Six Colors* (plate 5). Below the saxophone player lie the harsh realities for blacks in the urban North—the darkened shapes of the weary traveler and the fleeing figure, with ominous, clutching hands hovering above and behind them. Jazz and the sax player stand for economic, social, and artistic promise for African Americans, already somewhat diminished by the grim conditions of the Depression. Douglas presents jazz as the music of the modern Harlem, a momentary, exultant note of joy, already nostalgic by 1934.

The Harlem Renaissance did not advocate racial separatism; Douglas wanted to see blacks become part of an American culture. "Every aspect" of African American art, he wrote, should be identified, labeled, and then "offered to American culture to be used, to be integrated with that of all other groups making up our common American cultural heritage."[84] Jazz itself was promoted as a fully integrated cultural product, a mix of the African American and the American. J. A. Rogers had written of the components of jazz as "one part American and three parts American Negro." Douglas's jazz saxophonist too is part African American, part American: he draws together types and tropes from throughout African American and white art, literature, and music and forms from them a new definition of the modern American. The musician plays a tune heard by multiple audiences and serves as a cultural mediator. Whereas Paul Whiteman used jazz as a metaphor for the melting pot in order to imagine an American whose ethnic origins were erased, Douglas used this same figure to imagine a more fully realized and inclusive metaphor, the New Negro. This jazz musician possesses a dual identity—a "double-consciousness" that merges the American and the Negro selves not only of a black Harlem resident in 1930, but for all viewers.

All music, any organization of sounds is then a tool for the creation or consolidation of a community, of a totality.

Jacques Attali, 1985

# CONCLUSION

## MODERNISM, MUSIC, AND AMERICAN IDENTITY

*Song of the Towers* (plate 8) summarizes the issues presented throughout this book. As in Marin's 1911–13 cityscapes, Stella's *New York Interpreted,* and Davis's *Hot Still Scape for Six Colors* (plates 1, 4, 5, figs. 9–13), in Douglas's painting the themes of music and the city intersect. The saxophonist plays jazz among the towers of New York, while reverberating, abstract color circles suggest the sounds made by both the musician and his city. Through the jazz musician and the Statue of Liberty, Douglas makes music and the city signifiers of cultural identity. These paired figures together constitute a representation of Americanness, with its necessary ethnic and racial inflections. The saxophonist moves between two worlds; he is connected to things American—the Statue of Liberty—and things African American—Harlem, jazz, music. As in the work of Marin, Stella, Dove, and Davis, the goal is the definition of a new kind of artistic and political identity.

But *Song of the Towers* also argues the fragility, instability, and mutability of identity. When Douglas painted this work in 1934, the jazz musician was already a construction of the past—that is, the New Negro of the 1920s; the weary figure on the left stood for the blues and for the experience of American blacks during the Depression. In modernist American art the fluid nature of music, whether jazz, avant-garde, or noise music, served as an ideal form for containing these ever-shifting notions of cultural identity. For Marin, the city made a music expressive of the modern American spirit. Stella saw a new polyphony and new musical spaces in the technology and invention of the new world, while Dove and Davis imagined the speed and energy of modern America as jazz, and Douglas, working from a perhaps more skeptical position as a partial outsider, saw elements of all these musical and urban connections, but claimed jazz—or reclaimed it—for his own black city of Harlem. The theorist Jacques Attali has posited that all music serves as a tool for consolidating community; music as represented in pre–World War II modernist art functioned as an instrument for defining various identities and affiliations—ethnic, racial, national.

This examination of music and the musical city in early modernist art challenges the notion of an absolute, fixed concept of national identity and argues for the importance of ethnic and racial awareness in changing constructs of Americanness. The art historian Lowery Stokes Sims has written, "Over the last four hundred years, 'American'. . . has come to mean European-derived, relegating a succession of 'others' to exclusion or marginalization. . . . It is clear that the history of art in general and that of modernism in particular needs to be reworked after the model of encounters rather than conquests, so that mutual interactions between Europe and Africa, America and Africa, Asia and Europe, Africa and Asia, and America and Asia are acknowledged."[1] Just as Paul Gilroy criticizes the "unthinking assumption that cultures always flow into patterns congruent with the borders of essentially homogeneous nation states,"[2] we must redefine our concept of cultural identity *within* a

nation's borders. In early twentieth-century modernism as in other aspects of national life, Americanness was not defined from the top down, hegemonically, but rather at the meeting places between distinct groups: working and middle classes, Europe and America, white and black. The colonized were shaped by the colonizers, but the colonizers were equally shaped by the colonized. Evidence of the "encounters" and "mutual interactions" that Sims writes about abound in early twentieth-century American art. With new technologies and the rise of popular culture, boundaries between social and cultural groups were contested and renegotiated. This intermixing shaped modernism, for artists, more than most people, could travel with ease between worlds, both literally and in their work: from the middle class to the working class, from the artistic milieu of New York to that of Paris, from Italy to the Lower East Side, from concert halls to the jazz clubs of Harlem and Hoboken. For Marin, Stella, Dove, Davis, and Douglas, such journeys, or encounters, helped to form their notions of art and American identity.

Stella viewed America from his position as a European immigrant; he operated in the space where the old world and the new world met. His image of America was informed by his connection to immigrant locales—that is, immigrant working-class culture and international avant-garde circles in New York. He saw America as a culture of diversity and used the musical term *polyphony* to evoke this multiplicity. For Dove, the new music and sound technologies—the phonograph, radio, movies—served as instruments for his encounters. Through these machines he listened to the music of Gershwin and Berlin, which had in their turn already been shaped by an interaction between European art music, popular songs, and African American sounds. Davis encountered African American music directly in Hoboken jazz bars and through his acquaintances with jazz musicians. These exchanges helped him define a national identity that was blackened, even though the presence of black per-formers and blackness was erased from the American-ness of his canvases. Douglas too strode across bound-aries. In *Song of the Towers* he drew from images in mainstream American and African American cultures. His jazz musician was whitened, just as Dove's and Davis's jazz paintings were blackened, though Douglas did not erase racial identities or disguise the process of intermixing.

In defining such encounters, this study takes partic-ular note of the importance of race in constructs of national identity. We cannot talk about Americanness absent from race or ethnicity; black culture and white culture are categories within Americanness, though by no means stable or fixed ones. W. E. B. Du Bois understood this: "Our song, our toil, our cheer and warning have been given to this nation in blood-brotherhood. . . . Would America have been America without her Negro people?"[3] More recently, the writer Toni Morrison has discussed the centrality of the black presence as both subject and aesthetic mode in American literature, arguing cogently that neither black nor white writers can avoid racially inflected language in the racialized society of the United States.[4] The literary critic Eric J. Sundquist also recon-structs American literature by looking at the ways that black culture has shaped it, but sees white and black culture as inextricably intertwined: "White American culture," he states, "simply cannot be imagined apart from black American culture."[5] The cultural historian Ann Douglas uses the term "mongrel Manhattan" to characterize the intermixing of black and white in 1920s New York. She notes, "White consciousness of the Negro's rights and gifts . . . and black confidence that Negroes could use white models and channels of power to achieve their own ends . . . reached a peak of intensity in the 1920s."[6]

Art historians have much to learn from these studies. Could American modernism have broken free of the European model without the resource and

influence of African American culture? General histo-ries of modernism in the visual arts have rarely under-stood the centrality of black culture to the American modernist enterprise; what has long been obvious in American music studies and has garnered recent attention in literary studies is still largely absent from art-historical and curatorial surveys. Attention to African American presence in modern art has com-monly been limited to discussion of the Harlem Renaissance—most often presented as a separate and marginalized movement. While some recent studies of Abstract Expressionism have relocated African Ameri-can artists and black culture as important to this movement, studies of early twentieth-century American modernism have largely ignored the role of African American art and culture.[7] The work of African American artists must be analyzed in connec-tion to that of white artists, and vice versa. The con-sideration of jazz in the present study is intended to provoke thought about the centrality of black culture to American modernism and the relation between the Harlem Renaissance and what has typically been called mainstream modernism. African American music shaped the form and subject matter of mod-ernist art in the United States. For Stuart Davis, jazz initially signified the real in American life and was later a specific metaphor for modern America and the painter's own abstract style. It is clear that attention to the work of Aaron Douglas informs our understand-ing of that of his contemporaries Dove and Davis: all three were engaged with a form of abstraction modi-fied by figuration, and all adopted music and musical analogies to define their cultural identity.

A broader point can also be made here: that music itself is central to American modernism. As Paul Gilroy states, "The contemporary debates over moder-nity and its possible eclipse . . . have largely ignored music. This is odd given that the modern differentia-tion of the true, the good, and the beautiful was con-veyed directly in the transformation of public use of culture in general and the increased public importance of all kinds of music."[8] Using music as an explicit model for their painting, Marin, Stella, Dove, Davis, and Douglas created an art built on abstract forms, flat patterns, brilliant colors, and dynamic line. These abstract elements were not merely formal arrangements, but were full of meaning. Music was understood as a nondescriptive, non-narrative art, deeply connected to modern American culture—especially urban music and the urban culture. For Marin, music embodied the energy of the city; for Stella, it captured the multiple and diverse sounds of urban life. Dove, Davis, and Douglas all used jazz to imagine modern America—its speed, dynamism, joy. Thus, music did not simply serve as a formal model for modernism, but expressed the complex layers of meanings of this artistic mode, particularly its Americanness.

Jazz was *the* modern and American music; black music—or rather, a music with roots in southern African American culture—came to signify modernity and Americanness. The black figure too was viewed as the exemplary modern, Western personality: fragmented, alienated, decentered.[9] Many literary and cultural critics have seen doubleness as central to the modern self—with or without a perception of its presence in black identity. We see this splitting in action in all the artists examined in this study. The white American artists Dove and Davis adopted an African American music, or mask, to fabricate their modern American identity. Douglas used the same trick in reverse: the black jazz saxophonist in *Song of the Towers* can be read as the universal fragmented self, embodying not only African American identity, but the modern self in the West.

By studying their images of music and the musical city, we see the early modernist painters Marin, Stella, Dove, Davis, and Douglas producing an art shaped by the intermixing of cultures and placing high value on national identity. All five artists used music to signify the Americanness of modernist art, with some giving it its full racial dimensions. The issues of modernism and national cultural identity continued to be played out in post–World War II American art. The image of music and the musical city persisted as a signifier of identity, although the terms of that identity changed in new historical contexts.

Abstract Expressionist artists, for example, abandoned the literal image of American urban vitality in favor of what they saw as universal symbols, yet they continued to use music, especially jazz, as an artistic inspiration. Although the role of jazz in this art has often been noted, the impact of the music's Americanness on the production and reception of Abstract Expressionist painting has not been examined. In December 1946 the Samuel Kootz Gallery in New York hosted an exhibition, "Homage to Jazz," that included, among many works by New York School painters, Adolph Gottlieb's *Mood Indigo* and *Black and Tan Fantasy* and William Baziotes's *"That Evening Sun Goes Down."* The show's subtitle was "[a] colorful tribute in paint to a great American art."[10] In the catalog, Barry Ulanov linked jazz with the emergent Abstract Expressionist style:

> Jazz to take the traditional formulations of the diatonic scale and make another sense of them, playing minor thirds against major, minor sevenths against major, and all without changing key. Jazz to spring new colors from plumbers' plungers and loosened, softened, spittled reeds. And to ears accustomed only to the conventional tonal relationships the new sounds were chaos incarnate. It was like noise, they said, it was superficial and without perspective. Without perspective, two dimensional. Even as the painters had robbed parallel lines of their converging point, even as they flattened houses and faces and guitars, jazzmen had reduced the values of notes, flattened them. And to ears which would hear, a richer music was made, a broader art, neck-deep in tonal resources and *relentlessly of our time and place.*

Ineluctably, *our painters came to our music. Our painters?* Those who made the great discovery that their medium was inherently two-dimensional. *Our music?* The music of conflict and confusion and new order constructed from the intrinsic sounds of the instruments and from the rhythm native to the instrumentalists. I've seen a large number of jazz musicians stand admiringly before the work of their opposite numbers in painting; I've seen their own primitive paintings, so much like others in spirit and feeling if not in technique. And now I've seen the paintings of jazz and jazzmen and the jazzmen of the new painters. They have discovered each other, the painters and the jazzmen, and their mutual discoveries about the function of art, as they had to. *For these are the pre-eminent arts of this era in this country, the provocative, the original arts* [emphasis added].[11]

Ulanov connects the innovative sounds of jazz to the innovative two-dimensional art of American modernism. He creates a story about the emergence of the abstract manner of Baziotes, Robert Motherwell, Gottlieb, and others that ignores European modernism as well as earlier twentieth-century American modernism. Ulanov instead identifies jazz, which during the 1940s and 1950s was becoming increasingly abstract and improvisatory in the hands of John Coltrane, Miles Davis, and others, as the source of this new American visual art.

Jackson Pollock's work had already been compared to jazz in a 1945 review by the critic Alfred Frankenstein: "The flare and spatter and fury of his paintings are emotional rather than formal, and like the best jazz, one feels that much of it is the result of inspired improvisation rather than conscious planning."[12] Other parallels have been proposed between Pollock's drip paintings, such as *Autumn Rhythm (No. 30)* (fig. 97), and jazz: both depended on a search for the primitive or invocation of the unconscious; the large-scale paintings shared with 1940s bebop an emphasis on solo improvisation, accelerated rhythm,

and long, legato compositions; Pollock's working method, like that of a jazz musician, employed improvisation and active use of the whole body. Jazz improvisation possessed the expressive freedom that Pollock desired in his own art and was an influence on his improvisatory style. The painter often listened to jazz, which played on the soundtrack for his action-painting films.[13] Lee Krasner commented that Pollock "would get into grooves of listening to his jazz records—not just for days—day and night, day and night for three days running, until you thought you would climb the roof! . . . Jazz? He thought it was the only other really creative thing happening in this country."[14] Like Davis and Dove before him Pollock turned to a music whose origins and major contemporary practitioners were black as a guide to formulating his modernist style. And in Pollock's paintings, as in those by Dove and Davis, the blackness of this American identity was once again erased in the name of a universal message.

By the 1940s jazz had already received international acclaim for its innovation and modernity, often equated with Americanness both in the United States and abroad. Jazz-inspired images, moreover, often made a connection between jazz and democracy. Davis gave his *Hot Still Scape for Six Colors—Seventh Avenue Style* (plate 5) the alternate title *Art of an Urban Democracy, 7th Avenue,* while Douglas coupled his jazz saxophonist with the Statue of Liberty in *Song of the Towers* (plate 8). Abstract Expressionism was exported in the triumphant postwar years as an American product embodying the same qualities associated with jazz improvisation—democracy, freedom, individual expression. Throughout the 1950s the New York School was showcased in international exhibitions sponsored by the CIA and the Museum of Modern Art.[15] These cultural exhibitions became instruments of American postwar policy in Europe. At home and abroad, Abstract Expressionism came to represent bold courage, energy, and especially freedom—a politically

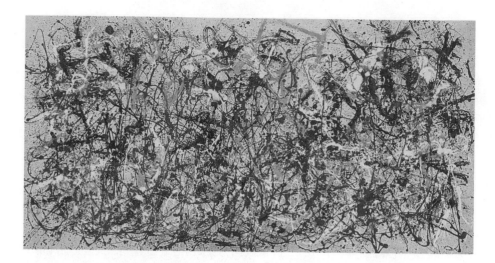

Figure 97

Jackson Pollock, *Autumn Rhythm (No. 30),* 1950. Oil on canvas, 105 × 207 in. (266.7 × 525.8 cm). New York, Metropolitan Museum of Art (George A. Hearn Fund, 1957, 57.92. All rights reserved. © 1997 Pollock-Krasner Foundation/Artists Rights Society [ARS], New York).

charged word that became common in writing about the art. Alfred H. Barr, Jr., clearly stated the connection between Abstract Expressionism and American democracy in his catalog introduction for the traveling exhibition "The New American Painting," organized by the Museum of Modern Art's International Council and sent to Europe in 1958: "[The Abstract Expressionists] defiantly reject the conventional values of the society which surrounds them, but they are not politically engagés even though their paintings have been praised and condemned as symbolic demonstrations of freedom in a world in which freedom connotes a political attitude."[16]

In post-World War II America the watchword in the visual arts, particularly among the Abstract Expressionists, was universalism. Yet despite this heroic, internationalist language, the art was still received as a national, distinctly American style. Pollock was represented as a latter-day cowboy or tough guy in the manner of popular heroes like James Dean; the painter himself talked of the bigness of the Western landscape as a parallel to his own big canvases. As in so much that concerns American

identity, this style was also shaped by race, as artists of the New York School turned to so-called American primitives, both Native Americans and African Americans for inspiration.[17] How did African Americans respond to this aesthetic of universalism presented by the white world? What role did the subject of their music play in their own art?

A black member of the New York School, the painter Norman Lewis (1909–79) began his career dedicated to Social Realism. During the 1930s and early 1940s he remained committed to the artistic project of the Harlem Renaissance as articulated by Alain Locke; he directed his art away from abstraction and painted the figure, focusing on the lives of urban black workers and their families. Lewis's post-World War II work took a different direction. He moved away from creating a racially articulated art and began to think of himself as an American artist who happened to be black, writing in 1946: "I have been concerned not only with my own creative and technical development but with the limitations which every American Negro who is desirous of a broad kind of development must face—namely, the limitations

Figure 98

Norman Lewis, *Jazz Musicians,* 1948. Oil on canvas, 50 × 42 in. (127 × 106.7 cm). Estate of Norman Lewis.

which come under the names, 'African Idiom,' 'Negro Idiom,' or 'Social Painting.' I have been concerned therefore with greater freedom for the individual to be publicly first an artist (assuming merit) and incidentally, a Negro."[18] Like his New York School colleagues, he was committed to universalism, believing that art should add to a "universal knowledge of aesthetics" that "exists for one form of expression or another in all men."[19]

Lewis moved toward abstraction but produced partially nonrepresentational works containing figures of black musicians, thus interweaving African American experience into abstract patterns signifying the universal. Following this revised notion of a racial art, he began to adopt various modes of semiabstract European modernism in which references to the figure continued to appear until around 1946. Even after this time, he occasionally returned to earlier representational subjects, especially images of music and of Harlem.[20] In *Jazz Musicians* (fig. 98), skeletal stick figures resembling those of Paul Klee cluster in a black and red ground. Much like the abstracted forms in Dove's *Swing Music (Louis Armstrong)* (plate 7), these figures of black musicians surface as a seemingly immaterial presence within a style in which racial difference has supposedly been erased. Lewis grafted African American life and experience onto the universal, yet the black figure appears—and is lost—in these abstract signs.

Also working in New York after the war, Romare Bearden (1911–88), like Lewis, used music and particularly the figure of the black musician to construct racial identity in his paintings. He rejected the notion of racial identity that Douglas had proposed—that is, the merged Negro and American. In fact, like Lewis, Bearden distanced himself from the Harlem Renaissance, which he considered trite and derivative, suffering from the paternalism of white patrons.[21] Yet while he criticized the art of the Harlem Renaissance, Bearden confronted many of the same issues in his

Figure 99

Romare Bearden, *Alto Composite,* from the Of the Blues series, 1974. Collage with acrylic and lacquer on board, 50 × 44 in. (127 × 111.8 cm). Private collection (courtesy the Estate of Romare Bearden).

own art. Like Douglas, he challenged stereotypes of blacks and created a fresh vision of African American identity, often by appropriating and collaging fragmentary images from art history and popular magazines into his paintings. He explained his goals: "I did the new work out of a response and need to redefine the image of man in terms of the Negro experience I know best. I felt that the Negro was becoming too much of an abstraction rather than the reality that art can give a subject. . . . What I've attempted to do is establish a world through art in which the validity of my Negro experience could live and make its own logic."[22] Lee Stephens Glazer has analyzed Bearden's process of validating his experience in his Projections series (1964). According to Glazer, Bearden employed three strategies: he established the importance of ritual in black vernacular practices as distinctively African American; he challenged journalistic stereotypes through revision; and he alluded to art-historical images in his collages of black life, thereby defining the history of art as a "visual system that could accommodate and affirm African American identity."[23] Like Lewis, Bearden sought to knit African American experience into a conception of the universal.

Bearden adopted music, especially jazz, as a central theme in his art. With its abstracted, fragmented musician holding a violin, *A Blue Note* (c. 1946), which appeared in the 1946 "Homage to Jazz" exhibition, is not only akin to Davis's Cubist manner but marks an early example of Bearden's use of jazz. Bearden often described the process of making his art, especially his collages, as parallel to jazz performance: "You do something, and then you improvise."[24] He explained: "All of the [collages] that I did here, I didn't begin that way. . . . I just started putting something down to see what would happen. Jazz is improvisation, and you've got to get some feeling of that."[25] While Bearden painted numerous abstract images of music, as in *A Portrait of Max: In Sounds, Rhythms, Colors and Silences* (1985), many of his music paintings deal quite

concretely with the black musician in the African American community, in ritual, and in history, as in his three series Of the Blues (1975), Of the Blues: Second Chorus (1976), and Jazz (1979). In the Blues works, Bearden presented a narrative history of jazz from its roots in sacred and secular folk music to its urban form, with its performers and its abstract sounds. As Douglas did in *Song of the Towers,* Bearden portrays the musician as solitary and heroic in such works as *Alto Composite* (fig. 99), from Of the Blues. Bearden does not represent his figure as a merged American and Negro, as Douglas did, but suggests the fragmentation of the black self through the medium of collage, building the figure from magazine cutouts. It is the formal language of *Alto Composite* that suggests African American identity—fragmented, reformed, and composed of references to prior images in both African American culture and modernist art.

In even a few quick examples we may see that in post-1940 American modernism music, and especially urban jazz, continued to serve art and to contribute to its construction of racial and national identity. Images of jazz and jazz musicians have remained popular in later twentieth-century art—Franz Kline's *Hot Jazz (Bleecker Street Tavern)* (1940); Jacob Lawrence's *Café Comedian* (1957); Jean-Michel Basquiat's *Discography II* (1983); and Larry Rivers's *Jazz Musician* (1958), *Ikon Hands* (1988), and *Dick Schwartz, Umber Blues* (1987) are just a sampling. This music continues to be used to imagine national identity, not only in the art world but in the wider culture. Sheldon Hackney, director of the National Endowment for the Humanities, has recently written in an article discussing his project, "A National Conversation": "A member of the group eloquently offered jazz as the ideal metaphor for America. It is a truly indigenous art form, he argued, evolved out of the interaction of European and African cultures in the New World. As befits a democratic society, it was created from the bottom up, is nonhierarchical in both its performance and appeal, and began as a disdained expression of a marginal group, slowly being taken into the mainstream. Most importantly, jazz emphasizes the improvisation of individual performers within a group setting."[26]

The image of New York as the musical city too has survived in American popular culture. The jazz musician roaming the streets of New York like a cool Pied Piper appears in advertisements selling the excitement of New York to tourists.[27] Woody Allen's 1979 film *Manhattan* sets scenes of skyscrapers and the Brooklyn Bridge to the sounds of Gershwin's *Rhapsody in Blue.* These images have clearly been shaped by early twentieth-century American modernist painting, especially John Marin's dancing skyscrapers and Aaron Douglas's Harlem jazz saxophonist. These works helped to define notions of cultural identity in their time and continue to shape and present New York as the ultimate modern American city, full of energy, motion, and music. Painting the musical city and jazz, Marin, Stella, Dove, Davis, and Douglas invented a vision of America that has defined its identity in the modern world.

# Notes

*Introduction*

1. See, for example, Gail Levin, "Die Musik in der frühen amerikanischen Abstraktion," in Karin von Maur, ed., *Vom Klang der Bilder: Die Musik in der Kunst des 20. Jahrhunderts,* exh. cat. (Munich: Prestel and Stuttgart Staatsgalerie, 1985), 368–71; Howard Risatti, "Music and the Development of Abstraction in America: The Decades Surrounding the Armory Show," *Art Journal* 39 (Fall 1979): 8–13; and Judith Zilczer, "'Color Music': Synaesthesia and Nineteenth-Century Sources for Abstract Art," *Artibus et Historiae* 16, no. 7 (1987): 101–26.

2. Eric J. Hobsbawm, "Introduction: Inventing Traditions," in *The Invention of Tradition*, ed. Eric J. Hobsbawm and Terence Ranger (Cambridge, Eng.: Cambridge University Press, 1985), 1–14, and idem, *Nations and Nationalism since*

*1780: Programme, Myth, Reality* (Cambridge, Eng.: Cambridge University Press, 1990), 101–62.

3. Van Wyck Brooks, *The Wine of the Puritans: A Study of Present-Day America* (1908; repr. Folcroft, Pa.: Folcroft Press, 1969), 136.

4. Werner Sollors, *Beyond Ethnicity: Consent and Descent in American Culture* (New York: Oxford University Press, 1986), 254. The central character in Zangwill's *The Melting Pot* is the musician David Quixano, whose aim is to compose an American symphony that will express the merging and re-forming of the many races and ethnic groups in American society. At the play's end Quixano performs his symphony at a settlement house in New York.

5. Waldo Frank, *The Re-discovery of America: An Introduction to a Philosophy of American Life* (New York: Scribner's, 1929), 259–60.

6. Undated manuscript, repr. in Cleve Gray, ed., *John Marin by John Marin* (New York: Holt, Rinehart and Winston, 1970), 161, hereafter Gray, ed., *Marin by Marin.*

7. W. E. B. Du Bois, *The Souls of Black Folk* (1903), in W. E. B. Du Bois, *W. E. B. Du Bois: Writings* (New York: Literary Classics of the United States, 1986), 364–65.

8. On modernism and the city, for example, see Anna C. Chave, "'Who Will Paint New York?': 'The World's New Art Center' and the Skyscraper Paintings of Georgia O'Keeffe," *American Art* 5, nos. 1–2 (Winter–Spring 1991): 86–107; Merrill Schleier, *The Skyscraper in American Art, 1890–1931,* Studies in the Fine Arts: The Avant-Garde, no. 53 (Ann Arbor: UMI Research Press, 1986); William Sharpe, "New York, Night, and Cultural Mythmaking," *Smithsonian Studies in American Art* 2, no. 3 (Fall 1988): 2–21; and Dickran Tashjian, *Skyscraper Primitives: Dada and the American Avant-Garde, 1910–25* (Middletown, Conn.: Wesleyan University Press, 1975). On modernism and music, see Levin, "Die Musik in der frühen amerikanischen Abstraktion," 368–71; Risatti, "Music and the Development of Abstraction in America"; and Zilczer, "'Color Music.'" On modernism and nationalism, see Matthew Baigell, "American Art and National Identity: The 1920s," *Arts* 61 (February 1987): 48–55; Wanda Corn, "Toward a Native Art," *Wilson Quarterly* 5 (Summer 1981): 166–77; and Arthur F. Wertheim, *The New York Little Renaissance: Iconoclasm, Modernism, and Nationalism in American Culture, 1908–1917* (New York: New York University Press, 1976).

9. Paul Gilroy, *The Black Atlantic: Modernity and Double Consciousness* (Cambridge, Mass.: Harvard University Press, 1993).

10. Quoted in Melinda Boyd Parsons, *To All Believers— The Art of Pamela Colman Smith,* exh. cat. (Wilmington, Del.: Delaware Art Museum, 1974), n.p.

11. Letter, Marsden Hartley to Norma Berger, December 30, 1912, quoted in Barbara Haskell, *Marsden Hartley,* exh. cat. (New York: Whitney Museum of American Art and New York University Press, 1980), 139–40, n. 74.

12. Letter, Hartley to Alfred Stieglitz, received December 20, 1912, quoted in Haskell, *Marsden Hartley,* 28.

13. For Hartley, Bach's music embodied an otherworldliness. He would later write, "I was listening to a Bach partita played on the harpsichord by an expert, and the thought came, how could it have been otherwise, so completely and loftily impersonal as all great art is." Marsden Hartley, *On Art,* ed. Gail R. Scott (New York: Horizon Press, 1982), 291. The scalloped arch, seated Buddhalike figure, eight-pointed

stars, and interlocking rings in *Musical Theme (Oriental Symphony)* all refer to Eastern religious sources; see [Sandra] Gail Levin, "Wassily Kandinsky and the American Avant-Garde, 1912–50" (Ph.D. diss., Rutgers University, 1976), vol. 1, 89–106, and Haskell, *Marsden Hartley,* 27.

## Chapter 1: John Marin and the "Great Music" of the City

1. See Stephen Kern, *The Culture of Time and Space, 1880–1918* (Cambridge, Mass.: Harvard University Press, 1983), 109–30, and Cecelia Tichi, *Shifting Gears: Technology, Literature, Culture in Modernist America* (Chapel Hill: University of North Carolina Press, 1987), 231, 240.

2. Undated manuscript, repr. in Cleve Gray, ed., *John Marin by John Marin* (New York: Holt, Rinehart and Winston, 1970), 19, hereafter Gray, ed., *Marin by Marin.*

3. Letter, John Marin, Jr., to the author, July 26, 1985. The artist's son commented on his father's interest in music: "For him music was not just a hobby; it was a love, like you love a person." According to his son, Marin disliked French composers, especially Debussy. The painter wrote: "There was a man Orlando Gibbons—15th century—in his music I hear the bells of Heaven a ringing up there aloft . . . music— modern music—most of it not for me—Jazz—music I can accept—for there the instruments are on a real honest drunk are having fun. . . . Yes I realize the Greatness of Beethoven and Mozart and Bach but there was a man not much played—he was a lover too—led quite a happy life— I'll say again and again not fully appreciated—dear Haydn sheer music." Letter, Marin to Louis Kalonyme, July 7, 1953, repr. in Gray, ed., *Marin by Marin,* 171. Clippings in Marin's scrapbook also suggest his musical tastes: a *New York World-Telegram* announcement of an all-Russian concert, an essay on Greek mime and music, and articles on Gibbons, Tureck, and a Bach, Schumann, and Poulenc concert. See John Marin Papers, Archives of American Art, Smithsonian Institution, Washington, D.C. (hereafter AAA), reel N60–11, frames 9, 18–21, 54, 61, 180.

4. Herbert J. Seligmann, "Marin at Cape Split: A Reminiscence of One of Maine's Greatest Painters," *Down East* 1 (Winter 1955): 23–26; clipping in Marin Papers, AAA, reel N60–10, frame 633. For other comments on Marin's piano playing, see Matthew Josephson, "Profiles— Leprechaun on the Palisades," *New Yorker* 18 (March 14, 1942): 26–35, clipping in Marin Papers, AAA, reel N60–11, frame 484, and Dorothy Norman's comments from a round-

table discussion on Marin, held after his death, Downtown Gallery Papers, AAA, reel ND34, frame 196.

5. Letter, John Marin to Alfred Stieglitz, August 31, 1940, Alfred Stieglitz Archive, Yale Collection of American Literature, Beinecke Rare Book and Manuscript Library, Yale University (hereafter YCAL).

6. Undated manuscript, repr. in Gray, ed., *Marin by Marin,* 148.

7. Marin stated, "The paint is put on in such a way that you feel that it went in and was made by paint fingers." Dorothy Norman, "Conversation with Marin," clipping in Marin Papers, AAA, reel N60–10, frame 605. Also see John Marin, "Can a Photograph Have the Significance of Art?" *Manuscripts* 4 (December 1922): 11. Mackinley Helm, *John Marin* (Boston: Pellegrini and Cudahy, 1948), 33, describes Marin's ambidextrous painting technique and, p. 19, n. 13, suggests a connection between this technique and his piano playing. Also see Duncan Phillips, "Retrospective at the Venice Biennale," *Art News* 49 ( June 1950): 20–21, Marin Papers, AAA, reel N60–10, frame 565, and Van Deren Coke, *Marin in New Mexico, 1929 and 1930,* exh. cat. (Albuquerque: University Art Museum and the University of New Mexico Press, 1968), 6–7.

8. John Marin, "A Few Notes," *Twice-a-Year 2* (Spring–Summer 1939): 177.

9. Undated manuscript, repr. in Gray, ed., *Marin by Marin,* 107.

10. Letter, Marin to Duncan and Marjorie Phillips, c. 1950, repr. in Gray, ed., *Marin by Marin,* 118. Marin also stated, "I think that Haydn and Bach and those fellows before Haydn's time—those English fellows like Purcell and Orlando Gibbons—gave their music real action. I try to make the parts of my picture move the same way—only I always try to make them move back and forth from the center of the paper or canvas—like notes leaving and going back to middle C on the keyboard." From an interview with Marin, recorded in Helm, *John Marin,* 95.

11. Marin wrote, for example: "There will be the big quiet forms there will be all sorts of movements and rhythm beats   one-two-three—two-two-three—three-one-one—all sorts—all seen and expressed in color weights." Marin, "John Marin by Himself," *Creative Art 2* (October 1928): xxxvi. Line could communicate this rhythm and movement too: "Drawing is the path of all movement Great and Small. . . . Drawing is the path made visible." *John Marin Drawings and Water Colors* (New York: Twin Editions, 1950), n.p.

12. "Review of John Marin Exhibition," *Camera Work* 42–43 (April–July 1913): 24.

13. Videotape, *John Marin's New York* (New York: V.I.E.W., 1993). Carol Jay composed the original score.

14. Quoted in *John Marin's New York,* exh. cat. (New York: Kennedy Galleries, 1981), n.p.

15. *John Marin Drawings and Water Colors,* n.p.

16. For discussions of the theme of New York in American modernism, see Wanda Corn, "The New New York," *Art in America* 61 ( July–August 1973): 58–65; Merrill Schleier, *The Skyscraper in American Art, 1890–1931,* Studies in the Fine Arts: The Avant-Garde, no. 53 (Ann Arbor: UMI Research Press, 1986); and Arthur F. Wertheim, *The New York Little Renaissance: Iconoclasm, Modernism, and Nationalism in American Culture, 1908–1917* (New York: New York University Press, 1976), 201–12.

17. Sidney Allan [Sadakichi Hartmann], "The 'Flat-Iron' Building.—An Esthetical Dissertation," *Camera Work* 4 (October 1903): 36–40. Also see Alvin Langdon Coburn, "The Relation of Time to Art," *Camera Work* 36 (October 1911): 72, and Joseph A. Keiley, "Landscape: A Reverie," *Camera Work* 4 (October 1903): 45–46.

18. For reproductions of photographs published in *Camera Work,* see Marianne Fulton Margolis, ed., *Camera Work: A Pictorial Guide* (New York: Dover, 1978). See Schleier, *The Skyscraper in American Art,* 41–63, for a discussion of urban iconography and the Stieglitz circle.

19. In 1905, in Paris, Arthur B. Carles had introduced Marin to Edward Steichen, who then introduced him to Stieglitz, owner of the innovative Gallery 291 in New York, around 1909. Stieglitz opened the Little Galleries of the Photo-Secession, or Gallery 291, in 1905. Although his initial goal was to exhibit photography as a fine art, by 1908 he had turned his attention to bringing examples of European modernism to the American public. His early exhibitions included the works of Rodin, Matisse, Toulouse-Lautrec, and Cézanne. By 1910, with his "Young American Painters" exhibition, Stieglitz also began supporting American artists working in the new mode. He guaranteed Marin an income until his works began to sell and offered him an annual one-person exhibition. He had a show at Gallery 291 with Alfred Maurer in 1909 and a one-person show there in February 1910. For more on Marin's early career, see Ruth E. Fine, *John Marin,* exh. cat. (Washington, D.C.: National Gallery of Art and New York: Abbeville Press, 1990), 75–106, and William Innes Homer, *Alfred Stieglitz and the American Avant-Garde* (Boston: New York Graphic Society, 1977), 88–108.

20. Letter, Marin to Stieglitz, October 11, 1910, YCAL.

21. See *43 Watercolors, 20 Pastels, and 8 Etchings by John Marin,* exh. cat. (New York: Gallery 291, February 7–19, 1910), John Marin File, New York Public Library Papers, AAA, reel N53, frame 941.

22. Marin wrote of the skyscrapers, "I have just started some Downtown stuff and to pile these great houses one upon another with paint as they do pile themselves up there so beautiful so fantastic at times one is afraid to look at them but feel like running away." Letter, Marin to Stieglitz, 1911, YCAL.

23. See Homer, *Stieglitz and the American Avant-Garde,* 104–6; Sheldon Reich, *John Marin: A Stylistic Analysis and Catalogue Raisonné,* vol. 1 (Tucson: University of Arizona Press, 1970), 56–62; and idem, "John Marin: Paintings of New York, 1912," *American Art Journal* 1 (Spring 1969): 43–52.

24. See Marin's paintings of the Singer Building and Broadway listed and/or reproduced in Reich, *Marin: A Stylistic Analysis and Catalogue Raisonné,* vol. 2, 342, 343, 351, 362.

25. Coburn, "The Relation of Time to Art," 72.

26. Both Reich, in *Marin: A Stylistic Analysis and Catalogue Raisonné,* vol. 1, 57, and Schleier, in *The Skyscraper in American Art,* 51, see direct connections between Marin's cityscapes and photography.

27. *An Exhibition of Watercolors—New York, Berkshire and Adirondack Series—and Oils by John Marin,* exh. cat. (New York: Gallery 291, January 20–February 15, 1913), Marin File, New York Public Library Papers, AAA, reel N53, frame 941. This catalog essay also appeared in "Notes on '291'— Water-Colors by John Marin," *Camera Work* 42–43 (April– July 1913): 18, and was later reprinted in Dorothy Norman, ed. and intro., *The Selected Writings of John Marin* (New York: Pellegrini and Cudahy, 1949), 4–5.

28. See n. 23

29. See Gordon Craig, *46 Drawings and Etchings by Gordon Craig,* exh. cat. (New York: Gallery 291, December 14, 1910–January 12, 1911), quoted in Homer, *Stieglitz and the American Avant-Garde,* 306; Andrew Kagan, "Paul Klee's *Polyphonic Architecture* (1930)," *Arts* 54 (January 1980): 154–55; and Wolfgang Stechow, "Problems of Structure in Some Relations between the Visual Arts and Music," *Journal of Aesthetics and Art Criticism* 11 (June 1953): 324–33.

30. Abraham A. Davidson, "John Marin: Dynamism Codified," *Artforum* 9 (April 1971): 37.

31. See Stechow, "Problems of Structure in Some Relations between the Visual Arts and Music," 324–33. The comparison of architecture to music was formulated by Friedrich Wilhelm Joseph von Schelling; see his *The Philosophy of Art,* ed. and trans. Douglas W. Stott (Minneapolis: University of Minnesota Press, 1989), 166, 170–80.

32. "Review of John Marin Exhibition," 24, 41.

33. See Schleier, *The Skyscraper in American Art,* 57.

34. See Kern, *The Culture of Time and Space,* and Daniel Joseph Singal, "Towards a Definition of American Modernism," in Daniel Joseph Singal, ed., *Modernist Culture in America* (Belmont, Calif.: Wadsworth, 1991), 1–27.

35. For more on Bergson and his American public, see Thomas Quirk, "Bergson in America," *Prospects: An Annual of American Culture Studies,* vol. 11, ed. Jack Salzman (Cambridge, Eng.: Cambridge University Press, 1987), 453–90, and Wertheim, *The New York Little Renaissance,* 7. For a brief discussion of Marin and Bergson, see Debra Bricker Balken, *John Marin's Berkshire Landscapes,* exh. cat. (Pittsfield, Mass.: Berkshire Museum, 1985), n.p.

36. Henri Bergson, *An Introduction to Metaphysics* (1903), discussed and quoted in Kern, *The Culture of Time and Space,* 25–26.

37. Henri Bergson, *Time and Free Will: An Essay on the Immediate Data of Consciousness,* trans. F. L. Pogson (1910; repr. New York: Macmillan, 1959), 100. For more on Bergson and music, see Mark Antliff, *Inventing Bergson: Cultural Politics and the Parisian Avant-Garde* (Princeton: Princeton University Press, 1993), 65–66, and Gabriel Marcel, "Bergsonism and Music," *La Revue musicale* 6 (1925): 219–29, repr. in *Reflections on Art: A Source Book of Writings by Artists, Critics, and Philosophers,* ed. Susanne K. Langer (Baltimore: Johns Hopkins University Press, 1958), 144.

38. Henri Bergson, "What Is the Object of Art?" *Camera Work* 37 (January 1912): 24. Also see idem, "An Extract from Bergson," *Camera Work* 36 (October 1911): 20–21. If Marin did not know Bergson's ideas firsthand, he may have known them from writings about Cubism, most notably Albert Gleizes's and Jean Metzinger's *Du cubisme* (1912). See Antliff, *Inventing Bergson,* 39–66, for a discussion of Bergson's *durée* and Cubism.

39. "Is Photography a New Art?" *Camera Work* 21 (June 1908): 17–18.

40. Lauvrik wrote, "Generically, these two arts—music and the plastic arts—are at variance with one another, and what gives life to one is the death of the other. The first is fluent and transitory while the latter is static and enduring."

See J. Nilsen Lauvrik, "Is It Art? Post-Impressionism, Cubism, Futurism" (New York: International Press, 1913), 26, repr. in *The Armory Show International Exhibition of Modern Art, 1913,* vol. 3 (New York: Arno Press, 1972).

41. Wassily Kandinsky, *Concerning the Spiritual in Art* (1912), trans. and intro. M. T. H. Sadler (1914; repr. New York: Dover, 1977), 19. *Concerning the Spiritual in Art* was first published in December 1911 by Reinhard Piper in Munich, although it was dated 1912. The first English translation appeared in 1914. See Wassily Kandinsky, *Kandinsky: Complete Writings on Art,* vol. 1 (1901–21), ed. Kenneth C. Lindsay and Peter Vergo (Boston: G. K. Hall, 1982), 114–15, and Peg Weiss, *Kandinsky in Munich: The Formative Jugendstil Years* (Princeton: Princeton University Press, 1979), 139–40.

42. Willard Huntington Wright, *Modern Painting: Its Tendency and Meaning* (New York: John Lane, 1915), 18, 312, 250, 300.

43. Morgan Russell, "Individual Introduction," *Les Synchromistes S. Macdonald-Wright et Morgan Russell,* exh. cat. (Paris: Bernheim-Jeune, October 27–November 8, 1913), repr. in Gail Levin, *Synchromism and American Color Abstraction,* exh. cat. (New York: Whitney Museum of American Art and George Braziller, 1978), 130.

44. From Russell's notebook, September 1912, quoted in Levin, *Synchromism and American Color Abstraction,* 18.

45. See James M. Baker, "*Prometheus* in America: The Significance of the World Premiere of Scriabin's *Poem of Fire* as Color-Music, New York, 20 March, 1915," in *Over Here! Modernism, The First Exile, 1914–1919,* exh. cat. (Providence: David Winton Bell Gallery, Brown University, 1989), 90–109; "Color Music," *Literary Digest* 46 (June 21, 1913): 1378–79; and Stark Young, "The Color Organ," *Theatre Arts* 6, no. 1 (January 1922): 20–32. Color organs appeared as early as 1877 in the United States with Bainbridge Bishop and were especially popular in the early twentieth century. See Sherrye Cohn, *Arthur Dove: Nature as Symbol,* Studies in the Fine Arts: The Avant-Garde, no. 49 (Ann Arbor: UMI Research Press, 1985), 53, 66–67, and Linda Dalrymple Henderson, *The Fourth Dimension and Non-Euclidean Geometry in Modern Art* (Princeton: Princeton University Press, 1983), 186–201.

46. Quoted in *Max Weber: Retrospective Exhibition, 1907–1930,* intro. Alfred Barr, exh. cat. (New York: Museum of Modern Art, 1930), 17.

47. See Georgia O'Keeffe, *Georgia O'Keeffe* (New York: Viking Press, 1976), n.p., on her work and the musical analogy.

48. Max Weber, "The Fourth Dimension from a Plastic Point of View," *Camera Work* 31 (July 1910): 25. For more on Weber and the fourth dimension, see Willard Bohn, "In Pursuit of the Fourth Dimension: Guillaume Apollinaire and Max Weber," *Arts* 54 (June 1980): 166–69, and Henderson, *The Fourth Dimension and Non-Euclidean Geometry,* 167–82.

49. Max Weber, "On the Brooklyn Bridge," unpublished essay, 1912; quoted in Percy North, *Max Weber: American Modern,* exh. cat. (New York: Jewish Museum, 1982), 56.

50. Abraham Walkowitz Papers, AAA, reel D303, frame 915. For more on Walkowitz's early art, see Sheldon Reich, "Abraham Walkowitz: Pioneer of American Modernism," *American Art Journal* 3 (Spring 1971): 72–82, and Martica Sawin, *Abraham Walkowitz, 1878–1965,* exh. cat. (Salt Lake City: Utah Museum of Fine Arts, 1975).

51. Walkowitz Papers, AAA, reel D303, frame 1628.

52. Quoted by A. L. Chanin, 1949; clipping in Walkowitz Papers, AAA, reel D303, frame 1702.

53. Abraham Walkowitz, *Improvisations of New York: A Symphony in Lines* (Girard, Kansas: Haldeman-Julius Publications, 1948), n.p.

54. *An Exhibition of Watercolors—New York, Berkshire and Adirondack Series—and Oils by John Marin,* Marin File, New York Public Library Papers, AAA, reel N53, frame 941.

55. This print is reproduced in Walkowitz, *Improvisations of New York,* n.p.

56. See Eric J. Hobsbawm, "Introduction: Inventing Traditions," in *The Invention of Tradition,* ed. Eric J. Hobsbawm and Terence Ranger (Cambridge, Eng.: Cambridge University Press, 1985), 1–14, for a discussion of this notion of "invented traditions."

57. Marius de Zayas, "From '291,'" *Camera Work* 48 (October 1916): 69–70.

58. Letter, Stieglitz to Paul Rosenfeld, September 3, 1923; quoted in Sarah Greenough and Juan Hamilton, *Alfred Stieglitz, Photographs and Writings,* exh. cat. (Washington, D.C.: National Gallery of Art, 1983), 212.

59. For more on nationalism in the 1910s and 1920s, see Matthew Baigell, "American Art and National Identity: The 1920s," *Arts* 61 (February 1987): 48–55, and Wanda Corn, "Toward a Native Art," *Wilson Quarterly* 5 (Summer 1981): 166–77.

60. See Judith Zilczer, "The Armory Show and the American Avant-Garde: A Re-evaluation," *Arts* 53 (September 1978): 126–30.

61. See, for example, Randolph Bourne, "Our Cultural Humility," *Atlantic Monthly* 114 (October 1914): 506.

62. Huntington Wright explained in the catalog introduction, "The pictures here shown give us an unusual opportunity for coming into touch with the more important modern American painters." See *The Forum Exhibition of Modern American Painters,* exh. cat. (1916; repr. New York: Arno Press, 1968), 41.

63. Brooks coined the term *usable past* in 1918, although he and his *Seven Arts* colleagues were interested in discovering America's cultural history well before this date; see Wertheim, *The New York Little Renaissance,* 181. Also see "Editorial Statement," *Seven Arts* 1 (November 1916): 52–53, and James Oppenheim, "The Story of the *Seven Arts,"* *American Mercury* 20 (June 1930): 156. On other cultural nationalist magazines, see Wertheim, *The New York Little Renaissance,* 169–72, 196–97.

64. Paul Rosenfeld, *Port of New York,* intro. Sherman Paul (1924; repr. Urbana: University of Illinois Press, 1961), xxxiv.

65. Marius de Zayas, "On New York," *291* 5–6 (July–August 1915): n.p.

66. See Judith Zilczer, "Robert J. Coady: Forgotten Spokesman for Avant-Garde Culture in America," *American Art Review* 2 (September–October 1975): 77–89.

67. Matthew Josephson, "The Great American Billposter," *Broom* 3, no. 4 (November 1922): 305. Also see idem, "Made in America," *Broom* 2, no. 3 (June 1922): 270.

68. Paul Strand, "John Marin," unpublished manuscript, 5, quoted in Balken, *John Marin's Berkshire Landscapes,* n.p.

69. Letter, Marin to Stieglitz, November 23, 1919, YCAL.

70. Letter, Marin to Duncan and Marjorie Phillips, February 18, 1937, repr. in Norman, ed., *The Selected Writings of John Marin,* 172.

71. Marin believed that American art would come naturally from Americans. He stated, "When we grow potatoes in the country we use American soil and when we paint pictures I guess we use something like it." *New York Herald Tribune,* October 18, 1936, repr. in Gray, ed., *Marin by Marin,* 128. He also wrote, "This weather of ours here in America—cussed alluring and repellent all in the same breath. Let our people live here long enough and they'll get like the weather, then some—things—great—will happen." Undated manuscript, repr. in Gray, ed., *Marin by Marin,* 152.

72. Timothy Robert Rodgers, "False Memories: Alfred Stieglitz and the Development of the Nationalist Aesthetic," in *Over Here! Modernism,* 60–61.

73. J. Nilsen Lauvrik, "Review of John Marin Exhibition," *Camera Work* 42–43 (April–July 1913): 41.

74. J. Edgar Chamberlain, "Review of John Marin

Exhibition," *Camera Work* 42–43 (April–July 1913): 23.

75. Allan, "The 'Flat-Iron' Building," 36, 39–40, and Stieglitz, quoted in Dorothy Norman, *Alfred Stieglitz: An American Seer* (New York: Random House, 1960), 45.

76. Arthur Cravan, "New York," *Soil* 1 (December 1916): 36. See also "Artistic Aspects of the Skyscraper," *Current Opinion* 54, no. 4 (April 1913): 321, and Francis Picabia, "How New York Looks to Me," *New York American,* March 30, 1913, magazine section, 11.

77. Waldo Frank, *Our America* (1919; repr. New York: AMS Press, 1972), 171.

78. Claude Bragdon, "The Shelton Hotel, New York," *Architectural Record* 58, no. 1 (July 1925): 1.

79. Benjamin de Casseres, "The Ironical in Art," *Camera Work* 38 (April 1912): 17–18.

80. Antliff, *Inventing Bergson,* 168–84. Filippo Tommaso Marinetti wrote, for example, "It is in Italy that we launch this manifesto of violence, destructive and incendiary, by which we this day found 'Futurism,' because we would deliver Italy from its canker of professors, archaeologists, cicerones and antiquaries." From *Initial Manifesto of Futurism,* February 20, 1909, repr. in Joshua C. Taylor, *Futurism,* exh. cat. (New York: Doubleday and the Museum of Modern Art, 1961), 124.

81. Marin, "John Marin by Himself," xxxv.

82. Letters, Marin to Stieglitz, September 24, 1924 and September 12, 1923, YCAL. Marin's writings attest to his liking for jazz: "I imagine if we were familiar with their [Eastern and American Indian] music and had not been fed up with German and Italian music of the period and even after—and heard one of the Eastern music—we'd get a kick—and feel a basic rightness. Why we get (though we hate to admit it) a kick out of JAZZ and I am sure that has some of the Eastern flavor." Undated manuscript, repr. in Gray, ed., *Marin by Marin,* 148. John Marin, Jr., wrote in a letter to the author, July 26, 1985: "He also felt that way about some American Jazz. George Gershwin appealed to him. However, I don't recall him mentioning any particular band leaders or musicians. I know he liked some Black jazz bands of the vaudeville days."

83. Contemporary critics saw the restlessness and energy of Marin's art as a direct jazz equivalent. See Edwin Alden Jewell, "New Art of Marin Put on Exhibition," newspaper clipping with handwritten source and date as *Art News,* December 21, 1933, Marin File, New York Public Library Papers, AAA, reel N53, frame 955.

84. One theory about the origin of the word *jazz* holds

that it was slang for *speed;* see Kern, *The Culture of Time and Space,* 123–24.

## Chapter 2: Joseph Stella, the New Art, and Noise Music

1. Henry W. Nevinson, "The Impulse to Futurism," *Atlantic Monthly* 114 (November 1914): 630.

2. Henry Blake Fuller, *The Cliff Dwellers* (1893), quoted in Merrill Schleier, *The Skyscraper in American Art, 1890–1931,* Studies in the Fine Arts: The Avant-Garde, no. 53 (Ann Arbor: UMI Research Press, 1986), 12; Sidney Allan [Sadakichi Hartmann], "The 'Flat-Iron' Building—An Esthetical Dissertation," *Camera Work* 4 (October 1903): 39–40.

3. Kurt Weill, quoted in Peter Conrad, *The Art of the City: Views and Versions of New York* (New York: Oxford University Press, 1984), 118.

4. T. J. Jackson Lears, "From Salvation to Self-Realization: Advertising and the Therapeutic Roots of the Consumer Culture, 1880–1930," in Richard Wrightman Fox and T. J. Jackson Lears, eds., *The Culture of Consumption: Critical Essays in American History, 1880–1930* (New York: Pantheon, 1983), 8–9.

5. "Pressing Forward into Space," *Nation* 94 (April 11, 1912): 356.

6. For references to *Factory Music,* see Arthur Dove Papers, AAA, reel 2803, frame 726, and Ann Lee Morgan, *Arthur Dove, Life and Work, with a Catalogue Raisonné* (Newark, Del.: University of Delaware Press, 1984), 129. For a discussion of Demuth's painting and Williams's poem, see Barbara Haskell, *Charles Demuth,* exh. cat. (New York: Whitney Museum of American Art and Harry N. Abrams, 1987), 183–85.

7. See reference to Stella's *Self-Portrait, Singing* in a memorandum from John I. H. Baur to Miss McKellar, June 26, 1963; Joseph Stella File, Whitney Museum of American Art Papers, AAA, reel N689, frame 402. See also Louise Varèse, *Varèse: A Looking-Glass Diary, 1883–1928* (New York: W. W. Norton, 1972), 158, on Stella's singing. See Barbara Haskell, *Joseph Stella,* exh. cat. (New York: Whitney Museum of American Art and Harry N. Abrams, 1994), 47, 56–57, on Stella and music.

8. Anna C. Chave, "'Who Will Paint New York?': 'The World's New Art Center' and the Skyscraper Paintings of Georgia O'Keeffe," *American Art* 5, nos. 1–2 (Winter–Spring 1991): 86–107.

9. Stella, quoted in B. J. Kospoth, "Joseph Stella's Exposition," untitled newspaper, European edition, Paris, June 28, 1931, clipping in Joseph Stella Papers, AAA, reel 347, frame 216.

10. Joseph Stella, "Discovery of America: Autobiographical Notes," *Art News* 59 (November 1960): 42, 64. Also see typescript of Stella's "Autobiographical Notes," given to Lloyd Goodrich, February 1946, Stella File, Whitney Museum Papers, AAA, reel N689, frames 196–206.

11. Stella, "Discovery of America," 64. See Haskell, *Joseph Stella,* 31–35, and Irma B. Jaffe, *Joseph Stella* (Cambridge, Mass.: Harvard University Press, 1970), 24–38, for discussions of Stella in Paris.

12. Stella used the phrase "new art" to describe modernism; see Joseph Stella, "The New Art," *Trend* 5 (June 1913): 392–95.

13. Futurist art was first exhibited in the United States in 1915 at the Panama-Pacific Exposition in San Francisco and again in 1917 at an exhibition of Severini's works at Gallery 291.

14. For more on Futurism and American art, see John O. Hand, "Futurism in America," *Art Journal* 41 (Winter 1981): 337–42, and Howard Anthony Risatti, "American Critical Reaction to European Modernism, 1908 to 1917" (Ph.D. diss., University of Illinois at Urbana–Champaign, 1978), 39–42.

15. See Arthur Jerome Eddy, *Cubists and Post-Impressionists* (Chicago: A. C. McClurg, 1914), 166, and Nevinson, "The Impulse to Futurism," 630. Futurist music was performed at the concert "The Art of Noises and the Great Futurist Concert of Noises" at the London Coliseum, June 15, 1914; see ibid., 631. By the early 1920s the machine and its music were objects of fascination and were much discussed in such journals as *Broom.* See Carl Engel, "The Mansion of Peace," *Broom* 2, no. 1 (April 1922): 36–37, and Enrico Prampolini, "The Aesthetic of the Machine and Mechanical Introspection in Art," *Broom* 3, no. 3 (October 1922): 235–37.

16. Stella, "The New Art," 394–95.

17. *Der Rosenkavalier (The Knight of the Rose),* a three-act comic opera by Richard Strauss, with libretto by Hugo von Hofmannsthal, was first performed in Dresden in January 1911. Stella perhaps saw the New York premiere at the Metropolitan Opera House, December 9, 1913. Strauss was popular in New York modernist circles: he visited the city in 1904, was mentioned in *Camera Work,* and was photographed by Edward Steichen.

18. Sadakichi Hartmann, "Rodin's *Balzac*," *Camera Work* 34–35 (April–June 1911): 21.

19. Gabrielle Buffet, "Modern Art and the Public," *Camera Work* special number (June 1913): 12–13.

20. Letter, Georgia O'Keeffe to Anita Pollitzer, June 1915, in Anita Pollitzer, *A Woman on Paper: Georgia O'Keeffe* (New York: Simon and Schuster, 1988), 6.

21. Umberto Boccioni, Carlo D. Carrà, Luigi Russolo, Giacomo Balla, and Gino Severini, *Futurist Painting: Technical Manifesto,* April 11, 1910, repr. in Joshua C. Taylor, *Futurism,* exh. cat. (New York: Doubleday and the Museum of Modern Art, 1961), 126.

22. Boccioni (1910), quoted in Taylor, *Futurism,* 35.

23. Carlo Carrà's "La Pittura dei suoni, rumori, odori" is dated August 11, 1913, and was published in *Lacerba* 1, no. 17 (September 1, 1913); quoted in Marianne W. Martin, *Futurist Art and Theory, 1909–1915* (1968; repr. New York: Hacker Art Books, 1978), 136.

24. Filippo Tommaso Marinetti, *Initial Manifesto of Futurism,* February 20, 1909, repr. in Taylor, *Futurism,* 124. Other painters influenced by the Futurists wrote about the musical city. The German Expressionist Ludwig Meidner, for example, stated in 1913: "Let us paint what is close to us, our city world! The tumultuous streets, the elegance of iron suspension bridges, gasometers, which hang like mountains of white clouds, the shouting coloration of buses and fast locomotives, the waving telephone wires (are they not like songs?)." Quoted in Theda Shapiro, "The Metropolis in the Visual Arts: Paris, Berlin, New York, 1890–1940," *Metropolis, 1890–1940,* ed. Anthony Sutcliffe (Chicago: University of Chicago Press, 1984), 105.

25. For a discussion of these paintings, see Taylor, *Futurism,* 45, 52.

26. Stella, "Discovery of America," 65.

27. See John F. Kasson, *Amusing the Million: Coney Island at the Turn of the Century* (New York: Hill and Wang, 1978), 8.

28. Albert Bigelow Paine, "The New Coney Island," *Century* 68 (August 1904): 535; quoted in Kasson, *Amusing the Million,* 63.

29. Stella, "Discovery of America," 65. Stella later wrote of *Battle of Lights, Coney Island:* "I felt that 'Coney Island' should be shown too: it makes a strong contrast to the 'Bridge': this pictures the drama, while 'Coney' is the 'comedy' of modern machinery." Letter, Stella to Katherine Dreier, September 26, 1926, Joseph Stella File, Société Anonyme Collection, YCAL.

30. Francis Picabia, "A Post-Cubist's Impressions of New York," *New York Tribune,* March 9, 1913, part 2, 1.

31. Francis Picabia, "How New York Looks to Me," *New York American,* March 30, 1913, magazine section, 11.

32. Theorists, scientists, and aestheticians from Plato to Isaac Newton have made this connection between the musical scale and the color spectrum.

33. Jan Thompson, "Picabia and His Influence on American Art, 1913–1917," *Art Journal* 39 (Fall 1979): 20. Both Stella and Picabia were associated with the Arensberg circle. Picabia's machine drawings have been discussed as a source for Stella's machine style in works such as *New York Interpreted.* For more on Picabia and Stella, see William Agee, "New York Dada, 1910–1930," *Art News Annual 34: The Avant Garde,* ed. Thomas B. Hess and John Ashbery (New York: Macmillan, 1968), 110, and Thompson, "Picabia and His Influence," 19–20. Thompson, p. 20, also comments on the likeness between Picabia's *Music is like painting* and Stella's *Song of the Nightingale.* For more on New York Dada, see Francis M. Naumann, *New York Dada, 1915–23* (New York: Harry N. Abrams, 1994).

34. Quoted in John I. H. Baur, *Joseph Stella,* exh. cat. (New York: Whitney Museum of American Art and Shorewood, 1963), 23.

35. Stella, "Discovery of America," 65.

36. Joseph Stella, "The Brooklyn Bridge (A Page of My Life)," *Transition* 16–17 (June 1929): 86–88.

37. Quoted in Conrad, *The Art of the City,* 239.

38. Stella, "Discovery of America," 65.

39. Ibid., 71.

40. From Frank E. W. Freund, "Joseph Stella," *Cicerone* 16 (October 1924), repr. in *Jahrbuch der jungen Kunst,* ed. Georg Biermann (Leipzig: Klinghardt und Biermann, 1924), 310.

41. Quoted in Freund, "Joseph Stella," 313.

42. The quoted passages are, respectively, in Jaffe, *Joseph Stella,* 77, 78; Freund, "Joseph Stella," 310–13; Stella, "Discovery of America," 66; Stella's comments on *New York Interpreted,* repr. in *Joseph Stella,* exh. cat. (Newark, N.J.: Newark Museum, April 23, 1939), in Joseph Stella Papers, AAA, reel 347, frame 91; Stella, "Discovery of America," 66.

43. Stella, "The New Art," 395.

44. Romain Rolland, "America and the Arts," *Seven Arts* 1 (November 1916): 47.

45. Ann Douglas, *Terrible Honesty: Mongrel Manhattan in the 1920s* (New York: Farrar, Straus and Giroux, 1995), 179–88.

46. Stella, "The Brooklyn Bridge (A Page of My Life)," 88.

47. See Wanda Corn, "In Detail: Joseph Stella and *New York Interpreted*," *Portfolio* 1 (January–February 1982): 43, and Jaffe, *Joseph Stella*, 69–70, for more on Stella's religious imagery.

48. Stella, "Discovery of America," 66.

49. See George Cotkin, *Reluctant Modernism: American Thought and Culture, 1880–1900* (New York: Twayne, 1992), for a discussion of the dialectic between tradition and modernism in turn-of-the-century American culture.

50. Waldo Frank stated that the journal forged a "national programme after Whitman, by which America shall become a creative force in the modern world." Frank, *The Re-discovery of America: An Introduction to a Philosophy of American Life* (New York: Scribner's, 1929), 318.

51. Malcolm Cowley, "Pascin's America," *Broom* 4 (January 1923): 36, quoted in Matthew Baigell, "Walt Whitman and Early Twentieth-Century American Art," in *Walt Whitman and the Visual Arts,* ed. Geoffrey M. Sill and Roberta K. Tarbell (New Brunswick: Rutgers University Press, 1992), 121.

52. Wanda M. Corn, "Postscript: Walt Whitman and the Visual Arts," in *Whitman and the Visual Arts,* 168, 171.

53. Quoted in Justin Kaplan, *Walt Whitman: A Life* (New York: Simon and Schuster, 1980), 179.

54. Quoted in Kaplan, *Walt Whitman,* 241. Musicians were also inspired by Whitman's poetry; see F. O. Matthiesen, *American Renaissance: Art and Expression in the Age of Emerson and Whitman* (New York: Oxford University Press, 1941), 363, and Henry O. Osgood, *So This Is Jazz* (Boston: Little, Brown, 1926), 159.

55. Matthiesen, *American Renaissance,* 559, 561. See Louise Pound, "Walt Whitman and Italian Music," *American Mercury* 6, no. 21 (September 1925): 58–63, and Basil de Sélincourt, *Walt Whitman: A Critical Study* (London: Martin Secker, 1914), 104–11.

56. James Oppenheim, "Lazy Verse," *Seven Arts* 1 (November 1916): 71.

57. Walt Whitman, *The Portable Walt Whitman,* ed. Mark Van Doren and Malcolm Cowley (New York: Viking Press, 1973), 60–61.

58. Ibid., 326.

59. Stella, "The Brooklyn Bridge (A Page of My Life)," 87, and "For the American Painting," in *Stella, 1943,* exh. cat. (New York: ACA Gallery, 1943), Joseph Stella File, YCAL.

60. Stella wrote in "Discovery of America," 41, "After my classical education in Italy, I came to New York in 1896 and with the greatest admiration for Walt Whitman." Charmion von Wiegand stated, "[Stella] can quote endlessly from Walt Whitman and Edgar Allan Poe," in "Joseph Stella—Painter of the Brooklyn Bridge," unpublished essay, 1939, Joseph Stella Papers, AAA, reel 346, frame 1389. See also Baigell, "Walt Whitman and Early Twentieth-Century American Art," in *Whitman and the Visual Arts,* 127–29; William Innes Homer, *Robert Henri and His Circle* (Ithaca: Cornell University Press, 1969), 76, 145, 158–60; and Bennard B. Perlman, *The Immortal Eight* (New York: Exposition Press, 1962), 17, 55, 63–64, 122, on Henri and Whitman.

61. Stella, "For the American Painting," Joseph Stella File, YCAL.

62. Stella, "The New Art," 395.

63. See Baigell, "Walt Whitman and Early Twentieth-Century American Art," 132–34, for a discussion of Stella and Whitman. Benjamin de Casseres also linked Whitman with European modernism; see Baigell, "Walt Whitman and Early Twentieth-Century American Art," 134.

64. Marinetti, *Initial Manifesto of Futurism,* repr. in Taylor, *Futurism,* 124.

65. This poetic and musical transformation of ordinary noise also appeared in at least one contemporary literary representation of the modern American city. Hart Crane's *The Bridge* (1923) presents the Brooklyn Bridge as a harp with choiring strings, surrounded by the music and noises of New York harbor. It catalogs other sounds of the modern city: radio, the music of Bert Williams and the minstrels, trains whistling, headlights "rushing with sound," a "world of whistles, wire, and steam," singing popular songs, machines that sing, a serenading escalator. Crane's use of musical language and awareness of sound as part of the modern American experience parallels Stella's; as Irma B. Jaffe has pointed out, the poet was indebted to Stella in this work. See Jaffe, "Joseph Stella and Hart Crane: The Brooklyn Bridge," *American Art Journal* 1 (Fall 1969): 98–107.

66. Werner Sollors, *Beyond Ethnicity: Consent and Descent in American Culture* (New York: Oxford University Press, 1986), 254.

67. Israel Zangwill, *The Melting Pot: A Drama in Four Acts* (1925 ed.; repr. New York: AMS Press, 1969), 33.

68. Horace Kallen, "Democracy versus the Melting-Pot" (1915), quoted in Sollors, *Beyond Ethnicity,* 97.

69. Rolland, "America and the Arts," 49–50.

70. "The Shipbuilders as Sketched by Joseph Stella," *Survey* 41 (November 30, 1918): 259–62.

71. Balilla Pratella, *Technical Manifesto of Futurist Music,* March 11, 1911, trans. in Nicolas Slonimsky, *Music since 1900,*

5th ed. (New York: Schirmer Books, 1994), 1019.

72. Luigi Russolo, *The Art of Noises,* March 11, 1913, trans. in Slonimsky, *Music since 1900,* 1020.

73. Russolo, *The Art of Noises,* in Slonimsky, *Music since 1900,* 1021. For more on Futurist music, see Rodney J. Payton, "The Music of Futurism," *Musical Quarterly* 62 (January 1976): 25–45.

74. Most of Russolo's noise instruments were destroyed in World War I, although photographs of them have survived. See Giovanni Lista, "Klang und Polyphonie der Stadt bei den Futuristen," in Karin von Maur, ed., *Vom Klang der Bilder: Die Musik in der Kunst des 20. Jahrhunderts,* exh. cat. (Munich: Prestel and Stuttgart Staatsgalerie, 1985), 380–83.

75. See Alan Howard Levy, *Musical Nationalism: American Composers' Search for Identity* (Westport, Conn.: Greenwood Press, 1983), 64–65, and Gunther Schuller, *Early Jazz: Its Roots and Musical Development* (New York: Oxford University Press, 1968), 164.

76. See, for example, Douglas, *Terrible Honesty,* 179–88, and Paul Rosenfeld, *Modern Tendencies in Music* (New York: Caxton Institute, 1927), 8–9, 47–49, on the equation of *modern* with *American.*

77. For a discussion of Varèse's association with the avant garde, especially visual artists, see Jonathan W. Bernard, *The Music of Edgard Varèse* (New Haven: Yale University Press, 1987), 1–2; William Innes Homer, *Alfred Stieglitz and the American Avant-Garde* (Boston: New York Graphic Society, 1977), 182; Bram Dijkstra, *Cubism, Stieglitz, and the Early Poetry of William Carlos Williams* (Princeton: Princeton University Press, 1969), 38; Olivia Mattis, "Edgard Varèse and the Visual Arts" (Ph.D. diss., Stanford University, 1992); and Naumann, *New York Dada,* 105–8.

78. Varèse, quoted in Bernard, *The Music of Edgard Varèse,* 1.

79. Varèse, "The Liberation of Sound," quoted in Bernard, *The Music of Edgard Varèse,* 7.

80. See Mattis, "Edgard Varèse and the Visual Arts," 19–93, 122–69. The composer's wife, Louise Varèse, wrote: "While poets were juggling words on a page and painters were producing curious juxtapositions of noses, ears, eyes, and breasts in the name of simultaneism, Varèse was beginning to wonder how it might be obtained musically. He believed that, given the means, simultaneism was literally possible in music." Louise Varèse, *A Looking-Glass Diary,* 104–5. Also see Bernard, *The Music of Edgard Varèse,* 1–38.

81. Varèse, "The Liberation of Sound," quoted in Mattis, "Edgard Varèse and the Visual Arts," 8.

82. See Ferruccio Busoni, "Sketch of a New Aesthetic of Music," in *Three Classics in the Aesthetic of Music* (New York: Dover, 1962), 95.

83. From a statement in the *Christian Science Monitor,* July 1922, quoted in Fernand Ouellette, *Edgard Varèse,* trans. Derek Coltman (1966; repr. London: Calder and Boyars, 1973), 76. Varèse exclaimed, in a manifesto published in 1917: "Our alphabet is poverty-stricken and illogical. The music that ought to be living and vibrating at this moment needs new means of expression, and only science can infuse it with youthful sap." Edgar[d] Varèse, "Que la musique sonne," *391* 5 (June 1917): n.p.

84. From a lecture by Edgard Varèse, quoted in Louise Varèse, *A Looking-Glass Diary,* 42. Also see Edgar[d] Varèse, "The Music of Tomorrow," *London Evening News,* June 14, 1924, 4.

85. From a lecture by Edgard Varèse, quoted in Louise Varèse, *A Looking-Glass Diary,* 105. For more on *Hyperprism,* see Ouellette, *Edgard Varèse,* 38–39.

86. Quoted in Louise Varèse, *A Looking-Glass Diary,* 230.

87. Paul Rosenfeld, *An Hour with American Music* (Philadelphia: J. B. Lippincott, 1929), 171, and idem, *Discoveries of a Music Critic* (New York: Vienna House, 1936), 260.

88. Jaffe, *Joseph Stella,* xi, writes that Varèse was Stella's closest friend in the years after the Armory Show. For other references to the Stella–Varèse friendship, see Baur, *Joseph Stella,* 32, and Judith Zilczer, *Joseph Stella,* exh. cat. (Washington, D.C.: Smithsonian Institution Press, 1983), 13. Varèse befriended Stella and Picabia and contributed poetry to Picabia's magazine *391;* his poem "Oblation" appeared in *391* 5 (June 1917): n.p. Also see letters from Varèse to Louise Norton [Varèse], New York, June 22 and July 15, 1921, Varèse Archive, New York; I want to thank Olivia Mattis for sharing this material with me. Pietro Lazzari remembered seeing Stella and Varèse together at Romany Marie's: "Around a small table in a Greenwich Village tea shop were sitting three people. In the center was Stella. . . . Next to him, on his right, was art dealer Valentine Dudensing; on his left, Varèse, the composer. . . . Stella and Varèse were all the time together." From "Recollections of Stella" (1926), Stella File, Whitney Museum Papers, AAA, reel N689, frames 5–6. Also see Mattis, "Edgard Varèse and the Visual Arts," 122–48, 152, 157; Ruth Phelps and Henri Morane, "Artistes d'avant-garde en Amérique," *Figaro hebdomadaire* [New York?], July 25, 1928, 8–9; and Louise Varèse, *A Looking-Glass Diary,* 98.

89. Throughout his career, Varèse was committed to the musical education of the public. In the late 1910s and 1920s

he founded and supported organizations such as the New Symphony Orchestra, International Composers' Guild, and Pan-American Association of Composers to advance the performance of modern music by American orchestras. The International Composers' Guild published a manifesto in *Broom* 1, no. 1 (November 1921): 94–95. Juliana Force and Gertrude Vanderbilt Whitney supported Varèse's New Symphony and the ICG. In fact, Varèse received a monthly allowance of two hundred dollars from Whitney so that he could proceed with plans for the ICG. See Mattis, "Edgard Varèse and the Visual Arts," 146–86, and Louise Varèse, *A Looking-Glass Diary,* 153–55.

90. Louise Varèse, *A Looking-Glass Diary,* 157–58.

91. Ibid.

92. Ibid., 20.

93. Stella, "Discovery of America," 66. Despite his faith and optimism in the United States, Stella remained ambivalent toward technology. Although he marveled at monuments of American engineering such as the Brooklyn Bridge, he feared the hellish aspects of industrialization. He compared Pittsburgh's steel mills to the "infernal regions sung by Dante" and wrote of the "great evils" and contrasts in the American city, its "unheard of riches" and "frightful poverty." See Jaffe, *Joseph Stella,* 19, 25, 77–79. For more on Stella's negative attitudes toward the city, see Corn, "In Detail," 45; Haskell, *Joseph Stella,* 23; and Schleier, *The Skyscraper in American Art,* 102–3.

94. Olivia Mattis, "Edgard Varèse's 'Progressive' Nationalism: *Amériques* Meets *Américanisme,*" in *Edgard Varèse: Die Befreiung des Klangs,* ed. Helga de La Motte-Haber (Hofheim, Germany: Wolke, 1992), 154.

95. Louise Varèse, *A Looking-Glass Diary,* 150. For more on the scoring of *Amériques,* see 56.

96. Note to a young music student, Odile Vivier, quoted in Ouellette, *Edgard Varèse,* 56. Varèse also explained: "A title is generally given after the score is written in order to catalogue the work, or it may occur to me while I am composing, but it always derives from some association of ideas in relation to the score, and has, needless to say, an imaginative appeal to me personally." From "My Titles," unpublished text, quoted in Ouellette, *Edgard Varèse,* 55.

97. From an interview in the *Evening Bulletin* (Philadelphia), April 12, 1926, quoted in Ouellette, *Edgard Varèse,* 57. Rosenfeld described *Amériques:* "The raucous sluggish symphony, with its immense metallic sonorities, sharply appreciated vulgarities, and over-delicate contrasts, actually borders on the caricatural. . . . The title, eternal symbol of

new worlds awaiting discovery, is beautifully justified by it. . . . There is a distinct quality about it; the style being both metallic and strident, and aerial and delicate, like the reflection of a prairie sunset on steel rails." Rosenfeld, *An Hour with American Music,* 169.

98. Quoted in Ouellette, *Edgard Varèse,* 56.

99. Rosenfeld, *Modern Tendencies in Music,* 102–3.

100. *Amériques* was first performed in April 1926 by Leopold Stokowski and the Philadelphia Orchestra in Philadelphia and then New York.

101. Edgard Varèse, quoted in Louise Varèse, *A Looking-Glass Diary,* 211.

102. Rosenfeld, *An Hour with American Music,* 174.

103. Stella, "Discovery of America," 65.

104. From an unpublished recorded interview with Varèse by Gilbert Chase, c. 1961, quoted in Mattis, "Edgard Varèse's 'Progressive Nationalism,' " 149.

105. Harold A. Loeb, "Foreign Exchange," *Broom* 2, no. 2 (May 1922): 178.

106. Antonio Aniante, quoted in Haskell, *Joseph Stella,* 9. Stella also saw his art in terms of his connection to two places. He said in a 1928 interview: "Vous voyez dans mon oeuvre deux éléments qui contrastent, se soutiennent, dus à ma formation de jeunesse italienne et à l'emploi des matériaux américains." Phelps and Morane, "Artistes d'avant-garde en Amérique," 8.

*Chapter 3: The Abstract Art of Arthur Dove and Stuart Davis*

1. "Artistic Aspects of the Skyscraper," *Current Opinion* 54, no. 4 (April 1913): 321, and Claude Bragdon, "The Shelton Hotel, New York," *Architectural Record* 58, no. 1 (July 1925): 1.

2. George Gershwin, "The Composer in the Machine Age," in *Revolt in the Arts,* ed. Oliver M. Sayler (New York: Brentanos, 1930), 266.

3. See Eric Lott, *Love and Theft: Blackface Minstrelsy and the American Working Class* (New York: Oxford University Press, 1995), 18, 92, for a discussion of earlier forms of black music as a site of the contestation of American cultural identity.

4. For the origins of the term *jazz,* see Burton W. Peretti, *The Creation of Jazz: Music, Race, and Culture in Urban America* (Urbana: University of Illinois Press, 1992), 22, 133; Frank Tirro, *Jazz: A History* (New York: W. W. Norton, 1977),

51; and "Why 'Jazz' Sends Us Back to the Jungle," *Current Opinion* 65 (September 1918): 165.

5. For the sources, development, and definitions of jazz, see Kathy J. Ogren, *The Jazz Revolution: Twenties America and the Meaning of Jazz* (New York: Oxford University Press, 1989), 14–18; Peretti, *The Creation of Jazz;* and Gunther Schuller, *Early Jazz: Its Roots and Musical Development* (New York: Oxford University Press, 1968), 18.

6. See Ted Gioia, *The Imperfect Art: Reflections on Jazz and Modern Culture* (New York: Oxford University Press, 1988), and Peretti, *The Creation of Jazz.*

7. Peretti, *The Creation of Jazz,* 44–45.

8. See Paul Gilroy, *The Black Atlantic: Modernity and Double Consciousness* (Cambridge, Mass.: Harvard University Press, 1993), xi, 95–96.

9. For a fuller discussion of the cultural meanings of jazz, see Mark S. Harvey, "Jazz and Modernism: Changing Conceptions of Innovation and Tradition," in Reginald T. Buckner and Steven Weiland, eds., *Jazz in Mind: Essays on the History and Meaning of Jazz* (Detroit: Wayne State University Press, 1991), 134–35, and Ogren, *The Jazz Revolution,* 111–61. On the German perception of jazz, see Beeke Sell Tower, "Jungle Music and Song of Machines: Jazz and American Dance in Weimar Culture," in *Envisioning America: Prints, Drawings, and Photographs by George Grosz and His Contemporaries, 1915–1933,* exh. cat. (Cambridge, Mass.: Busch-Reisinger Museum, 1990), 87–105.

10. For other discussions of the connection between modernism and black culture, see Ann Douglas, *Terrible Honesty: Mongrel Manhattan in the 1920s* (New York: Farrar, Straus and Giroux, 1995); Gilroy, *The Black Atlantic;* Richard J. Powell, *The Blues Aesthetic: Black Culture and Modernism,* exh. cat. (Washington, D.C.: Washington Project for the Arts, 1989); and Eric J. Sundquist, *To Wake the Nations: Race in the Making of American Literature* (Cambridge, Mass.: Harvard University Press, 1993), 457–625.

11. Emanuel Julius, "Night Life in Newark," *New York Call,* magazine section, Sunday, May 30, 1915, 8.

12. See Emily Farnham, *Charles Demuth: Behind a Laughing Mask* (Norman: University of Oklahoma Press, 1971), 102–5, and Barbara Haskell, *Charles Demuth,* exh. cat. (New York: Whitney Museum of American Art and Harry N. Abrams, 1987), 56–58.

13. Gioia, *The Imperfect Art,* 22; see 19–49 on jazz and the primitive.

14. "Appeal of the Primitive Jazz," *Literary Digest* 55 (August 25, 1917): 28–29; "Why 'Jazz' Sends Us Back to the Jungle," 165.

15. See William S. Rubin, ed., *"Primitivism" in 20th Century Art: Affinity of the Tribal and the Modern,* exh. cat., 2 vols. (New York: Museum of Modern Art, 1984).

16. Darius Milhaud, who had heard jazz in Harlem, regarded it as African: "This authentic music had its roots in the darkest corners of the Negro soul, the vestigial traces of Africa, no doubt." Quoted in Mona Hadler, "Jazz and the Visual Arts," *Arts* 57 ( June 1983): 92.

17. For more on Harlem and white audiences, see Douglas, *Terrible Honesty;* Lewis A. Erenberg, *Steppin' Out: New York Nightlife and the Transformation of American Culture, 1890–1930* (Westport, Conn.: Greenwood Press, 1981), 256–57; and David Levering Lewis, *When Harlem Was in Vogue* (New York: Alfred A. Knopf, 1981), 99.

18. For a description of these murals, see clipping from *Opportunity,* November 1927, 319, Aaron Douglas Papers, Fisk University Special Collections, AAA, reel 4523. Alain Locke, *Negro Art: Past and Present* (1936; repr. New York: Arno Press, 1969), 68, also mentions Douglas's Club Ebony murals. Douglas discusses the opening of the club in his essay "The Harlem Renaissance," 13–14, Aaron Douglas Papers, AAA, reel 4520.

19. See Erenberg, *Steppin' Out,* 256–57, and Ogren, *The Jazz Revolution,* 75–76, for descriptions of the primitive atmosphere of jazz clubs.

20. This connection can also be seen in many German artists' renderings of jazz themes in the 1920s; see Tower, "Jungle Music and Song of Machines," 87–105.

21. See Jontyle Theresa Robinson and Wendy Greenhouse, *The Art of Archibald J. Motley, Jr.,* exh. cat. (Chicago: Chicago Historical Society, 1991), 89, 108. His *Stomp* (1927), *Syncopation* (1924), and *Black and Tan Cabaret* (c. 1921) feature the black-and-tan clubs operated for both blacks and whites in Bronzeville, Chicago's South Side black neighborhood.

22. Usually dated 1944, *Primitive Music* can be assigned to December 1943, as notes in Dove's diary apparently refer to it, describing its color scheme, zigzags, and musical theme: "Did RYOWBlk—more like music /\/\/\/\" (December 13, 1943), "Painted and finished /\/\/\/\ _____" (December 31). See Arthur Dove Papers, AAA, reel 725, frames 1022, 1028.

23. See Sherrye Cohn, *Arthur Dove: Nature as Symbol,* Studies in the Fine Arts: The Avant-Garde, no. 49 (Ann Arbor: UMI Research Press, 1985), 104, and Sasha Newman, *Arthur Dove and Duncan Phillips: Artist and Patron*, exh. cat. (Washington, D.C.: Phillips Collection and New York: George Braziller, 1982), 44. Other works in this series include *Indian Summer* (1941), *Silver Chief* (1942), and *Indian One* (1943).

24. Howard Devree, "Brief Comment on Some Recently Opened Shows—Dove," *New York Times,* March 26, 1944, clipping in Downtown Gallery Papers, AAA, reel ND31, frame 536.

25. J. A. Rogers, "Jazz at Home," in Alain Locke, ed., *The New Negro* (1925; repr. New York: Atheneum, 1992), 217.

26. Ibid., 222–23, 217. George Antheil also saw jazz as a post–World War I music; see Alain Locke, *The Negro and His Music* (1936; repr. New York: Arno Press, 1969), 89.

27. H. A. L. (Harold A. Loeb), "The Mysticism of Money," *Broom* 3, no. 2 (September 1922): 124; Locke, *The Negro and His Music,* 89; Sadakichi Hartmann, *White Chrysanthemums—Literary Fragments and Pronouncements,* ed. George Knox and Harry Lawton (New York: Herder and Herder, 1971), 80 (this excerpt is undated); Waldo Frank, *In the American Jungle* (1937; repr. Freeport, N.Y.: Books for Libraries Press, 1968), 118–19. Frank, 122–23, criticized jazz as a folk expression that simply reproduced modern sounds and did not transform them into art: "[Jazz] expresses well a mass response to our world of piston rods, cylinders and mechanized laws. The response is of the folk and is passive. . . . Since the rhythm of our age is not transfigured in jazz, as in truly creative art, . . . the elements of the age itself which we may disapprove will appear also in jazz."

28. Le Corbusier, quoted in Peter Conrad, *The Art of the City: Views and Versions of New York* (New York: Oxford University Press, 1984), 138; Blaise Cendrars, Paul Hindemith, and Maurice Vlaminck quoted in Hadler, "Jazz and the Visual Arts," 91, 96.

29. See Tower, "Jungle Music and Song of Machines," 94–95, for illustration and discussion of the art work; Bertolt Brecht quoted in Hadler, "Jazz and the Visual Arts," 96.

30. "Two Views of Ragtime: Hiram Kelly Moderwell, 'A Modest Proposal,' and Charles L. Buchanan, 'Ragtime and American Music,'" *Seven Arts* 9 (July 1917): 370.

31. Le Corbusier quoted in Conrad, *The Art of the City,* 138.

32. Florine Stettheimer quoted in Hadler, "Jazz and the Visual Arts," 96.

33. Undated manuscript, repr. in Cleve Gray, ed., *John Marin by John Marin* (New York: Holt, Rinehart and Winston, 1970), 148.

34. Stuart Davis, "The Place of Painting in Contemporary Culture: The Easel is a Cool Spot at an Arena of Hot Events," *Art News* 56 (Summer 1957): 29.

35. Mark Tobey described New York as having "sirens, dynamic lights, brilliant parades." *Retrospective Exhibition of Paintings by Mark Tobey* (San Francisco, 1951), quoted in Eliza E. Rathbone, *Mark Tobey: City Paintings,* exh. cat. (Washington, D.C.: National Gallery of Art, 1984), 32.

36. Francis Picabia, "How New York Looks to Me," *New York American,* March 30, 1913, magazine section, 11.

37. See "Mr. Picabia Paints 'Coon Songs,'" *New York Herald,* March 18, 1913, 12. For other reviews of Picabia's jazz paintings, see Maurice Aisen, "The Latest Evolution in Art and Picabia," *Camera Work* special number (June 1913): 19; Gabrielle Buffet, "Modern Art and the Public," *Camera Work* special number (June 1913): 12; and Samuel Swift, "Review of Picabia's Paintings at 291 from the *New York Sun,*" *Camera Work* 42–43 (April–July 1913): 48. Albert Gleizes adopted vaudeville and jazz themes in works such as *On a Vaudeville Theme* (1917) and *Jazz* (1915); see Daniel Robbins, *Albert Gleizes, 1881–1953,* exh. cat. (New York: Solomon R. Guggenheim Museum of Art, 1964).

38. Tower, "Jungle Music and Song of Machines," 87–105.

39. "Two Views of Ragtime," 378, 382.

40. Gilbert Seldes, "Toujours Jazz," *Dial* 75 (August 1923): 151–52.

41. Henry O. Osgood, *So This Is Jazz* (Boston: Little, Brown, 1926), 27.

42. Frank Jewett Mather, Jr., Charles Rufus Morey, and William James Henderson, *The American Spirit in Art* (New Haven: Yale University Press, 1927), 342–43.

43. James Weldon Johnson, ed., *The Book of American Negro Poetry* (1922; 2d ed., New York: Harcourt, Brace, 1931), 10, 19.

44. Rogers, "Jazz at Home," 219–20.

45. Undated letter, Robert Coady to Mabel Dodge, quoted in Judith Katy Zilc32er, "The Aesthetic Struggle in America, 1913–1918: Abstract Art and Theory in the Stieglitz Circle" (Ph.D. diss., University of Delaware, 1975), 147.

46. Mather, Morey, and Henderson, *The American Spirit in Art,* 342–43.

47. Matthew Josephson, "The Great American Billposter," *Broom* 3, no. 4 (November 1922): 305. He also wrote: "An instance of this search for fresh booty is the strong leaning for purely American elements in the new literature. The contemporary American flora and fauna are collected, in an arbitrary fashion, out of the inimitable films, the newspaper accounts, the jazz band, on the hunch that the world is on its way to being Americanized in the next two decades." "After and beyond Dada," *Broom* 2, no. 4 (July 1922): 347.

48. Robert Coady, "American Art," *Soil* 1 (December 1916): 3.

49. For diary references to popular music and musical

events, see Helen Torr Dove Papers, AAA, reel N70/52, frames 110, 112–22, 144, 156, 174, 175 (December 15, 1925; notes at the end of 1925 diary; March 27, 1926; May 16, 1926; July 25, 1926; July 31, 1926); reel 38, frames 170, 404, 432, 451–52 (November 29, 1930; September 8, 1932; December 25, 1933; February 2–3, 1933); reel 39, frames 292, 324 (January 26, 1936; March 31, 1936); reel 40, frames 58, 120 (November 22, 1938; June 18, 1939); and Arthur Dove Papers, reel 725, frame 630 (February 16, 1941).

50. See Arthur Dove Papers, AAA, reel 725, frames 951, 954, 1029–30 (June 27–28, 1943; July 4, 1943; end of 1943 diary).

51. See, for example, Theodore E. Stebbins, Jr., and Carol Troyen, *The Lane Collection: 20th-Century Paintings in the American Tradition,* exh. cat. (Boston: Museum of Fine Arts, 1983).

52. For more on Dove's music paintings, see Donna M. Cassidy, "Arthur Dove's Music Paintings of the Jazz Age," *American Art Journal* 20, no. 1 (1988): 4–23; idem, "The Painted Music of America in the Works of Arthur G. Dove, John Marin, and Joseph Stella: An Aspect of Cultural Nationalism" (Ph.D. diss., Boston University, 1988), 107–70; Cohn, *Arthur Dove,* 15–16, 69–71; Barbara Haskell, *Arthur Dove,* exh. cat. (Boston: New York Graphic Society, 1974), 28–29; Ann Lee Morgan, *Arthur Dove, Life and Work, with a Catalogue Raisonné* (Newark, Del.: University of Delaware Press, 1984), 47, 69, nn. 35–36; Newman, *Arthur Dove and Duncan Phillips,* 43–44; Suzanne Mullett Smith and Gordon H. Smith, "Music of the Eye: The Development of an Idea," talk delivered at American University, Washington, D.C., Department of Music, 1950 (re-edited 1976), Suzanne Mullett Smith Papers, AAA, reel 1043, frames 1269–74; Frederick S. Wight, *Arthur G. Dove,* exh. cat. (Berkeley: University of California Press, 1958), 54–56; and Judith Zilczer, "Synaesthesia and Popular Culture: Arthur Dove, George Gershwin, and the 'Rhapsody in Blue,'" *Art Journal* 44 (Winter 1984): 361–66.

53. Letter, Alfred Stieglitz to Arthur B. Carles, April 11, 1913, quoted in William A. Camfield, *Francis Picabia: His Art, Life, and Times* (Princeton: Princeton University Press, 1979), 56.

54. Samuel Swift writes in the *New York Sun,* March 1913 (repr. in Swift, "Review of Picabia's Paintings at 291," 48), "[Picabia's watercolors] conveyed to [Dove] as definite a meaning, in terms of emotion, as any formula might have done that had been readily accepted the world over."

55. William Innes Homer, *Alfred Stieglitz and the American Avant-Garde* (Boston: New York Graphic Society, 1977), 210, and Arlette Jean Klaric, "Arthur G. Dove's Abstract Style of 1912: Dimensions of the Decorative and Bergsonian Realities" (Ph.D. diss., University of Wisconsin, Madison, 1984), 185, also link Dove's *Music* to Duchamp's *Nude Descending a Staircase,* on view at the Armory Show.

56. Newspaper clipping with handwritten title, *Chicago Evening Post,* 1913, Downtown Gallery Papers, AAA, reel ND70, frame 557. Picabia's *Chanson Negre I* was among four studies purchased by Stieglitz from Picabia's 1913 show at 291. Samuel Swift reported in the *New York Sun:* "Picabia did not know, it seems, that purple was the favorite color of most negroes, but as he has told Mr. Stieglitz, who afterward conveyed this fact to him, purple was the inevitable and dominating hue that sprang to the Frenchman's consciousness." Swift, "Review of Picabia's Paintings at 291," 48.

57. Arthur Jerome Eddy, *Cubists and Post-Impressionists* (Chicago: A. C. McClurg, 1914), 128.

58. See *Catalogue of Victor Records* (Camden, N.J.: Victor Talking Machine Company, 1921), n.p. Other early modernists dealt with Oriental themes; see Marsden Hartley's *Musical Theme (Oriental Symphony)* (1912–13), Max Weber's *Chinese Restaurant* (1915), and Joseph Stella's *Chinatown* (1917). Also see Henry Bellaman's poem "Decorations for an Imaginary Ballet," *Broom* 1, no. 2 (December 1921): 116–18, for a contemporary description of Chinese music.

59. Dove recorded the color scheme of *Factory Music* as silver, yellow, indian-red, and blue, similar to that in *Chinese Music;* see Arthur Dove Papers, AAA, reel 2803, frame 726.

60. Rosenfeld, for instance, described Dove's earlier work as Whitmanesque—a "*Leaves of Grass* through pigment." Paul Rosenfeld, *Port of New York,* intro. Sherman Paul (1924; repr. Urbana: University of Illinois Press, 1961), 169.

61. See Arthur Dove Papers, AAA, roll 954, frame 761, for a copy of the exhibition catalog.

62. Helen Torr Dove writes, "A. to NY on 8:09. . . . A. heard Paul Whiteman." Helen Torr Dove Papers, reel N70/52, frame 110, entry for December 15, 1925. Entry July 31, 1926 (frame 175), reads: "Got records, one 'Rhapsody in Blue' by Gershwin and 4 jazz. . . ." Entry for August 2, 1926 (frame 176), states: "Up early and [Arthur] put records on at 7:30. A. quite amused by Gershwin." Besides the six exhibited paintings, Dove produced drawings and studies from the phonograph recordings; see entries for December 1 and 29, 1926, and January 8, 1927 (frames 206, 213, 219). Reds purchased more Gershwin albums for Dove on January 8, 1927: "A. painting big, jazy, beautiful. I to Huntington tried to get

Gershwin or Stravinsky records. . . . Later I put on records and A. did 6 things from them." At the same time, Dove purchased recordings of Igor Stravinsky's music and did a painting from the fourth movement of the *Firebird Suite,* now lost; see entries for January 8 and 20, 1927, and November 30, 1927 (frames 219, 222, 301). Dove preferred jazz and Gershwin, finding the Russian composer too sad; see entry March 2, 1927 (frame 232).

63. The 1924 Whiteman–Gershwin recording of *Rhapsody in Blue* (Victor 55225) was rereleased in 1927; see *Catalogue of Victor Records* (1927), n.p. For a recording of the 1924 version of *Rhapsody in Blue* as well as "I'll Build a Stairway to Paradise" and "An Orange Grove in California," see *An Experiment in Modern Music: Paul Whiteman at Aeolian Hall,* sound recording, Smithsonian Institution Collection, 1981, RCA special products.

64. Undated letter, Dove to Stieglitz and Georgia O'Keeffe, Alfred Stieglitz Archive, YCAL. Ann Lee Morgan dates this letter to October 30, 1926; see her *Dear Stieglitz, Dear Dove* (Newark, Del.: University of Delaware Press, 1988), 128–29.

65. See Helen Torr Dove Papers, AAA, reel N70/52, entry for December 5, 1924. Dove wrote to Stieglitz, c. 1926–27, YCAL: "Perhaps with all that was going on the photograph of the clouds, you know the one I mean, made me feel like having it pass through me the most." He later purchased one of these "equivalents"; see letter, Dove to Stieglitz, July 6, 1942, YCAL.

66. Arthur G. Dove, "An Idea," in untitled exh. cat. (New York: Intimate Gallery, December 12, 1927–January 11, 1928) n.p., in Arthur Dove Papers, AAA, reel 954, frame 761.

67. Dove wrote, "The future seems to be gone through by a spiral spring from the past." Letter, Dove to Stieglitz, August 18, 1925, YCAL. Cohn, *Arthur Dove,* 32, 60, points out that the spiral became a common conceit to visualize time in the early twentieth century.

68. In "Synaesthesia and Popular Culture," Zilczer argues that both *Rhapsody in Blue* and Dove's painting of it represent the union of the fine arts and popular culture. Following this argument, the painting *I'll Build a Stairway to Paradise* and Gauthier's concert can be also associated with this union, for in this concert the singer introduced American popular music in her classical program. Whiteman got the idea for *An Experiment in Modern Music* from Gauthier's concert; see James Lincoln Collier, *The Reception of Jazz in America: A New View* (New York: Institute for Studies in American Music, 1988), 17. "I'll Build a Stairway to

Paradise" was rereleased by Victor in 1925; see *Catalogue of Victor Records,* n.p.

69. Helen Torr Dove Papers, AAA, reel N70/52, frame 242.

70. "An Orange Grove in California" is listed in the program for *An Experiment in Modern Music* as "An Orange Blossom in California," perhaps confused with Victor Herbert's contemporary show, *Orange Blossoms.* For more on *The Music Box Revue of 1923,* see Jack Burton, *The Blue Book of Tin Pan Alley* (Watkins Glen, N.Y.: Century House, 1951), 154, and Osgood, *So This Is Jazz,* 225.

71. Dove purchased five jazz recordings, including *Rhapsody in Blue,* on July 31, 1926, as well as Gershwin and Stravinsky albums on January 8, 1927, but "Orange Grove" is not named in the diary; see Helen Torr Dove Papers, AAA, reel N70/52. RCA Victor first released a recording of "An Orange Grove in California" in October 1923 (Victor 55226), with subsequent releases through the 1920s by both Whiteman and John Steel; see *Catalogue of Victor Records* (1923), n.p.

72. "Rhythm Rag" was a 1927 recording by Paul Whiteman and his Orchestra (Victor 19773); see *Catalogue of Victor Records* (1927), n.p. The Whiteman recording is at the Motion Picture, Broadcasting and Recorded Sound Division, Library of Congress. In a letter to Dove, January 7, 1928, Stieglitz wrote that "[the collector Duncan Phillips] wanted *Something in Brown, Carmine, and Blue, Rhythm Rag,* and *Just Painting*—but felt that he was going beyond his depth in taking one." See Arthur Dove Papers, AAA, reel 725, frame 135. Reds records, on January 5, 1928, "A. called Stieglitz . . . *Rhythm Rag* sold." See Helen Torr Dove Papers, AAA, reel N70/52, frame 313. Marguerite Mergantine was identified as the original buyer of this work; see Arthur Dove Papers, AAA, reel 2803, frame 735.

There are discrepancies in the spelling of *Improvision.* Morgan lists it as *Improvisation,* but in the Dove files and exhibition catalog it is listed as *Improvision.* See Arthur Dove Papers, AAA, reel 954, frame 761, and reel 2803, frame 729; Downtown Gallery Papers, AAA, reel ND31, frames 182–83; and Suzanne Mullett Smith Papers, AAA, reel 1043, frame 577.

73. Homer, *Alfred Stieglitz and the American Avant-Garde,* 209.

74. Dove, "An Idea," n.p.

75. Record of a fragment of a conversation in Halesite Yacht Club, among Dove, Reds, and Alfred Maurer, c. 1930–32; quoted in Wight, *Arthur G. Dove,* 62, and Suzanne

Mullett, "Arthur G. Dove: A Study in Contemporary Art" (master's thesis, American University, 1944), 20–21, in Suzanne Mullett Smith Papers, AAA, reel 1043.

76. Dove, "An Idea," n.p.

77. Quoted in Samuel M. Kootz, *Modern American Painters* (Norwood, Mass.: Plimpton Press, 1930), 38.

78. Jewell wrote to Dove: "Mr. Stieglitz says you already know that he has given me your *Orange Grove in California*. It is a very beautiful picture, and seemed to me one of the finest things in your recent show. . . . I want you to know how deeply I appreciate having it and how genuinely interested I am in the work you are doing." Letter, Stieglitz to Dove, January 25, 1928, Arthur Dove Papers, AAA, reel 954, frame 459. Written on the back of *An Orange Grove in California,* in pencil, is "To E. A. Jewell; appreciation from the Room, Jan 13/28." When Jewell later wrote on Dove's music paintings, he defended *An Orange Grove in California:* "It belongs to a certain period which I have always considered, in its way, Dove's 'top'! He has never to my knowledge done anything else like it." Quoted in Wight, *Arthur G. Dove,* 55–56.

79. Edwin Alden Jewell, *Americans* (New York: Alfred A. Knopf, 1930), 25, 19.

80. See Edward Jablonski and Lawrence D. Stewart, *The Gershwin Years* (Garden City, N.Y.: Doubleday, 1973), 90, and Zilczer, "Synaesthesia and Popular Culture," 363, for more on the title of *Rhapsody in Blue* and its relation to Whistler. Gershwin himself was a painter by avocation. See "Gershwin's Compositions in Paint," *American Art* 7, no. 3 (Summer 1993): 92–94, and Marsden Hartley, "The Late George Gershwin's Hope for Painting," c. 1937, YCAL, also in Marsden Hartley Papers, AAA, reel 1371, frames 3642–44.

81. George Gershwin, quoted in Charles Schwartz, *Gershwin: His Life and Music* (New York: Bobbs-Merrill, 1973), 77.

82. Helen Torr Dove Papers, AAA, reel 39, frame 513, entry for April 2, 1937.

83. Music and sound continued to inform Dove's later art. He visualized sounds in *Fog Horns* (1929; fig. 87) and *Sounds and Seagulls of the Flat* (1932). Reds wrote, on July 6, 1932: "A. got two ideas for paintings, one of dawn, one of sound." On August 29, 1932, she wrote: "A. worked on painting *Sounds and Seagulls on the Flat.*" Helen Torr Dove Papers, AAA, reel 38, frame 402. In 1929 Dove painted *Primitive Jazz,* now lost; Reds wrote in her diary on November 18, 1929: "Arthur made frame for *Primitive Jazz.*" See Helen Torr Dove Papers, AAA, reel N70/52, frame 573. There are other references to music in the Doves' diaries

and letters. He scribbled a musical notation in his diary on September 7, 1943; see Arthur Dove Papers, reel 725, frame 979. On February 27, 1943, Dove talked to Stieglitz: "Am trying to add time to the idea," he noted. "Related gradation give the rhythm . . . sound with music rather rhythm"; and again: "Made pencil drawing in rhythmic c beat" (December 17, 1942) and "straight gouache in 1/2 time" (June 11, 1942); see Arthur Dove Papers, AAA, reel 725, frames 859, 760. He wrote to Stieglitz, May 4, 1942: "Including hoping that the timing idea in this show would be self-evident. It is comparable to music, but not the same. . . . It is coming out of space rather than drawing 'from the eye track' which is still a relic. It can come as a thought, a form, or sensation. Have a small one here that is even more evident." YCAL.

84. See J. Fred Macdonald, *Don't Touch That Dial! Radio Programming in American Life, 1920–1960* (Chicago: Nelson-Hall, 1979), 60–61.

85. Ogren, *The Jazz Revolution,* 104; and see 101–7 for a discussion of the impact of radio and motion pictures on the popularity of jazz.

86. See Helen Torr Dove Papers, AAA, reel 39, frames 449, 490–92, entries for December 2, 1936, and February 14–17, 1937. Reds's diary indicates that in late 1936 and early 1937 the painter was again very interested in music. The entry for November 15, 1936, reads, "In a.m. Arthur did an alive small music thing," and on January 14, 1937, she writes "swing," perhaps referring to swing music. Helen Torr Dove Papers, AAA, reel 39, frames 441, 475.

87. Morgan, *Arthur Dove,* 233. A copy of the exhibition catalog may be found in the Whitney Museum of American Art Papers, AAA, reel N653, frame 444, and Arthur Dove Papers, AAA, reel 954, frame 763.

88. See Roger D. Kinkle, *The Complete Encyclopedia of Popular Music and Jazz, 1900–1950,* vol. 1 (New Rochelle, N.Y.: Arlington House, 1974), 294.

89. Excerpt from Dove's unpublished notes; quoted in Wight, *Arthur G. Dove,* 58, and Suzanne Mullett Smith Papers, AAA, reel 1043, frame 1196.

90. For a discussion of the stylistic sources for the radio paintings, see Cassidy, "The Painted Music of America," 142–43.

91. On October 24, 1937, Reds wrote, "In afternoon both to see movie—Artists and Models—with Louis Armstrong as drawing power." *Swing Music (Louis Armstrong)* was completed between March 7 and 13, 1938. On March 12 Reds wrote, "Arthur worked on 'Louis Armstrong Music'—a perfect thing in mathematical beauty of color-

paint." See Helen Torr Dove Papers, AAA, reel 39, frames 610, 684. *Artists and Models,* a musical comedy set in the advertising world, starred Jack Benny, Ida Lupino, Gail Patrick, Richard Arlen, Martha Raye, and Connie Boswell; see Burton, *Blue Book of Tin Pan Alley,* 459, and David Meeker, *Jazz in the Movies* (New York: Da Capo Press, 1982), no. 161. For more on *Artists and Models,* see Marc H. Miller, ed., *Louis Armstrong: A Cultural Legacy,* exh. cat. (New York: Queens Museum of Art and Seattle: University of Washington Press, 1994), 161–63; for other images and portraits of Armstrong, see 10, 15, 45, 48.

92. See Max Jones and John Chilton, *The Louis Armstrong Story* (Boston: Little, Brown, 1971), 162; Louis Armstrong, *Swing That Music* (New York: Longmans, Green, 1936); and Hugues Panassié, *Louis Armstrong* (New York: Da Capo Press, 1971), 111.

93. Kandinsky writes, "In music, (light warm red) is a sound of trumpets, strong, harsh, and ringing." Wassily Kandinsky, *Concerning the Spiritual in Art* (1912), trans. and intro. M. T. H. Sadler (1914; repr. New York: Dover, 1977), 40.

94. A reviewer wrote, "The brilliant reds and blues, against more subdued purples and grays and browns, are the portrait of the Louis Armstrong he admires." *Springfield Sunday Union and Republic,* April 10, 1938; clipping in Downtown Gallery Papers, AAA, reel ND70, frame 437. (No author is listed, but it is most likely Elizabeth McCausland.) Other critics saw exotic elements in this work and one wrote about it as a "witch's holiday," recalling "that terrifying yet beautiful last scene in the opera 'Emperor Jones' when the voodoo devils finally triumphed over the unfortunate hero." See "Attractions in the Galleries," *New York Sun,* March 1938; clipping in Downtown Gallery Papers, AAA, reel ND31, frame 606.

95. Schuller, *Early Jazz: Its Roots and Musical Development,* 91.

96. Ibid.

97. "Swing: The Hottest and Best Kind of Jazz Reaches Its Golden Age," *Life* 5, no. 6 (August 8, 1938): 51.

98. Armstrong ignores the commercial aspects of swing music. While swing was promoted and labeled as "hot" in the 1930s, it was clearly a commercial, sweetened form of jazz.

99. Armstrong, *Swing That Music,* 30, 75.

100. Lott, *Love and Theft.*

101. "Two Views of Ragtime," 376.

102. Paul Whiteman, *Jazz* (New York: J. H. Sears, 1926), 99.

103. Lawrence W. Levine, "Jazz and American Culture," in *The Unpredictable Past: Explorations in American Cultural History* (New York: Oxford University Press, 1993), 184.

104. James Weldon Johnson and J. Rosamond Johnson, eds., *The Book of American Negro Spirituals* (1925, 1926; repr. New York: Da Capo Press, 1985), 16.

105. Peretti, *The Creation of Jazz,* 71.

106. Ibid., 189.

107. Seldes writes, "In words and music the negro side expresses something which underlies a great deal of America—our independence, our carelessness, our frankness, and gaiety." Seldes, "Toujours Jazz," 158.

108. Ibid., 158–63. This dichotomy between instinctive jazz and intellectual white European music appeared earlier, in Eddy, *Cubists and Post-Impressionists,* 84.

109. See Thomas A. De Long, *Pops: Paul Whiteman, King of Jazz* (Piscataway, N.J.: New Century, 1983), and Schwartz, *Gershwin: His Life and Music,* 73–74, for more on Whiteman.

110. Whiteman, *Jazz,* 237, writes: "My men are of every ancestry—Italian, German, French, English, Scandinavian. That does not matter. Nor does their religion, of which there are almost as many varieties as there are men. What does matter is that they are all American citizens and nearly all native born." On p. 22 he presents himself as a multiethnic American of the "good" immigrant variety: "I am a mixture of Irish, Scotch, English and Holland Dutch." See Peretti, *The Creation of Jazz,* 177–210, on jazz and the color line.

111. Whiteman, *Jazz,* 237. The stress on native birth, of course, reflects a white immigrant anxiety. Whiteman claims that only Americans can play jazz well. He writes, p. 74, of trying to teach jazz to the English: "Jazz was simply not in their blood. They lacked the spontaneity, the exuberance, the courage—I do not know what. The something, whatever it is we call American, the indefinable something that is jazz. They didn't have it."

112. See Frederick Lewis Allen, *Only Yesterday: An Informal History of the Nineteen-Twenties* (1931; repr. New York: Harper and Row, 1964), 56. See Douglas, *Terrible Honesty,* 49, and Walter Benn Michaels, "The Souls of White Folks," in *Literature and the Body: Essays on Populations and Persons,* ed. Elaine Scarry (Baltimore: Johns Hopkins University Press, 1988), 185–209, for an analysis of the "white American race" and early twentieth-century literature and culture.

113. See Jürgen Heinrichs, "Blackness in Weimar: German Art Practice as Cross-Cultural Translation of American Jazz and Dance" (paper presented at the annual meeting of the College Art Association, San Antonio, Tex., 1995), and Tower, "Jungle Music and Song of Machines," 96.

114. Examples include Gershwin's *Rhapsody in Blue*

(1924) and Aaron Copland's *Piano Concerto* (1929). For more on jazz and Americanism in early twentieth-century music, see Alan Howard Levy, *Musical Nationalism: American Composers' Search for Identity* (Westport, Conn.: Greenwood Press, 1983), and Barbara A. Zuck, *A History of Musical Americanism,* Studies in Musicology Series, no. 39 (Ann Arbor: UMI Research Press, 1978, 1980).

115. See Lott, *Love and Theft,* 50, 72, for a discussion of this same process in black minstrelsy. See also Michael Rogin, "Making America Home: Racial Masquerade and Ethnic Assimilation in the Transition to Talking Pictures," *Journal of American History* 79 (December 1992): 1050–77. Toni Morrison makes this connection between Africanism and American identity: "It was this Africanism, deployed as rawness and savagery, that provided the staging ground and arena for the elaboration of the quintessential American identity." In *Playing in the Dark: Whiteness and the Literary Imagination* (Cambridge, Mass.: Harvard University Press, 1992), 44.

116. *King of Jazz* drew upon the same melting-pot imagery used in Whiteman's book, *Jazz,* 8–9, 119. *King of Jazz* and *Jazz* also both relied on the image of the cowboy and cowgirl. By conflating jazz and Western icons Whiteman underscored the Americanness of his music and constructed his own identity as native. In turn-of-the-century America, the image of the cowboy was used to construct an Anglo-Saxon identity; see Alex Nemerov, "Doing the 'Old America,'" in *The West as America,* ed. William H. Truettner, exh. cat. (Washington, D.C.: National Museum of American Art and Smithsonian Institution Press, 1991), 298–301. German artists also used these icons to construct a romantic, long-distance notion of America; see Tower, "Jungle Music and Song of Machines."

117. Peretti, *The Creation of Jazz,* 39–40, 149.

118. Gioia, *The Imperfect Art,* 63–65, and Peretti, *The Creation of Jazz,* 151–63, 168–70.

119. For an analysis of Armstrong's *Swing That Music,* see William H. Kenney III, "Negotiating the Color Line: Louis Armstrong's Autobiographies," in Buckner and Weiland, eds., *Jazz in Mind,* 38–47.

120. Gioia, *The Imperfect Art,* 4.

121. Douglas, *Terrible Honesty,* 295, compares appropriation of black culture to abstraction.

122. Bonnie L. Grad, "Stuart Davis and Contemporary Culture," *Artibus et Historiae* 24 (1991): 187, and John R. Lane, *Stuart Davis: Art and Art Theory,* exh. cat. (New York: Brooklyn Museum, 1978), 146.

123. Miller, ed., *Louis Armstrong: A Cultural Legacy,* 127.

124. Stuart Davis, *Autobiography,* 1945, repr. in Diane Kelder, ed., *Stuart Davis* (New York: Praeger, 1971), 20–21. Davis's early training and experience shaped his later art, as he wrote: "The two dominant forces in my early art education were the teachings of Robert Henri whose school I attended and the Armory Show of modern European art in 1913." Stuart Davis, "How to Construct a Modern Easel Picture," lecture delivered at the New School for Social Research, 1941, repr. in Kelder, ed., *Stuart Davis,* 3.

125. See Sylvia L. Yount, "Consuming Drama: Everett Shinn and the Spectacular City," *American Art* 6, no. 4 (Fall 1992): 86–109.

126. Davis, *Autobiography,* repr. in Kelder, ed., *Stuart Davis,* 21. Davis was interested in other music as well; see his drawing of Igor Stravinsky in *Dial* 73 (August 1922): following 158.

127. Glenn O. Coleman, quoted in Julius, "Night Life in Newark," 9.

128. Julius, "Night Life in Newark," 8. Clement Wood's poem "Spoons" also accompanied this article; it sketched the portrait on an old spoons player who frequented one of the Newark barrel houses.

129. Lowery Stokes Sims argues that *The Back Room* depicted both blacks and whites in the same social space; see Sims et al., *Stuart Davis, American Painter,* exh. cat. (New York: Metropolitan Museum of Art and Harry N. Abrams, 1991), 118. While this club did allow racial mixing, it is not clear that there are whites in the painting. The figures with lightened faces may simply be light-skinned blacks, or Davis may have used the lighter tones to indicate those faces picking up light from the lamp—or he may have intended a certain ambiguity. Julius, "Night Life in Newark," 9, notes seeing a black prostitute with a powdered white face in one of the barrel houses.

130. This drawing was published in *Masses* 5 (February 1914): 14, with the caption "Life's Done Been Gettin' Monotonous Since Dey Bu'ned Down Ou'ah Church." See Rebecca Zurier, *Art for the Masses (1911–1917): A Radical Magazine and Its Graphics,* exh. cat. (New Haven: Yale University Art Gallery, 1985), 36–39.

131. See Marianne Doezema, *George Bellows and Urban America* (New Haven: Yale University Press, 1992), 77–82, on boxing, and Yount, "Consuming Drama," 104, on vaudeville.

132. Quoted in Sam Feinstein, "Stuart Davis: Always Jazz Music," *Art Digest* 28 (March 1, 1954): 14.

133. Stuart Davis, "The Cube Root," *Art News* (February

1, 1943), repr. in Kelder, ed., *Stuart Davis,* 130.

134. See John Lucas, "The Fine Art Jive of Stuart Davis," *Arts* 31 (September 1957): 35, and Stuart Davis, "Self-Interview, 1931," *Creative Art* 9 (September 1931): 208–11. The painter's admiration for jazz was so great that he even named his son George Earl after the pianist Earl Hines and drummer George Wettling; see Lane, *Stuart Davis: Art and Art Theory,* 146.

135. Statement by Stuart Davis, 1959, in Earl Davis, ed., *The Fine Art of Jazz: A Stuart Davis Centennial Celebration* (New York: privately printed, 1991), 13, quoted in Miller, ed., *Louis Armstrong: A Cultural Legacy,* 48.

136. Quoted in Lucas, "The Fine Art Jive of Stuart Davis," 33.

137. Davis, "Mural for Studio B, WNYC (working notes)," 1939, repr. in Kelder, ed., *Stuart Davis,* 92.

138. Davis's daybooks, 1932, repr. in Kelder, ed., *Stuart Davis,* 59–60. Davis also wrote: "A painting is made out of color which has certain inherent emotional properties and these colors by use in different proportions can be made to express an intended emotional message. That is the fact of painting. The painter has at hand a set of colors just as the musician has sounds and it is his business to compose the material that he starts out to work with." Davis, "Notebooks," December 30, 1922, repr. in Kelder, ed., *Stuart Davis,* 38.

139. Davis, *Autobiography,* repr. in Kelder, ed., *Stuart Davis,* 21.

140. Sims et al., *Stuart Davis,* 213.

141. Davis, "Mural for Studio B, WNYC (working notes)," repr. in Kelder, ed., *Stuart Davis,* 92.

142. Stuart Davis Papers, September 2, 1940, quoted in Sims et al., *Stuart Davis,* 72.

143. Davis, "Self-Interview," 211.

144. Quoted in Sims et al., *Stuart Davis,* 240. Also see Brian O'Doherty, *American Masters: The Voice and the Myth in Modern Art* (New York: E. P. Dutton, 1982), 93, for a discussion of the radio as a model of abstraction for Davis.

145. Walter Quirt Papers, quoted in Cécile Whiting, *Antifascism in American Art* (New Haven: Yale University Press, 1989), 84.

146. Arthur Dove, quoted in Wight, *Arthur G. Dove,* 64. Powell, *The Blues Aesthetic,* 28, discusses Dove's *Swinging in the Park* in relation to contemporary swing music.

147. Edwin Alden Jewell, "Concerning That Plea for Motion—Controversy about Abstraction Raises Question of 'Movement' in Painting," *New York Times,* September 19,

1937, Downtown Gallery Papers, AAA, reel N70–51, frame 435. Other critics commented on the exotic quality of *Swinging in the Park.* Henry McBride considered its color suggestive of the tropics or Africa; see the *New York Sun,* March 14, 1931, Downtown Gallery Papers, AAA, reel ND70, frame 1519.

148. Stuart Davis, "Hot Still-Scape for Six Colors—Seventh Avenue Style," *Parnassus* 12, no. 8 (December 1940): 6.

149. Artists have often compared colors to the sounds of musical instruments; see especially Kandinsky, *Concerning the Spiritual in Art,* 38–41.

150. See interview with Romare Bearden in Myron Schwartzman, *Romare Bearden: His Life and Art* (New York: Harry N. Abrams, 1990), 110–11.

151. See Grad, "Stuart Davis and Contemporary Culture," 182–88, for a discussion of the compositional structure of *Hot Still Scape.* Whiting, *Antifascism in American Art,* 89, discusses formal parallels between swing and *Hot Still Scape.*

152. See Lewis Kachur, "Stuart Davis's Word-Pictures," in Sims et al., *Stuart Davis,* 97–108, for a discussion of calligraphy and advertising in Davis's art. Davis saw himself as a product of the commercial culture: "I do not belong to the human race but am a product made by the American Can Co. and the New York *Evening Journal.*" Quoted in Grad, "Stuart Davis and Contemporary Culture," 169.

153. Kachur, "Stuart Davis's Word-Pictures," in Sims et al., *Stuart Davis,* 100–101.

154. Sims et al., *Stuart Davis,* 227. For more on Davis's *American Painting,* see Holliday T. Day and Hollister Sturges, eds., *Joslyn Art Museum: Painting and Sculpture from the European and American Collections* (Omaha: Joslyn Art Museum and University of Nebraska Press, 1987), 197–99.

155. Davis, "The Cube Root," repr. in Kelder, ed., *Stuart Davis,* 130.

156. Davis Papers, March 5, 1949, quoted in Kachur, "Davis's Word-Pictures," in Sims et al., *Stuart Davis,* 101.

157. See Whiting, *Antifascism in American Art,* 82–89. Also see Sims et al., "Stuart Davis in the 1930s: A Search for Social Relevance in Abstract Art," in Sims et al., *Stuart Davis,* 56–69. Davis even called sessions of the American Artists' Congress "jam sessions"; Schwartzman, *Romare Bearden,* 78.

158. Davis, "What about Modern Art and Democracy?" repr. in Kelder, ed., *Stuart Davis,* 136; see Grad, "Stuart Davis and Contemporary Culture," 176–77.

*Chapter 4: Aaron Douglas's* Song of the Towers

1. Stuart Davis abstracted the jazz performer in *For Internal Use Only* (1944–45), which contains fragments of jazz-club marquees, piano keys, and the black face and bow tie of the favorite boogie-woogie pianist of his fellow jazz fan Piet Mondrian; see John R. Lane, "Stuart Davis in the 1940s," in Lowery Stokes Sims et al., *Stuart Davis, American Painter,* exh. cat. (New York: Metropolitan Museum of Art and Harry N. Abrams, 1991), 74. The identity of the musician is reduced to black-face or a mask that Davis had earlier used in *ITLKSEZ* (1921).

2. W. E. B. Du Bois, *The Souls of Black Folk* (1903), in W. E. B. Du Bois, *W. E. B. Du Bois: Writings* (New York: Literary Classics of the United States, 1986), 364–65. James Weldon Johnson also defined African American identity in terms of this duality; see Johnson, *The Autobiography of an Ex-Coloured Man* (Boston: Sherman, French, 1912).

3. See Paul Gilroy, *The Black Atlantic: Modernity and Double Consciousness* (Cambridge, Mass.: Harvard University Press, 1993), and Eric J. Sundquist, *To Wake the Nations: Race in the Making of American Literature* (Cambridge, Mass.: Harvard University Press, 1993). Ann Douglas, *Terrible Honesty: Mongrel Manhattan in the 1920s* (New York: Farrar, Straus and Giroux, 1995), 105, writes of this black self in the 1920s: "The chosen mode of black Manhattan was one of contrasting, shifting rhythms as a fractured but infinite series of impersonations never culminating in the dénouement of unmasking."

4. After attending the debut of young black writers at the Civic Club in New York, Paul U. Kellog of the *Survey Graphic* decided to dedicate an entire issue to them. The March 1925 issue, entitled "Harlem—The Mecca of the New Negro," served as the basis of the *New Negro* anthology. For more on the influences on Douglas's style, see Amy Helene Kirschke, *Aaron Douglas: Art, Race, and the Harlem Renaissance* (Jackson: University Press of Mississippi, 1995), 14–31, 59–64. Douglas was familiar with the writings of Du Bois and the black magazines *The Crisis* and *Opportunity* before he came to New York in 1925, but until then he was not concerned with race in his art. The German artist Winold Reiss had come to the United States in 1913; he was known for his work as a muralist and as a delineator of folk types. See Robert Churchill, "Winold Reiss Paintings Given Fisk; Unveiling Set April 17," n.d., and "Biographical Sketch of Winold Reiss," n.d., in Aaron Douglas Papers, AAA, reel 4523.

5. Kirschke, *Aaron Douglas,* 55–70.

6. James Weldon Johnson, ed., *The Book of American Negro Poetry* (1922; 2d. ed. New York: Harcourt, Brace, 1931), 9. Du Bois coined the term in his essay, "The Talented Tenth," 1903, repr. in Du Bois, *W. E. B. Du Bois: Writings,* 842–61. The notion of African American identity proposed by the New Negro movement was shaped by the middle- and upper-class status of many of its participants.

7. For more on the Harlem Renaissance, see Jervis Anderson, *This Was Harlem: A Cultural Portrait, 1900–1950* (New York: Farrar, Straus and Giroux, 1981); Nathan Irvin Huggins, *Harlem Renaissance* (New York: Oxford University Press, 1971); and David Levering Lewis, *When Harlem Was in Vogue* (New York: Alfred A. Knopf, 1981).

8. For a list of Douglas's published illustrations, see *Harlem Renaissance: Art of Black America,* exh. cat. (New York: Studio Museum in Harlem and Harry N. Abrams, 1987), 192–93, and Kirschke, *Aaron Douglas,* 71–104.

9. For further biographical information, see "Aaron Douglas: An Autobiography," n.d., Aaron Douglas Papers, AAA, reel 4520; Theresa Dickason Cederholm, ed., *Afro-American Artists: A Bio-bibliographical Directory* (Boston: Boston Public Library, 1973), 80–81; and Bruce Kellner, ed., *The Harlem Renaissance: A Historical Dictionary for the Era* (Westport, Conn.: Greenwood Press, 1984).

10. Letter, Aaron Douglas to Langston Hughes, c. 1925; quoted in Richard J. Powell, *The Blues Aesthetic: Black Culture and Modernism,* exh. cat. (Washington, D.C.: Washington Project for the Arts, 1989), 24.

11. Douglas's style has been characterized as a combination of Synthetic Cubism and influence from Reiss and from African sculpture; see David Driskell, "The Flowering of the Harlem Renaissance: The Art of Aaron Douglas, Meta Warrick Fuller, Palmer Hayden, and William H. Johnson," in *Harlem Renaissance: Art of Black America,* 111, and Kirschke, *Aaron Douglas,* 71–91.

12. Locke set out his ideas in numerous essays and books, most notably "The Legacy of the Ancestral Arts," in Alain Locke, ed., *The New Negro* (1925; repr. New York: Atheneum, 1992), 254–67, and *Negro Art: Past and Present* (1936; repr. New York: Arno Press, 1969). Douglas's later lectures on the history of African American art restate Locke's ideas; see Aaron Douglas, "The Development of Negro Art in American Life," lecture, n.d.; Aaron Douglas Papers, AAA, reel 4520.

13. Locke, *Negro Art: Past and Present,* 12.

14. Ibid., 57. This emphasis on the figure in the works of

Harlem Renaissance artists is sometimes seen as a conservative element. See, for example, David C. Driskell, "The Evolution of a Black Aesthetic, 1920–1950," in *Two Centuries of Black American Art,* exh. cat. (New York: Alfred A. Knopf and Los Angeles: Los Angeles County Museum of Art, 1976), 59–79. This perspective depends on a view of abstraction and modernism as progressive, or advanced, and realism and American Scene painting as conservative. Yet it is perhaps more fruitful to see the use of figuration in the 1930s as following a separate but equally experimental trend, that of constructing a national identity through art.

15. This mural was funded through a New Deal art program. Driskell, in "The Flowering of the Harlem Renaissance," 49, describes it as a Works Progress Administration (WPA) project, and Kirschke, *Aaron Douglas,* 121, as a Public Works Administration (PWA) project. One anonymous writer characterized these murals as "graphic symbols of the Douglas philosophy as an artist . . . the power, variety, and substance of the African cultural heritage in American civilization and its dynamic in music, dance, and the graphic arts." From "In Memoriam: Aaron Douglas (1899–1979)," Memorial Chapel, Fisk University, Nashville, Tennessee; Aaron Douglas Papers, AAA, reel 4520.

16. Aaron Douglas, untitled essay, Aaron Douglas Papers, AAA, reel 4522.

17. See "African Art" and "Nubia," *Crisis* 30, no. 1 (May 1925): 38–39, and Kantiba Nerouy, "Tutankh-Amen and Ras Tafari," *Crisis* 29, no. 2 (December 1924): 64–68. These articles can also be found in the Aaron Douglas Papers, AAA, reel 4520. Douglas expressed admiration for the accomplishments of the Egyptians; see Aaron Douglas, "Art in Life," n.d., Aaron Douglas Papers, reel 4520.

18. Douglas, "Development of Negro Art," 2, Aaron Douglas Papers, AAA, reel 4520.

19. Also see Victor Arwas, *Art Deco* (New York: Harry N. Abrams, 1992), 91, 106–7, 170, 191.

20. Douglas used a number of devices from Art Deco vocabulary, including repeated circles, rays, and stylized foliage; see *Art Deco Designs and Motifs* (New York: Dover, 1972).

21. See Gilroy, *The Black Atlantic,* 127; Kirschke, *Aaron Douglas,* 77–78, 81; Sundquist, *To Wake the Nations,* 541, 553–65, on Egyptian art and pan-Africanism.

22. Sundquist, *To Wake the Nations,* 568, 570.

23. Douglas, "Development of Negro Art," 1, Aaron Douglas Papers, AAA, reel 4520.

24. Douglas wrote a commentary on Benton's *An Artist in America* (1937); see Aaron Douglas, comments on "An Artist in America, T. H. Benton," Aaron Douglas Papers, AAA, reel 4520. His papers also include a clipping from Margaret Just Butcher, "The Negro as Artist and in American Art," in *The Negro in American Culture* (New York: Alfred A. Knopf, 1956), which was based on notes, lectures, outlines, and other materials compiled by Alain Locke before his death in 1954; the author discussed Benton's positive representations of blacks: "[His work] has a revolutionary racial significance in that the Negro appears as an integral part of American activity with full justice accorded his share and relative position." See Aaron Douglas Papers, AAA, reel 4521.

25. For a discussion of Benton's images of blacks, see Henry Adams, *Thomas Hart Benton, An American Original,* exh. cat. (New York: Alfred A. Knopf, 1989), 211–13, 248–51; Alain Locke, *The Negro in Art* (1940; repr. New York: Hacker Art Books, 1969), 140; and Guy C. McElroy, *Facing History: The Black Image in American Art, 1710–1940,* exh. cat. (Washington, D.C.: Corcoran Gallery of Art, 1990), 125.

26. Driskell, "The Flowering of the Harlem Renaissance," 131.

27. Gilroy, *The Black Atlantic,* 90.

28. Sundquist, *To Wake the Nations,* 458.

29. See, for example, Alain Locke, quoted in Gilroy, *The Black Atlantic,* 91.

30. Published in the special issue on Harlem, *Survey Graphic* 6 (March 1925): 667.

31. Kirschke, *Aaron Douglas,* 72–73. *Roll, Jordan, Roll* introduced the music section in *The New Negro.*

32. Aaron Douglas, "Aspects of Negro Life," repr. in Cedric Dover, *American Negro Art* (Greenwich, Conn.: New York Graphic Society, 1960), back page. This description of the mural is based on a letter from Douglas to Dorothy Holmes [*sic,* Dorothy R. Homer], Branch Librarian, October 27, 1949, and his 1950 speech for the murals' rededication, repr. in "Aaron Douglas: An Autobiography," n.d., Aaron Douglas Papers, AAA, reel 4520.

33. Douglas, "Aspects of Negro Life."

34. On the illustrations, see Langston Hughes and Milton Meltzer, *Black Magic: A Pictorial History of the Negro in American Entertainment* (Englewood Cliffs, N.J.: Prentice-Hall, 1967), 8, 14.

35. Douglas, "Aspects of Negro Life."

36. Aaron Douglas, "Interpretation of *Songs of the Towers,*" c. 1966–67, Aaron Douglas Papers, AAA, reel 4522. Douglas copied the painting in 1966–67, at the height of the civil-

rights movement. He was commissioned by the local Wisconsin chapter of Links, Inc., a black women's service organization; they selected Douglas because they wanted a painting "to depict something of the historical contribution of the Negro to American life and give the people of Wisconsin a better appreciation of a Negro artist." See "Negro Art to Enhance Mansion," *Milwaukee Sentinel,* December 10, 1966, part 1, 1; clipping in Aaron Douglas Papers, AAA, reel 4523.

37. Douglas, "Interpretation of *Songs of the Towers.*"

38. Douglas identified this figure as a "jass musician" in "Interpretation of *Songs of the Towers.*"

39. Douglas ignored the experience of southern and working-class blacks, who enjoyed little of this prosperity. The interwar years were marked by riots, lynching, and the resurgence of the Ku Klux Klan. See Judith Stein, "Defining the Race, 1890–1930," in *The Invention of Ethnicity,* ed. Werner Sollors (New York: Oxford University Press, 1989), 98–101.

40. Douglas, "Interpretation of *Songs of the Towers,*" Aaron Douglas Papers, AAA, reel 4522.

41. Clement Alexander Price, "In Search of a People's Spirit: The Harmon Foundation and American Interest in Afro-American Artists," in Gary A. Reynolds and Beryl J. Wright, eds., *Against the Odds: African-American Artists and the Harmon Foundation,* exh. cat. (Newark, N.J.: Newark Museum, 1989), 77.

42. Alain Locke, *The Negro and His Music* (1936; repr. New York: Arno Press, 1969). Locke's education shaped his view of music and culture: he was a graduate of Harvard University and attended Oxford University with a Rhodes scholarship. He studied classics, German philosophy, and modern Greek literature.

43. The music historian Paul Burgett states that there was a "tendency among the Negro intelligentsia that sought the cultural transformation of black folk culture into a formal or high culture—an art of greater value." See his "Vindication as a Thematic Principle in the Writings of Alain Locke on the Music of Black Americans," in *Black Music in the Harlem Renaissance: A Collection of Essays,* ed. Samuel A. Floyd, Jr. (New York: Greenwood Press, 1990), 29.

44. Locke, *The Negro and His Music,* 4.

45. Ibid., 3.

46. Ibid., 72.

47. Ibid., 68.

48. Ibid., 65.

49. See Kathy J. Ogren, *The Jazz Revolution: Twenties*

*America and the Meaning of Jazz* (New York: Oxford University Press, 1989), 111–38, for a discussion of the views of Harlem Renaissance intellectuals on jazz.

50. J. A. Rogers, "Jazz at Home," in Locke, ed., *The New Negro,* 216.

51. Ibid., 219–20.

52. J. A. Rogers used a number of stereotypes to justify black ownership of jazz and to note the dangers of jazz for blacks. He wrote, for example: "The tired longshoreman, the porter, the housemaid and the poor elevator boy in search of recreation, seeking in jazz the tonic for weary nerves and muscles, are only too apt to find the bootlegger, the gambler and the demi-monde who have come there for victims and to escape the eyes of the police." See "Jazz at Home," 223.

53. Ibid., 221.

54. Hughes cited the black middle class's hesitancy to accept jazz and other racial expressions as evidence of its corruption by white culture. He wrote, "These common people are not afraid of spirituals, as for a long time their more intellectual brethren were, and jazz is their child. They [the folk] furnish a wealth of colorful, distinctive material for any artist because they still hold their own individuality in the face of American standardizations." Hughes, "The Negro Artist and the Racial Mountain," *Nation* 122 (June 23, 1926): 693.

55. See Ogren, *The Jazz Revolution,* 119–33, for Hughes's use of jazz.

56. Clipping, 1930s, Aaron Douglas Papers, AAA, reel 4523. One article gives *The Evolution of Jazz* as the title of this work; "Aaron Douglas Exhibit Will Stay Two More Weeks," untitled clipping, February 15, 1942, Aaron Douglas Papers, AAA, reel 4523. *Sketch for Bar Decoration,* Aaron Douglas Papers, AAA, reel 4520, is perhaps the sketch for this mural. The following description of these murals survives: "In warm blues, oranges and yellows he has depicted the Negro from jungle days on up to the modern jazz era. The figures are done in the characteristic Douglas manner and are extremely well-suited to the club." From *Opportunity,* November 1927, 319; clipping in Aaron Douglas Papers, AAA, reel 4523. Locke, *Negro Art: Past and Present,* 68, also mentions Douglas's Club Ebony murals. Douglas discusses the opening of this club in his essay "The Harlem Renaissance," unpublished manuscript, March 18, 1973, 13–14, Aaron Douglas Papers, AAA, reel 4520. Also see Kirschke, *Aaron Douglas,* 36, 109–10, and fig. 73.

57. Douglas, "The Harlem Renaissance," 8, Aaron Douglas Papers, AAA, reel 4520.

58. Aaron Douglas, untitled manuscript, Aaron Douglas Papers, AAA, reel 4522. Douglas wrote a short essay comparing music and painting; see Aaron Douglas, untitled essay, n.d., Aaron Douglas Papers, AAA, reel 4520. This essay not only discusses the iconography of music and musicians in the history of Western art, but also attempts to define visual equivalents of music. Douglas saw a shared formal language—rhythmic lines, harmonious color—in painting and music.

59. The Black Christ was an important trope in the New Negro movement and represented the black millennium, with revolution among the world's people of color; see Sundquist, *To Wake the Nations,* 591–96.

60. James Weldon Johnson, *God's Trombones: Seven Negro Sermons in Verse* (1927; repr. New York: Viking Press, 1969), 6–7.

61. Douglas, "Development of Negro Art," 7, Aaron Douglas Papers, AAA, reel 4520.

62. Johnson, *God's Trombones,* 53–54. Driskell, "The Flowering of the Harlem Renaissance," 129–39, links Douglas's paintings for *God's Trombones* to *Song of the Towers.*

63. The connection between the black jazz trumpeter and Gabriel was made overtly in Cole Porter's jazz- and gospel-inspired song "Blow Gabriel" from *Anything Goes* (1934) and in an editorial cartoon by Paul Conrad, published in the *Los Angeles Times,* July 7, 1971, in tribute to Louis Armstrong after his death. The latter shows Armstrong and Gabriel in heaven together, sounding their trumpets. See Marc H. Miller, ed., *Louis Armstrong: A Cultural Legacy,* exh. cat. (New York: Queens Museum of Art and Seattle: University of Washington Press, 1994), 225.

64. James Weldon Johnson and J. Rosamond Johnson, eds., *The Book of American Negro Spirituals* (1925, 1926; repr. New York: Da Capo Press, 1985), 185–87.

65. Weariness is a common trope in traditional black songs; see Sundquist, *To Wake the Nations,* 538. Du Bois used this same spiritual, "Cheer the Weary Traveler," as the closing for *The Souls of Black Folk.*

66. The smokestacks are most likely those of a power plant in Harlem, which Douglas painted in *Power Plant in Harlem* (n.d.).

67. Johnson and Johnson, eds., *The Book of American Negro Spirituals,* 64.

68. Langston Hughes, "The Fascination of Cities," *Crisis* 31, no. 3 (January 1926): 140.

69. Johnson and Johnson, eds., *The Book of American Negro Spirituals,* 11–12. "O Black and Unknown Bards" was first published in *Century Magazine,* 1908; see Sundquist, *To Wake the Nations,* 483.

70. Hughes, "The Negro Artist and the Racial Mountain," 694.

71. Ibid., 692–93. Hughes also writes: "But this is the mountain standing in the way of any true Negro art in America—this urge toward whiteness, the desire to pour racial individuality into the mold of American standardization, and to be as little Negro and as much American as possible. . . . A very high mountain indeed for the would-be artist to climb in order to discover himself and his people."

72. Ibid., 694.

73. Letter, Douglas to Homer, Aaron Douglas Papers, AAA, reel 4520.

74. The notion of a connection between jazz and democracy remains a powerful contemporary idea. The jazz trumpeter and historian Wynton Marsalis recently declared, "Louis Armstrong's trumpet speaks to the possibilities available to the individual in a democracy." Quoted in Burton W. Peretti, *The Creation of Jazz: Music, Race, and Culture in Urban America* (Urbana: University of Illinois Press, 1992), 1.

75. Gilroy, *The Black Atlantic,* 40. He also argues, 56–57, that music was often a substitute for political freedom.

76. Administrators of the federal project objected to Douglas's inclusion of a lynching in the panel *An Idyll in the Deep South;* see Kirschke, *Aaron Douglas,* 123. In 1964 Douglas mixed the two images of the clenched fist and the saxophone (as well as emblems of the other arts) in a program cover for the Fisk University Annual Festival of Music and Art; see copy in Aaron Douglas Papers, AAA, reel 4522.

77. Letter, Douglas to Homer, Aaron Douglas Papers, AAA, reel 4520.

78. Peretti, *The Creation of Jazz,* 53.

79. Ted Gioia, *The Imperfect Art: Reflections on Jazz and Modern Culture* (New York: Oxford University Press, 1988), 82, and Peretti, *The Creation of Jazz,* 71–73, 112. For more on Coleman Hawkins, see John Chilton, *The Song of the Hawk: The Life and Recordings of Coleman Hawkins* (Ann Arbor: University of Michigan Press, 1990), 76, and Kellner, ed., *The Harlem Renaissance: A Historical Dictionary for the Era,* 160–61.

80. See Christian Blanchet and Bertrand Dard, *Statue of Liberty: The First One Hundred Years,* trans. Bernard A. Weisberger (New York: American Heritage, 1985), 103–26.

81. Kirschke, *Aaron Douglas,* 21, notes, "[Alain] Locke compared Harlem's meaning for blacks to that of the Statue of Liberty for European immigrants." Other members of the

New Negro movement strove to distinguish blacks as non-immigrants, as part of the United States from its beginning; see Douglas, *Terrible Honesty,* 308. Douglas employs the same strategy here that Du Bois used in *The Souls of Black Folk,* when he wrote, "There are to-day no truer exponents of the pure human spirit of the Declaration of Independence than the American Negroes" (*W. E. B. Du Bois: Writings,* 370). *Song of the Towers* also recalls the concert scene in Israel Zangwill's *The Melting Pot,* in which the musician and composer David Quixano stands on the rooftop of a settlement house after he has just performed his American symphony; he is silhouetted against the New York skyline, which prominently (and rather ungeographically) features the Statue of Liberty.

82. See Beeke Sell Tower, "Jungle Music and Song of Machines: Jazz and American Dance in Weimar Culture," in *Envisioning America: Prints, Drawings, and Photographs by George Grosz and His Contemporaries, 1915–1933,* exh. cat. (Cambridge, Mass.: Busch-Reisinger Museum, 1990), 87–105.

83. In many of Douglas's paintings and drawings, the musician was a heroic figure and his musical instrument was a source of identity. In 1927 he made a drawing, *The Broken Banjo,* to illustrate the play of the same name by Willis Richardson, published in the anthology *Plays of Negro Life.* Douglas's work describes the physical power of Matt Turner, whose banjo is the source of liberation from his woes, although his attachment to the banjo also leads to his downfall. See Alain Locke and Montgomery Gregory, eds., *Plays of Negro Life: A Source-Book of Native American Drama* (1927; repr. Westport, Conn.: Negro Universities Press, 1976).

84. Douglas, "Development of Negro Art," 1, Aaron Douglas Papers, AAA, reel 4520. Writers of the New Negro movement often showed an inclination to demonstrate both the distinctiveness of blacks and their connection to the American mainstream; see, for example, E. Franklin Frazier, "Durham: Capital of the Black Middle Class" and James Weldon Johnson, "Harlem: The Culture Capital" in Locke, ed., *The New Negro,* 301–11, 333–49.

## Conclusion: Modernism, Music, and American Identity

1. Lowery Stokes Sims, "Subject/Subjectivity and Agency in the Art of African Americans," Art Bulletin 76, no. 4 (December 1994): 588, 590.

2. Paul Gilroy, *The Black Atlantic: Modernity and Double Consciousness* (Cambridge, Mass.: Harvard University Press, 1993), 5. Gilroy uses the image of travel and metaphor of a ship to explain cultural encounters and the dissolution of national borders.

3. W. E. B. Du Bois, *The Souls of Black Folk,* in W. E. B. Du Bois, *W. E. B. Du Bois: Writings* (New York: Literary Classics of the United States, 1986), 545.

4. Toni Morrison, *Playing in the Dark: Whiteness and the Literary Imagination* (Cambridge, Mass.: Harvard University Press, 1992).

5. Eric J. Sundquist, *To Wake the Nations: Race in the Making of American Literature* (Cambridge, Mass.: Harvard University Press, 1993), 4–5. Sundquist writes, p. 3, that mainstream American culture "had always been significantly black and southern, bearing the clear inflections of African-American language and creativity in popular as well as high culture."

6. Ann Douglas, *Terrible Honesty: Mongrel Manhattan in the 1920s* (New York: Farrar, Straus and Giroux, 1995), 5.

7. See, for example, Ann Gibson, *Abstract Expressionism: Race and Gender* (New Haven: Yale University Press, 1997), and Michael Leja, *Reframing Abstract Expressionism: Subjectivity and Painting in the 1940s* (New Haven: Yale University Press, 1993). Richard J. Powell, *The Blues Aesthetic: Black Culture and Modernism,* exh. cat. (Washington, D.C.: Washington Project for the Arts, 1989) is one of the few studies that argues for the influence of African American culture on early twentieth-century American modernist art. Numerous recent studies have expanded ways of thinking about twentieth-century African and African American art; see, for example, David C. Driskell, ed., *African American Visual Aesthetics: A Postmodernist View* (Washington, D.C.: Smithsonian Institution Press, 1995); idem, "The Flowering of the Harlem Renaissance: The Art of Aaron Douglas, Meta Warrick Fuller, Palmer Hayden, and William H. Johnson," in *Harlem Renaissance: Art of Black America,* exh. cat. (New York: Studio Museum in Harlem and Harry N. Abrams, 1987); Samella Lewis, *African American Art and Artists* (Berkeley: University of California Press, 1990); Richard J. Powell, *Homecoming: The Art and Life of William H. Johnson,* exh. cat. (Washington, D.C.: National Museum of American Art, 1991); and Susan Vogel et al., *Africa Explores: 20th Century African Art,* exh. cat. (New York: Center for African Art, 1991).

8. Gilroy, *The Black Atlantic,* 72.

9. See Douglas, *Terrible Honesty,* 105, and Gilroy, *The Black Atlantic,* 46.

10. Barry Ulanov, in *Homage to Jazz,* exh. cat. (New York: Samuel Kootz Gallery, December 3–21, 1946); Metropolitan Museum of Art Library, New York. The following is a selection of other works shown: William Baziotes's *Yellow Mood;* Romare Bearden's *"A Blue Note," "The Blues Got Me,"* and *Variation on a Blue Theme;* Byron Browne's *Jazz Trio, Hot Trumpet,* and *Man with a French Horn;* Adolph Gottlieb's *Jungle Dance;* Carl Holty's *Rhythm Man, Drum Break, Drum Riff,* and *Solo Flight;* and Robert Motherwell's *Flute, Homage to John Cage,* and *Suite in Three Movements.*

11. Ulanov, in *Homage to Jazz,* n.p.

12. Quoted in Francis O'Connor, *Jackson Pollock,* exh. cat. (New York: Museum of Modern Art, 1967), 38.

13. Andrew Kagan, "Improvisations: Notes on Jackson Pollock and the Black Contribution to American High Culture," *Arts* 53 (March 1979): 96–99; Chad Mandeles, "Jackson Pollock and Jazz: Structural Parallels," *Arts* 56 (October 1981): 139–41; and Powell, *The Blues Aesthetic,* 31.

14. Lee Krasner, quoted in Mandeles, "Jackson Pollock and Jazz," 139.

15. Eva Cockcroft, "Abstract Expressionism, Weapon of the Cold War," in *Pollock and After: The Critical Debate,* ed. Francis Frascina (New York: Harper and Row, 1985), 125–33. Also see Erika Doss, *Benton, Pollock, and the Politics of Modernism: From Regionalism to Abstract Expressionism* (Chicago: University of Chicago Press, 1991), 392–401, on freedom and Abstract Expressionism.

16. Quoted in Cockcroft, "Abstract Expressionism, Weapon of the Cold War," 131. Barr later argued that Social Realist art and totalitarianism went together; see Cockcroft, 131. Also see Robert Motherwell, "The Modern Artist's World," 1944, quoted in Max Kozloff, "American Painting during the Cold War," in *Pollock and After,* 111.

17. For discussions of Abstract Expressionism and primitivism, see Leja, *Reframing Abstract Expressionism,* 49–119, and W. Jackson Rushing, *Native American Art and the New York Avant-Garde: A History of Cultural Primitivism* (Austin: University of Texas Press, 1995), 121–190.

18. Norman Lewis, "Thesis," 1946, repr. in *Norman Lewis: From the Harlem Renaissance to Abstraction,* exh. cat. (New York: Kenkeleba Gallery, May 10–June 25, 1989), 63. Ann Gibson has commented that Lewis's "wartime experience . . . prompted him to question whether picturing 'the Negro' was the most effective means of expressing his own identity or of furthering the interests of the Black community." Ann Gibson, "Norman Lewis in the 1940s," in *Norman Lewis,* 11.

19. Lewis, "Thesis," in *Norman Lewis,* 63. Even the Harlem Renaissance critic Alain Locke revised his notion of racial art at this time; see Gibson, "Norman Lewis in the 1940s," 19.

20. Music surrounded Lewis in his Harlem studio, and he incorporated his response to it in his abstractions; see Julian Euell, "Thoughts about Norman Lewis," in *Norman Lewis,* 51–54, for more on Lewis and jazz.

21. Lee Stephens Glazer, "Signifying Identity: Art and Race in Romare Bearden's Projections," *Art Bulletin* 76, no. 3 (September 1994): 412, n. 10.

22. Bearden, quoted in Glazer, "Signifying Identity," 414.

23. Glazer, "Signifying Identity," 419, 426.

24. Myron Schwartzman, *Romare Bearden: His Life and Art* (New York: Harry N. Abrams, 1990), 30.

25. Ibid., 195.

26. Sheldon Hackney, "Organizing a National Conversation," *Chronicle of Higher Education* 11, no. 33 (April 20, 1994): A56.

27. See, for example, an advertisement for the Doral Tuscany Hotel in the *New Yorker* 65 (August 21, 1989): 13.

## Sources for Epigraphs

Chapter 1: John Marin, *An Exhibition of Watercolors—New York, Berkshire and Adirondack Series—and Oils by John Marin,* exh. cat. (New York: Gallery 291, January 20–February 13, 1913; and Marin, quoted in *John Marin Drawings and Water Colors,* 1950, n.p.

Chapter 2: Luigi Russolo, "The Art of Noises," 1913, in Slonimsky, *Music since 1900,* 1019, 1020; and Joseph Stella, "New York," n.d., quoted in Jaffe, *Joseph Stella,* 77–78.

Chapter 3: Paul Whiteman, *Jazz,* 1926, 132–33; and Stuart Davis, quoted in Lucas, "The Fine Art Jive of Stuart Davis," c. 1957, 33.

Chapter 4: Langston Hughes, "The Negro Artist and the Racial Mountain," 1926, 694; and Aaron Douglas, "Development of Negro Art," lecture, n.d., 10, Aaron Douglas Papers, AAA, reel 4520.

Conclusion: Jacques Attali, *Noise: The Political Economy of Music,* trans. Brian Massumi (Minneapolis: University of Minnesota Press, 1985), 6.

# WORKS CITED

Aaron Douglas Papers. Archives of American Art, Smithsonian Institution, Washington, D.C.

Abraham Walkowitz Papers. Archives of American Art, Smithsonian Institution, Washington, D.C.

Adams, Henry. *Thomas Hart Benton, An American Original*. Exh. cat. New York: Alfred A. Knopf, 1989.

"African Art." *Crisis* 30, no. 1 (May 1925): 38–39.

Agee, William. "New York Dada, 1910–1930." *Art News Annual 34: The Avant Garde*. Ed. Thomas B. Hess and John Ashbery. New York: Macmillan, 1968.

Aisen, Maurice. "The Latest Evolution in Art and Picabia." *Camera Work* special number (June 1913): 14–21.

Alfred Stieglitz Archive. Yale Collection of American Literature, Beinecke Rare Book and Manuscript Library, Yale University, New Haven, Conn.

Allan, Sidney [Sadakichi Hartmann]. "The 'Flat-Iron' Building.—An Esthetical Dissertation." *Camera Work* 4 (October 1903): 36–40.

Allen, Frederick Lewis. *Only Yesterday: An Informal History of the Nineteen-Twenties*. 1931. Repr. New York: Harper and Row, 1964.

Anderson, Jervis. *This Was Harlem: A Cultural Portrait, 1900–1950*. New York: Farrar, Straus and Giroux, 1981.

Antliff, Mark. *Inventing Bergson: Cultural Politics and the Parisian Avant-Garde.* Princeton: Princeton University Press, 1993.

"Appeal of the Primitive Jazz." *Literary Digest* 55 (August 25, 1917): 28–29.

*The Armory Show International Exhibition of Modern Art,* 1913. 3 vols. New York: Arno Press, 1972.

Armstrong, Louis. *Swing That Music.* New York: Longmans, Green, 1936.

*Art Deco Designs and Motifs.* New York: Dover, 1972.

Arthur Dove Papers. Archives of American Art, Smithsonian Institution, Washington, D.C.

"Artistic Aspects of the Skyscraper." *Current Opinion* 54, no. 4 (April 1913): 321–23.

Arwas, Victor. *Art Deco.* New York: Harry N. Abrams, 1992.

Attali, Jacques. *Noise: The Political Economy of Music.* Trans. Brian Massumi. Minneapolis: University of Minnesota Press, 1985.

Baigell, Matthew. "American Art and National Identity: The 1920s." *Arts* 61 (February 1987): 48–55.

———. "Walt Whitman and Early Twentieth-Century Art." In *Walt Whitman and the Visual Arts.* Ed. Geoffrey M. Sill and Roberta K. Tarbell. New Brunswick: Rutgers University Press, 1992.

Balken, Debra Bricker. *John Marin's Berkshire Landscapes.* Exh. cat. Pittsfield, Mass.: Berkshire Museum, 1985.

Baur, John I. H. *Joseph Stella.* Exh. cat. New York: Whitney Museum of American Art and Shorewood, 1963.

Bellamen, Henry. "Decorations for an Imaginary Ballet." *Broom* 1, no. 2 (December 1921): 116–18.

Bergson, Henri. "An Extract from Bergson." *Camera Work* 36 (October 1911): 20–21.

———. *Time and Free Will: An Essay on the Immediate Data of Consciousness.* Trans. F. L. Pogson. 1910. Repr. New York: Macmillan, 1959.

———. "What Is the Object of Art?" *Camera Work* 37 (January 1912): 22–26.

Bernard, Jonathan W. *The Music of Edgard Varèse.* New Haven: Yale University Press, 1987.

Blanchet, Christian, and Bertrand Dard. *Statue of Liberty: The First One Hundred Years.* Trans. Bernard A. Weisberger. New York: American Heritage, 1985.

Bohn, Willard. "In Pursuit of the Fourth Dimension: Guillaume Apollinaire and Max Weber." *Arts* 54 (June 1980): 166–69.

Bourne, Randolph. "Our Cultural Humility." *Atlantic Monthly* 114 (October 1914): 503–7.

Bragdon, Claude. "The Shelton Hotel, New York." *Architectural Record* 58, no. 1 (July 1925): 1–18.

Brooks, Van Wyck. *The Wine of the Puritans: A Study of Present-Day America.* 1908. Repr. Folcroft, Pa.: Folcroft Press, 1969.

"Broomides: Communications from Edgard Varèse." *Broom* 1, no. 1 (November 1921): 94–95.

Buckner, Reginald T., and Steven Weiland, eds. *Jazz in Mind: Essays on the History and Meanings of Jazz.* Detroit: Wayne State University Press, 1991.

Buffet, Gabrielle. "Modern Art and the Public." *Camera Work* special number (June 1913): 10–14.

Burgett, Paul. "Vindication as a Thematic Principle in the Writings of Alain Locke on the Music of Black Americans." In *Black Music in the Harlem Renaissance: A Collection of Essays.* Ed. Samuel A. Floyd, Jr. New York: Greenwood Press, 1990.

Burton, Jack. *The Blue Book of Tin Pan Alley.* Watkins Glen, N.Y.: Century House, 1951.

Busoni, Ferruccio. "Sketch of a New Aesthetic of Music." In *Three Classics in the Aesthetic of Music.* New York: Dover, 1962.

Butcher, Margaret Just. "The Negro as Artist and in American Art." In *The Negro in American Culture.* New York: Alfred A. Knopf, 1956.

Camfield, William A. *Francis Picabia: His Art, Life and Times.* Princeton: Princeton University Press, 1979.

Casseres, Benjamin de. "The Ironical in Art." *Camera Work* 38 (April 1912): 17–18.

Cassidy, Donna M. "Arthur Dove's Music Paintings of the Jazz Age." *American Art Journal* 20, no. 1 (1988): 4–23.

———. "The Painted Music of America in the Works of Arthur G. Dove, John Marin, and Joseph Stella: An Aspect of Cultural Nationalism." Ph.D. diss., Boston University, 1988.

*Catalogue of Victor Records.* Camden, N.J.: Victor Talking Machine Company, 1920–27.

Cederholm, Theresa Dickason, ed. *Afro-American Artists: A Bio-bibliographical Directory.* Boston: Boston Public Library, 1973.

Chave, Anna C. "'Who Will Paint New York?': 'The World's New Art Center' and the Skyscraper Paintings of Georgia O'Keeffe." *American Art* 5, nos. 1–2 (Winter–Spring 1991): 86–107.

Chilton, John. *The Song of the Hawk: The Life and Recordings of Coleman Hawkins.* Ann Arbor: University of Michigan Press, 1990.

Coady, Robert. "American Art." *Soil* 1 (December 1916): 3–4.

Coburn, Alvin Langdon. "The Relation of Time to Art." *Camera Work* 36 (October 1911): 72–73.

Cockcroft, Eva. "Abstract Expressionism, Weapon of the Cold War." In *Pollock and After: The Critical Debate.* Ed. Francis Frascina. New York: Harper and Row, 1985.

Cohn, Sherrye. *Arthur Dove: Nature as Symbol.* Studies in the Fine Arts: The Avant-Garde, no. 49. Ann Arbor: UMI Research Press, 1985.

Coke, Van Deren. *Marin in New Mexico, 1929 and 1930.* Exh. cat. Albuquerque: University Art Museum and the University of New Mexico Press, 1968.

Collier, James Lincoln. *The Reception of Jazz in America: A New View.* New York: Institute for Studies in American Music, 1988.

"Color Music." *Literary Digest* 46 (June 21, 1913): 1378–79.

Conrad, Peter. *The Art of the City: Views and Versions of New York.* New York: Oxford University Press, 1984.

Corn, Wanda M. "In Detail: Joseph Stella and *New York Interpreted.*" *Portfolio* 1 (January–February 1982): 40–45.

———. "The New New York." *Art in America* 61 (July–August 1973): 58–65.

———. "Postscript: Walt Whitman and the Visual Arts." In *Walt Whitman and the Visual Arts.* Ed. Geoffrey M. Sill and Roberta K. Tarbell. New Brunswick: Rutgers University Press, 1992.

———. "Toward a Native Art." *Wilson Quarterly* 5 (Summer 1981): 166–77.

Cotkin, George. *Reluctant Modernism: American Thought and Culture, 1880–1900.* New York: Twayne, 1992.

Cravan, Arthur. "New York." *Soil* 1 (December 1916): 36.

Davidson, Abraham A. "John Marin: Dynamism Codified." *Artforum* 9 (April 1971): 37–42.

Davis, Stuart. "Hot Still-Scape for Six Colors—Seventh Avenue Style." *Parnassus* 12, no. 8 (December 1940): 6.

———. "The Place of Painting in Contemporary Culture: The Easel Is a Cool Spot at an Arena of Hot Events." *Art News* 56 (June 1957): 29–30.

———. "Self-Interview, 1931." *Creative Art* 9 (September 1931): 208–11.

Day, Holliday T., and Hollister Sturges, eds. *Joslyn Art Museum: Painting and Sculpture from the European and American Collections.* Omaha: Joslyn Art Museum and University of Nebraska Press, 1987.

De Long, Thomas A. *Pops: Paul Whiteman, King of Jazz.* Piscataway, N.J.: New Century, 1983.

Dijkstra, Bram. *Cubism, Stieglitz, and the Early Poetry of William Carlos Williams.* Princeton: Princeton University Press, 1969.

Doezema, Marianne. *George Bellows and Urban America.* New Haven: Yale University Press, 1992.

Doss, Erika. *Benton, Pollock, and the Politics of Modernism: From Regionalism to Abstract Expressionism.* Chicago: University of Chicago Press, 1991.

Douglas, Ann. *Terrible Honesty: Mongrel Manhattan in the 1920s.* New York: Farrar, Straus and Giroux, 1995.

Dover, Cedric. *American Negro Art.* Greenwich, Conn.: New York Graphic Society, 1960.

Downtown Gallery Papers. Archives of American Art, Smithsonian Institution, Washington, D.C.

Driskell, David C. "The Evolution of a Black Aesthetic, 1920–1950." In *Two Centuries of Black American Art.* Exh. cat. New York: Alfred A. Knopf and Los Angeles: Los Angeles County Museum of Art, 1976.

———. "The Flowering of the Harlem Renaissance: The Art of Aaron Douglas, Meta Warrick Fuller, Palmer Hayden, and William H. Johnson." In *Harlem Renaissance: Art of Black America.* Exh. cat. New York: Studio Museum in Harlem and Harry N. Abrams, 1987.

Driskell, David C., ed. *African American Visual Aesthetics: A Postmodernist View.* Washington, D.C.: Smithsonian Institution Press, 1995.

Du Bois, W. E. B. *W. E. B. Du Bois: Writings.* New York: Literary Classics of the United States, 1986.

Eddy, Arthur Jerome. *Cubists and Post-Impressionists.* Chicago: A. C. McClurg, 1914.

"Editorial Statement." *Seven Arts* 1 (November 1916): 52–53.

Engel, Carl. "The Mansion of Peace." *Broom* 2, no. 1 (April 1922): 36–41.

Erenberg, Lewis A. *Steppin' Out: New York Nightlife and the Transformation of American Culture, 1890–1930.* Westport, Conn.: Greenwood Press, 1981.

Farnham, Emily. *Charles Demuth: Behind a Laughing Mask.* Norman: University of Oklahoma Press, 1971.

Feinstein, Sam. "Stuart Davis: Always Jazz Music." *Art Digest* 28 (March 1, 1954): 14.

Fine, Ruth E. *John Marin.* Exh. cat. Washington, D.C.: National Gallery of Art and New York: Abbeville Press, 1990.

*The Forum Exhibition of Modern American Painters.* Exh. cat. 1916. Repr. New York: Arno Press, 1968.

Frank, Waldo. *In the American Jungle.* 1937. Repr. Freeport, N.Y.: Books for Libraries Press, 1968.

———. *Our America.* 1919. Repr. New York: AMS Press, 1972.

———. *The Re-discovery of America: An Introduction to a Philosophy of American Life.* New York: Scribner's, 1929.

Freund, Frank E. W. "Joseph Stella." *Cicerone* 16 (October 1924): 963–72. Repr. in *Jahrbuch der jungen Kunst.* Ed. Georg Biermann. Leipzig: Klinkhardt und Biermann, 1924.

Gershwin, George. "The Composer in the Machine Age." In *Revolt in the Arts.* Ed. Oliver M. Sayler. New York: Brentanos, 1930.

"Gershwin's Compositions in Paint." *American Art* 7, no. 3 (Summer 1993): 92–94.

Gibson, Ann. *Abstract Expressionism: Race and Gender.* New Haven: Yale University Press, 1997.

Gilroy, Paul. *The Black Atlantic: Modernity and Double Consciousness.* Cambridge, Mass.: Harvard University Press, 1993.

Gioia, Ted. *The Imperfect Art: Reflections on Jazz and Modern Culture.* New York: Oxford University Press, 1988.

Glazer, Lee Stephens. "Signifying Identity: Art and Race in Romare Bearden's Projections." *Art Bulletin* 76, no. 3 (September 1994): 411–26.

Grad, Bonnie L. "Stuart Davis and Contemporary Culture." *Artibus et Historiae* 24 (1991): 165–91.

Gray, Cleve, ed. *John Marin by John Marin.* New York: Holt, Rinehart and Winston, 1970.

Greenough, Sarah, and Juan Hamilton. *Alfred Stieglitz, Photographs and Writings.* Exh. cat. Washington, D.C.: National Gallery of Art, 1983.

Hackney, Sheldon. "Organizing a National Conversation." *Chronicle of Higher Education* 11, no. 33 (April 20, 1994): A56.

Hadler, Mona. "Jazz and the Visual Arts." *Arts* 57 (June 1983): 91–101.

Hand, John O. "Futurism in America." *Art Journal* 41 (Winter 1981): 337–42.

*Harlem Renaissance: Art of Black America.* Exh. cat. New York: Studio Museum in Harlem and Harry N. Abrams, 1987.

Hartley, Marsden. *On Art.* Ed. Gail R. Scott. New York: Horizon Press, 1982.

Hartmann, Sadakichi. "Rodin's *Balzac.*" *Camera Work* 34–35 (April–June 1911): 19–21.

———. *White Chrysanthemums—Literary Fragments and Pronouncements.* Ed. George Knox and Harry Lawton. New York: Herder and Herder, 1971.

Haskell, Barbara. *Arthur Dove.* Exh. cat. Boston: New York Graphic Society, 1974.

———. *Charles Demuth.* Exh. cat. New York: Whitney Museum of American Art and Harry N. Abrams, 1987.

———. *Joseph Stella.* Exh. cat. New York: Whitney Museum of American Art and Harry N. Abrams, 1994.

———. *Marsden Hartley.* Exh. cat. New York: Whitney Museum of American Art and New York University Press, 1980.

Heinrichs, Jürgen. "Blackness in Weimar: German Art Practice as Cross-Cultural Translation of American Jazz and Dance." Paper presented at the annual meeting of the College Art Association, San Antonio, Tex., 1995.

Helen Torr Dove Papers. Archives of American Art, Smithsonian Institution, Washington, D.C.

Helm, Mackinley. *John Marin.* Boston: Pellegrini and Cudahy, 1948.

Henderson, Linda Dalrymple. *The Fourth Dimension and Non-Euclidean Geometry in Modern Art.* Princeton: Princeton University Press, 1983.

Hobsbawm, Eric J. "Introduction: Inventing Traditions." In *The Invention of Tradition.* Ed. Eric J. Hobsbawm and Terence Ranger. Cambridge, Eng.: Cambridge University Press, 1985.

———. *Nations and Nationalism since 1780: Programme, Myth, Reality.* Cambridge, Eng.: Cambridge University Press, 1990.

*Homage to Jazz.* Intro. Barry Ulanov. Exh. cat. New York: Samuel M. Kootz Gallery, December 3–21, 1946.

Homer, William Innes. *Alfred Stieglitz and the American Avant-Garde.* Boston: New York Graphic Society, 1977.

———. *Robert Henri and His Circle.* Ithaca: Cornell University Press, 1969.

Huggins, Nathan Irvin. *Harlem Renaissance.* New York: Oxford University Press, 1971.

Hughes, Langston. "The Fascination of Cities." *Crisis* 31, no. 3 (January 1926): 138–40.

———. "The Negro Artist and the Racial Mountain." *Nation* 122 (June 23, 1926): 692–94.

Hughes, Langston, and Milton Meltzer. *Black Magic: A Pictorial History of the Negro in American Entertainment.* Englewood Cliffs, N.J.: Prentice-Hall, 1967.

"Is Photography a New Art?" *Camera Work* 21 (June 1908): 17–18.

Jablonski, Edward, and Lawrence D. Stewart. *The Gershwin Years.* Garden City, N.Y.: Doubleday, 1973.

Jaffe, Irma B. *Joseph Stella*. Cambridge, Mass.: Harvard University Press, 1970.

———. "Joseph Stella and Hart Crane: The Brooklyn Bridge." *American Art Journal* 1 (Fall 1969): 98–107.

Jewell, Edwin Alden. *Americans*. New York: Alfred A. Knopf, 1930.

*John Marin Drawings and Water Colors*. New York: Twin Editions, 1950.

John Marin Papers. Archives of American Art, Smithsonian Institution, Washington, D.C.

*John Marin's New York*. Exh. cat. New York: Kennedy Galleries, 1981.

Johnson, James Weldon. *The Autobiography of an Ex-Coloured Man*. Boston: Sherman, French, 1912.

———. *God's Trombones: Seven Negro Sermons in Verse*. 1927. Repr. New York: Viking Press, 1969.

Johnson, James Weldon, ed. *The Book of American Negro Poetry*. 1922. 2d ed., New York: Harcourt, Brace, 1931.

Johnson, James Weldon, and J. Rosamond Johnson, eds. *The Book of American Negro Spirituals*. 1925, 1926. Repr. New York: Da Capo Press, 1985.

Jones, Max, and John Chilton. *The Louis Armstrong Story*. Boston: Little, Brown, 1971.

Josephson, Matthew. "After and beyond Dada." *Broom* 2, no. 4 (July 1922): 346–50.

———. "The Great American Billposter." *Broom* 3, no. 4 (November 1922): 304–12.

———. "Made in America." *Broom* 2, no. 3 (June 1922): 266–70.

Joseph Stella File. Société Anonyme Collection, Yale Collection of American Literature, Beinecke Rare Book and Manuscript Library, Yale University, New Haven, Conn.

Joseph Stella Papers. Archives of American Art, Smithsonian Institution, Washington, D.C.

Julius, Emanuel. "Night Life in Newark." *New York Call*, magazine section, Sunday, May 30, 1915, 8–9, 14.

Kagan, Andrew. "Improvisations: Notes on Jackson Pollock and the Black Contribution to American High Culture." *Arts* 53 (March 1979): 96–99.

———. "Paul Klee's *Polyphonic Architecture* (1930)." *Arts* 54 (January 1980): 154–57.

Kandinsky, Wassily. *Concerning the Spiritual in Art* (1912). Trans. and intro. M. T. H. Sadler. 1914. Repr. New York: Dover, 1977.

———. *Kandinsky: Complete Writings on Art*. Vol. 1 (1901–21). Ed. Kenneth C. Lindsay and Peter Vergo. Boston: G. K. Hall, 1982.

———. *Point and Line to Plane*. Ed. Hilla Rebay. 1947. Repr. New York: Dover, 1979.

Kaplan, Justin. *Walt Whitman: A Life*. New York: Simon and Schuster, 1980.

Kasson, John F. *Amusing the Million: Coney Island at the Turn of the Century*. New York: Hill and Wang, 1978.

Keiley, Joseph A. "Landscape: A Reverie." *Camera Work* 4 (October 1903): 45–46.

Kelder, Diane, ed. *Stuart Davis*. New York: Praeger, 1971.

Kellner, Bruce, ed. *The Harlem Renaissance: A Historical Dictionary for the Era*. Westport, Conn.: Greenwood Press, 1984.

Kern, Stephen. *The Culture of Time and Space, 1880–1918*. Cambridge, Mass.: Harvard University Press, 1983.

Kinkle, Roger D. *The Complete Encyclopedia of Popular Music and Jazz, 1900–1950*. New Rochelle, N.Y.: Arlington House, 1974.

Kirschke, Amy Helene. *Aaron Douglas: Art, Race, and the Harlem Renaissance*. Jackson: University Press of Mississippi, 1995.

Klaric, Arlette Jean. "Arthur G. Dove's Abstract Style of 1912: Dimensions of the Decorative and Bergsonian Realities." Ph.D. diss., University of Wisconsin, Madison, 1984.

Kootz, Samuel M. *Modern American Painters*. Norwood, Mass.: Plimpton Press, 1930.

Kozloff, Max. "American Painting during the Cold War." In *Pollock and After: The Critical Debate*. Ed. Francis Frascina. New York: Harper and Row, 1985.

Lane, John R. *Stuart Davis: Art and Art Theory*. Exh. cat. New York: Brooklyn Museum, 1978.

Lears, T. J. Jackson. "From Salvation to Self-Realization: Advertising and the Therapeutic Roots of the Consumer Culture, 1880–1930." In Richard Wrightman Fox and T. J. Jackson Lears, eds., *The Culture of Consumption: Critical Essays in American History, 1880–1930*. New York: Pantheon, 1983.

Leja, Michael. *Reframing Abstract Expressionism: Subjectivity and Painting in the 1940s*. New Haven: Yale University Press, 1993.

Levin, Gail. *Synchromism and American Color Abstraction, 1910–25*. Exh. cat. New York: Whitney Museum of American Art and George Braziller, 1978.

Levin, [Sandra] Gail. "Wassily Kandinsky and the American Avant-Garde, 1912–50." 2 vols. Ph.D. diss., Rutgers University, 1976.

Levine, Lawrence W. "Jazz and American Culture." In *The Unpredictable Past: Explorations in American Cultural*

*History*. New York: Oxford University Press, 1993.

Levy, Alan Howard. *Musical Nationalism: American Composers' Search for Identity*. Westport, Conn.: Greenwood Press, 1983.

Lewis, David Levering. *When Harlem Was in Vogue*. New York: Alfred A. Knopf, 1981.

Lewis, Samella. *African American Art and Artists*. Berkeley: University of California Press, 1990.

Locke, Alain. *The Negro and His Music*. 1936. Repr. New York: Arno Press, 1969.

———. *Negro Art: Past and Present*. 1936. Repr. New York: Arno Press, 1969.

———. *The Negro in Art*. 1940. Repr. New York: Hacker Art Books, 1969.

Locke, Alain, ed. *The New Negro*. 1925. Repr. New York: Atheneum, 1992.

Locke, Alain, and Montgomery Gregory, eds. *Plays of Negro Life: A Source-Book of Native American Drama*. 1927. Repr. Westport, Conn.: Negro Universities Press, 1976.

Loeb, Harold A. "Foreign Exchange." *Broom* 2, no. 2 (May 1922): 176–81.

———. [H. A. L.]. "The Mysticism of Money." *Broom* 3, no. 2 (September 1922): 115–30.

Lott, Eric. *Love and Theft: Blackface Minstrelsy and the American Working Class*. New York: Oxford University Press, 1995.

Lucas, John. "The Fine Art Jive of Stuart Davis." *Arts* 31 (September 1957): 34–37.

Macdonald, J. Fred. *Don't Touch That Dial! Radio Programming in American Life, 1920–1960*. Chicago: Nelson-Hall, 1979.

Mandeles, Chad. "Jackson Pollock and Jazz: Structural Parallels." *Arts* 56 (October 1981): 139–41.

Marcel, Gabriel. "Bergsonism and Music." *La Revue musicale* 6 (1925): 219–29. Repr. in *Reflections on Art: A Source Book of Writings by Artists, Critics, and Philosophers*. Ed. Susan K. Langer. Baltimore: Johns Hopkins University Press, 1958.

Margolis, Marianne Fulton, ed. *Camera Work: A Pictorial Guide*. New York: Dover, 1978.

Marin, John. "A Few Notes." *Twice-a-Year* 2 (Spring–Summer 1939): 176–80.

———. "Can a Photograph Have the Significance of Art?" *Manuscripts* 4 (December 1922): 10–11.

———. "John Marin by Himself." *Creative Art* 2 (October 1928): xxxv–xxxix.

Marsden Hartley Papers, Archives of American Art, Smithsonian Institution, Washington, D.C.

Martin, Marianne W. *Futurist Art and Theory, 1909–1915*. 1968. Repr. New York: Hacker Art Books, 1978.

Mather, Frank Jewett, Jr., Charles Rufus Morey, and William James Henderson. *The American Spirit in Art*. New Haven: Yale University Press, 1927.

Matthieson, F. O. *American Renaissance: Art and Expression in the Age of Emerson and Whitman*. New York: Oxford University Press, 1941.

Mattis, Olivia. "Edgard Varèse's 'Progressive' Nationalism: *Amériques* Meets *Américanisme*." In *Edgard Varèse: Die Befreiung des Klangs*. Ed. Helga de La Motte-Haber. Hofheim, Germany: Wolke, 1992.

———. "Edgard Varèse and the Visual Arts." Ph.D. diss., Stanford University, 1992.

Maur, Karin von, ed. *Vom Klang der Bilder: Die Musik in der Kunst des 20. Jahrhunderts*. Exh. cat. Munich: Prestel and Stuttgart Staatsgalerie, 1985.

*Max Weber: Retrospective Exhibition, 1907–1930*. Exh. cat. New York: Museum of Modern Art, 1930.

McElroy, Guy C. *Facing History: The Black Image in American Art, 1710–1940*. Exh. cat. Washington, D.C.: Corcoran Gallery of Art, 1990.

Meeker, David. *Jazz in the Movies*. New York: Da Capo Press, 1982.

Michaels, Walter Benn. "The Souls of White Folk." In *Literature and the Body: Essays on Populations and Persons*. Ed. Elaine Scarry. Baltimore: Johns Hopkins University Press, 1988.

Miller, Marc H., ed. *Louis Armstrong: A Cultural Legacy*. Exh. cat. New York: Queens Museum of Art and Seattle: University of Washington Press, 1994.

Morand, Paul. *Black Magic*. New York: Viking Press, 1929.

Morgan, Ann Lee. *Arthur Dove, Life and Work, with a Catalogue Raisonné*. Newark, Del.: University of Delaware Press, 1984.

Morgan, Ann Lee, ed. *Dear Stieglitz, Dear Dove*. Newark, Del.: University of Delaware Press, 1988.

Morrison, Toni. *Playing in the Dark: Whiteness and the Literary Imagination*. Cambridge, Mass.: Harvard University Press, 1992.

"Mr. Picabia Paints 'Coon Songs.'" *New York Herald,* March 18, 1913, 12.

Naumann, Francis M. *New York Dada, 1915–23*. New York: Harry N. Abrams, 1994.

Nemerov, Alex. "Doing the 'Old America.'" In *The West as America*. Ed. William H. Truettner. Exh. cat. Washington, D.C.: National Museum of American Art and Smithsonian Institution Press, 1991.

Nerouy, Kantiba. "Tutankh-Amen and Ras Tafari." *Crisis* 29, no. 2 (December 1924): 64–68.

Nevinson, Henry W. "The Impulse to Futurism." *Atlantic Monthly* 114 (November 1914): 626–33.

Newman, Sasha. *Arthur Dove and Duncan Phillips: Artist and Patron.* Exh. cat. Washington, D.C.: Phillips Collection and New York: George Braziller, 1982.

New York Public Library Papers (Art and Print Divisions). Archives of American Art, Smithsonian Institution, Washington, D.C.

Norman, Dorothy. *Alfred Stieglitz: An American Seer.* New York: Random House, 1960.

Norman, Dorothy, ed. and intro. *The Selected Writings of John Marin.* New York: Pellegrini and Cudahy, 1949.

*Norman Lewis: From the Harlem Renaissance to Abstraction.* Exh. cat. New York: Kenkeleba Gallery, May 10–June 25, 1989.

North, Percy. *Max Weber: American Modern.* Exh. cat. New York: Jewish Museum, 1982.

"Notes on '291'—Water Colors by John Marin." *Camera Work* 42–43 (April–July 1913): 18.

"Nubia." *Crisis* 30, no. 1 (May 1925): 38.

O'Connor, Francis. *Jackson Pollock.* Exh. cat. New York: Museum of Modern Art, 1967.

O'Doherty, Brian. *American Masters: The Voice and the Myth in Modern Art.* New York: E. P. Dutton, 1982.

Ogren, Kathy J. *The Jazz Revolution: Twenties America and the Meaning of Jazz.* New York: Oxford University Press, 1989.

O'Keeffe, Georgia. *Georgia O'Keeffe.* New York: Viking Press, 1976.

Oppenheim, James. "Lazy Verse." *Seven Arts* 1 (November 1916): 71.

———. "The Story of the *Seven Arts*." *American Mercury* 20 (June 1930): 156–64.

Osgood, Henry O. *So This Is Jazz.* Boston: Little, Brown, 1926.

Ouellette, Fernand. *Edgard Varèse.* Trans. Derek Coltman. 1966. Repr. London: Calder and Boyars, 1973.

*Over Here! Modernism, The First Exile, 1914–1919.* Exh. cat. Providence: David Winton Bell Gallery, Brown University, 1989.

Panassié, Hugues. *Louis Armstrong.* New York: Da Capo Press, 1971.

Parsons, Melinda Boyd. *To All Believers—The Art of Pamela Colman Smith.* Exh. cat. Wilmington, Del.: Delaware Art Museum, 1974.

Payton, Rodney J. "The Music of Futurism." *Musical Quarterly* 62 (January 1976): 25–45.

Peretti, Burton W. *The Creation of Jazz: Music, Race, and Culture in Urban America.* Urbana: University of Illinois Press, 1992.

Perlman, Bennard B. *The Immortal Eight.* New York: Exposition Press, 1962.

Phelps, Ruth, and Henri Morane. "Artistes d'avant-garde en Amérique." *Figaro hebdomadaire* [New York?], July 25, 1928, 8–9.

Picabia, Francis. "A Post-Cubist's Impressions of New York." *New York Tribune,* March 9, 1913, part 2, 1.

———. "How New York Looks To Me." *New York American,* March 30, 1913, magazine section, 11.

Pollitzer, Anita. *A Woman on Paper: Georgia O'Keeffe.* New York: Simon and Schuster, 1988.

Pound, Louise. "Walt Whitman and Italian Music." *American Mercury* 6, no. 21 (September 1925): 58–63.

Powell, Richard J. *The Blues Aesthetic: Black Culture and Modernism.* Exh. cat. Washington, D.C.: Washington Project for the Arts, 1989.

———. *Homecoming: The Art and Life of William H. Johnson.* Exh. cat. Washington, D.C.: National Museum of American Art, 1991.

Prampolini, Enrico. "The Aesthetic of the Machine and Mechanical Introspection in Art." *Broom* 3, no. 3 (October 1922): 235–37.

Pratella, Balilla. *Technical Manifesto of Futurist Music.* 1911. Trans. in Nicolas Slonimsky, *Music since 1900.* 5th ed. New York: Schirmer Books, 1994.

"Pressing Forward into Space." *Nation* 94 (April 11, 1912): 356.

Quirk, Thomas. "Bergson in America." *Prospects: An Annual of American Culture Studies.* Vol. 11. Ed. Jack Salzman. Cambridge, Eng.: Cambridge University Press, 1987.

Rathbone, Eliza E. *Mark Tobey: City Paintings.* Exh. cat. Washington, D.C.: National Gallery of Art, 1984.

Reich, Sheldon. "Abraham Walkowitz: Pioneer of American Modernism." *American Art Journal* 3 (Spring 1971): 72–82.

———. "John Marin: Paintings of New York, 1912." *American Art Journal* 1 (Spring 1969): 43–52.

———. *John Marin: A Stylistic Analysis and Catalogue Raisonné.* 2 vols. Tucson: University of Arizona Press, 1970.

"Review of John Marin Exhibition." *Camera Work* 42–43 (April–July 1913): 22–43.

Reynolds, Gary A., and Beryl J. Wright, eds. *Against the Odds: African-American Artists and the Harmon Foundation.*

Exh. cat. Newark, N.J.: Newark Museum, 1989.

Risatti, Howard Anthony. "American Critical Reaction to European Modernism, 1908 to 1917." Ph.D. diss., University of Illinois at Urbana–Champaign, 1978.

———. "Music and the Development of Abstraction in America: The Decades surrounding the Armory Show." *Art Journal* 39 (Fall 1979): 8–13.

Robbins, Daniel. *Albert Gleizes, 1881–1953*. Exh. cat. New York: Solomon R. Guggenheim Muscum of Art, 1964.

Robinson, Jontyle Theresa, and Wendy Greenhouse. *The Art of Archibald J. Motley, Jr.* Exh. cat. Chicago: Chicago Historical Society, 1991.

Rogin, Michael. "Making America Home: Racial Masquerade and Ethnic Assimilation in the Transition to Talking Pictures." *Journal of American History* 79 (December 1992): 1050–77.

Rolland, Romain. "America and the Arts." *Seven Arts* 1 (November 1916): 47–51.

Rosenfeld, Paul. *An Hour with American Music*. Philadelphia: J. B. Lippincott, 1929.

———. *Discoveries of a Music Critic*. New York: Vienna House, 1936.

———. *Modern Tendencies in Music*. New York: Caxton Institute, 1927.

———. *Port of New York*. Intro. Sherman Paul. 1924. Repr. Urbana: University of Illinois Press, 1961.

Rubin, William S., ed. *"Primitivism" in 20th Century Art: Affinity of the Tribal and the Modern*. Exh. cat. 2 vols. New York: Museum of Modern Art, 1984.

Rushing, W. Jackson. *Native American Art and the New York Avant-Garde*. Austin: University of Texas Press, 1995.

Russolo, Luigi. *The Art of Noises*. 1913. Trans. in Nicolas Slonimsky, *Music since 1900*. 5th ed. New York: Schirmer Books, 1994.

Sawin, Martica. *Abraham Walkowitz, 1878–1965*. Exh. cat. Salt Lake City: Utah Museum of Fine Arts, 1975.

Schelling, Friedrich Wilhelm Joseph von. *The Philosophy of Art*. Ed. and trans. Douglas W. Stott. Minneapolis: University of Minnesota Press, 1989.

Schleier, Merrill. *The Skyscraper in American Art, 1890–1931*. Studies in the Fine Arts: The Avant-Garde, no. 53. Ann Arbor: UMI Research Press, 1986.

Schuller, Gunther. *Early Jazz: Its Roots and Musical Development*. New York: Oxford University Press, 1968.

Schwartz, Charles. *Gershwin: His Life and Music*. New York: Bobbs-Merrill, 1973.

Schwartzman, Myron. *Romare Bearden: His Life and Art*. New York: Harry N. Abrams, 1990.

Seldes, Gilbert. "Toujours Jazz." *Dial* 75 (August 1923): 151–66.

Sélincourt, Basil de. *Walt Whitman: A Critical Study*. London: Martin Secker, 1914.

Shapiro, Theda. "The Metropolis in the Visual Arts: Paris, Berlin, New York." In *Metropolis, 1890–1940*. Ed. Anthony Sutcliffe. Chicago: University of Chicago Press, 1984.

Sharpe, William. "New York, Night, and Cultural Mythmaking." *Smithsonian Studies in American Art* 2, no. 3 (Fall 1988): 2–21.

"The Shipbuilders as Sketched by Joseph Stella." *Survey* 41 (November 30, 1918): 259–62.

Sims, Lowery Stokes, et al. *Stuart Davis, American Painter*. Exh. cat. New York: Metropolitan Museum of Art and Harry N. Abrams, 1991.

———. "Subject/Subjectivity and Agency in the Art of African Americans." *Art Bulletin* 76, no. 4 (December 1994): 587–90.

Singal, Daniel Joseph. "Towards a Definition of American Modernism." In *Modernist Culture in America*. Ed. Daniel Joseph Singal. Belmont, Calif.: Wadsworth, 1991.

Smith, Suzanne Mullett, and Gordon H. Smith. "Music of the Eye: The Development of An Idea." Paper presented at American University, Washington, D.C., Department of Music, 1950; reedited 1976.

Société Anonyme Papers. Yale Collection of American Literature, Beinecke Rare Book and Manuscript Library, Yale University, New Haven, Conn.

Sollors, Werner. *Beyond Ethnicity: Consent and Descent in American Culture*. New York: Oxford University Press, 1986.

Stebbins, Theodore E., Jr., and Carol Troyen. *The Lane Collection: 20th-Century Paintings in the American Tradition*. Exh. cat. Boston: Museum of Fine Arts, 1983.

Stechow, Wolfgang. "Problems of Structure in Some Relations between the Visual Arts and Music." *Journal of Aesthetics and Art Criticism* 11 (June 1953): 324–33.

Stein, Judith. "Defining the Race, 1890–1930." In *The Invention of Ethnicity*. Ed. Werner Sollors. New York: Oxford University Press, 1989.

Stella, Joseph. "The Brooklyn Bridge (A Page of My Life)." *Transition* 16–17 (June 1929): 86–88.

———. "Discovery of America: Autobiographical Notes." *Art News* 59 (November 1960): 41–43, 64–67.

———. "The New Art." *Trend* 5 (June 1913): 392–95.

Sundquist, Eric J. *To Wake the Nations: Race in the Making of American Literature*. Cambridge, Mass.: Harvard University Press, 1993.

*Survey Graphic* 6 (March 1925).

Suzanne Mullett Smith Papers. Archives of American Art, Smithsonian Institution, Washington, D.C.

Swift, Samuel. "Review of Picabia's Paintings at 291 from the *New York Sun*." *Camera Work* 42–43 (April–July 1913): 48–50.

"Swing: The Hottest and Best Kind of Jazz Reaches Its Golden Age." *Life* 5, no. 6 (August 8, 1938): 50–60.

Tashjian, Dickran. *Skyscraper Primitives: Dada and the American Avant-Garde, 1910–25*. Middletown, Conn.: Wesleyan University Press, 1975.

Taylor, Joshua C. *Futurism*. Exh. cat. New York: Doubleday and the Museum of Modern Art, 1961.

Thompson, Jan. "Picabia and His Influence on American Art, 1913–1917." *Art Journal* 39 (Fall 1979): 14–21.

Tichi, Cecelia. *Shifting Gears: Technology, Literature, Culture in Modernist America*. Chapel Hill: University of North Carolina Press, 1987.

Tirro, Frank. *Jazz: A History*. New York: W. W. Norton, 1977.

Tower, Beeke Sell. "Jungle Music and Song of Machines: Jazz and American Dance in Weimar Culture." In *Envisioning America: Prints, Drawings, and Photographs by George Grosz and His Contemporaries, 1915–1933*. Exh. cat. Cambridge, Mass.: Busch-Reisinger Museum, 1990.

"Two Views of Ragtime: Hiram Kelly Moderwell, 'A Modest Proposal,' and Charles L. Buchanan, 'Ragtime and American Music'" *Seven Arts* 9 (July 1917): 368–82.

Varèse, Edgar[d]. "The Music of Tomorrow." *London Evening News*, June 14, 1924, 4.

_____. "Oblation," "Verbe," and "Que la musique sonne." *391* 5 (June 1917): n.p.

Varèse, Louise. *Varèse: A Looking-Glass Diary, 1883–1928*. New York: W. W. Norton, 1972.

Vogel, Susan, et al. *Africa Explores: 20th Century African Art*. Exh. cat. New York: Center for African Art, 1991.

Walkowitz, Abraham. *Improvisations of New York: A Symphony in Lines*. Girard, Kansas: Haldeman-Julius Publications, 1948.

Weber, Max. "The Fourth Dimension from a Plastic Point of View." *Camera Work* 31 (July 1910): 25.

Weiss, Peg. *Kandinsky in Munich: The Formative Jugendstil Years*. Princeton: Princeton University Press, 1979.

Wertheim, Arthur F. *The New York Little Renaissance: Iconoclasm, Modernism, and Nationalism in American Culture, 1908–1917*. New York: New York University Press, 1976.

Whiteman, Paul. *Jazz*. New York: J. H. Sears, 1926.

Whiting, Cécile. *Antifascism in American Art*. New Haven: Yale University Press, 1989.

Whitman, Walt. *The Portable Walt Whitman*. Ed. Mark van Doren and Malcolm Cowley. New York: Viking Press, 1973.

Whitney Museum of American Art Papers. Archives of American Art, Smithsonian Institution, Washington, D.C.

"Why 'Jazz' Sends Us Back to the Jungle." *Current Opinion* 65 (September 1918): 165.

Wight, Frederick S. *Arthur G. Dove*. Exh. cat. Berkeley: University of California Press, 1958.

Wright, Willard Huntington. *Modern Painting: Its Tendency and Meaning*. New York: John Lane, 1915.

Young, Stark. "The Color Organ." *Theatre Arts* 6, no. 1 (January 1922): 20–32.

Yount, Sylvia L. "Consuming Drama: Everett Shinn and the Spectacular City." *American Art* 6, no. 4 (Fall 1992): 86–109.

Zangwill, Israel. *The Melting Pot: A Drama in Four Acts*. 1925 ed. Repr. New York: AMS Press, 1969.

Zayas, Marius de. "From '291.'" *Camera Work* 48 (October 1916): 69–70.

_____. "On New York." *291* 5–6 (July–August 1915): n.p.

Zilczer, Judith [Katy]. "The Aesthetic Struggle in America, 1913–1918: Abstract Art and Theory in the Stieglitz Circle." Ph.D. diss., University of Delaware, 1975.

_____. "The Armory Show and the American Avant-Garde: A Re-evaluation." *Arts* 53 (September 1978): 126–30.

_____. "'Color Music': Synaesthesia and Nineteenth-Century Sources for Abstract Art." *Artibus et Historiae* 16, no. 7 (1987): 101–26.

_____. *Joseph Stella*. Exh. cat. Washington, D.C.: Smithsonian Institution Press, 1983.

_____. "Robert J. Coady: Forgotten Spokesman for Avant-Garde Culture in America." *American Art Review* 2 (September–October 1975): 77–89.

_____. "Synaesthesia and Popular Culture: Arthur Dove, George Gershwin, and the 'Rhapsody in Blue.'" *Art Journal* 44 (Winter 1984): 361–66.

Zuck, Barbara A. *A History of Musical Americanism*. Studies in Musicology Series, no. 39. Ann Arbor: UMI Research Press, 1978, 1980.

Zurier, Rebecca. *Art for the Masses (1911–1917): A Radical Magazine and Its Graphics*. Exh. cat. New Haven: Yale University Art Gallery, 1985.

# INDEX